AF577202

MICROWAVE COOKING: IT'S NOT MAGIC

Compiled and Edited
by
John and Sharon Foltz
and
John and Tuppi Long
with
the assistance
of
Marcia Schwall

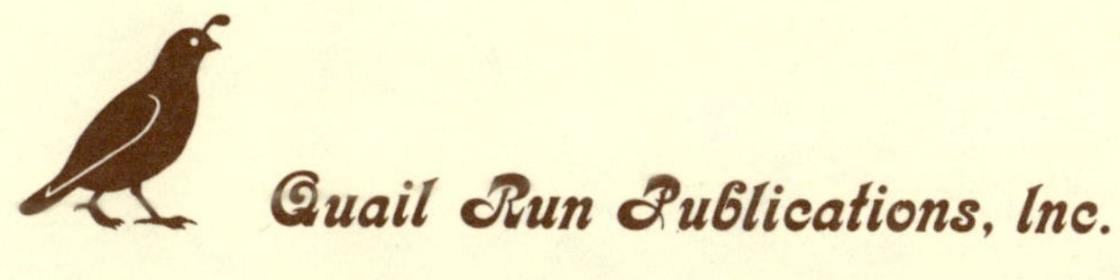

Paradise Valley, Arizona

PRECAUTIONS TO AVOID POSSIBLE EXPOSURE TO EXCESSIVE MICROWAVE ENERGY

(a) Do not attempt to operate oven with the door open since open-door operation can result in harmful exposure to microwave energy. It is important not to defeat or tamper with the safety interlocks.

(b) Do not place any object between the oven front face and the door or allow soil or cleaner residue to accumulate on sealing surfaces.

(c) Do not operate the oven if it is damaged. It is particularly important that the oven door close properly and that there is no damage to the: (1) Door (bent), (2) Hinges and latches (broken or loosened), (3) Door seals and sealing surfaces.

(d)The oven should not be adjusted or repaired by anyone except properly qualified service personnel.

The above is printed in compliance with the Food and Drug Administration, Department of Health, Education, and Welfare, Performance Standards for Microwave and Radio Frequency Emitting Products, 21 CFR 1030.10.

MICROWAVE COOKING: IT'S NOT MAGIC

Published by Quail Run Publications, Inc.
5221 North Quail Run Place, Paradise Valley, Arizona

ISBN 0-930380-03-7

Library of Congress Catalog Number 77-20466

Photography by A. F. Payne Photographic
Phoenix, Arizona

Illustrated by Diana Sheridan

Manufactured in U.S.A. by Ray Buse Printing and Advertising, Phoenix, Arizona

CONTENTS

INTRODUCTION

Marcia Bowlsby Schwall

Marcia Bowlsby Schwall,
HOME ECONOMIST

The last decade has seen a tremendous increase in consumer awareness and interest in the area of microwave oven cooking. The speed, efficiency and energy-saving features of microwave ovens are obvious attractions to people across the nation today. This collection of recipes will assist you in taking full advantage of all the energy-saving benefits of microwaves and give you an opportunity to taste good food.

This cookbook has been designed to help people enjoy their microwave oven more and provide them with good family and creative recipes of interest to all age levels. There is nothing magical about microwave cooking but its flavor and speed and ease with which anyone can turn out a delicious meal. Children and senior citizens find flash-cooking to be fantastic for their special needs. Those people whose diets are varied, and often restricted, also find that this type of food preparation provides them with the opportunity to cook and eat foods that normally might not be available to them.

"It's Not Magic" is a how-to-entertain cookbook as well as a superb collection of kitchen-tested recipes. Whether you want to cook quick-to-prepare foods or those created from scratch, the cookbook will direct you on how it should be done. Cooking hints and charts have been added to each chapter to aid in easy reference and can be used as tools in changing conventional recipes to microwave cooking times.

Microwave ovens come in assorted shapes and sizes. Offering a time savings of one-fourth to one-half when compared to conventional cooking. The directions in this book gives three power settings; high, medium and low. These settings, known as multiple-power, are designed to regulate the power level on your microwave just as you do on your conventional oven. The highest level on your microwave is noted as *high* in this cookbook. This setting is 100% power and is ideal for cooking vegetables, fish and beverages. *Medium* is equal to 60% power and is used for starting cakes and quick breads, stews and soups, roasts, meat loaves and ham, and for defrosting large meat items. Finally, *low,* 30% power, is the setting used in defrosting frozen foods and cooking rice, pastas, baked custards, softening chocolate and taking the chill off fruits. To check the power percentages on your oven, check with the instruction manual that came with your oven.

It is our feeling that microwave cooking will increase in popularity and practicality at an astonishing speed due to the fact that we are used to more leisure time, more travel, more entertainment sources, and can not afford the time it takes to prepare a meal in the conventional manner.

The easy and energy-saving recipes included in this cookbook will offer you the guidance you need to have success in microwave cooking.

PREFACE

CONGRATULATIONS!

You've arrived! You're finally going to experience the thrill of microwave cooking. The dream of enjoying a roast from freezer to table in just a few minutes; the four minute baked potato is here.

Today, microwave cooking is considered to be a necessity by the budget-minded family. How else can the working cook prepare a meal from scratch in the few minutes between his or her arrival home and the appointed dinner hour? How else can day-old rolls and leftovers be brought alive? How else can defrosting and cooking of the meat left in the freezer be accomplished so quickly?

It's true! Microwave cooking may change your cooking habits as a result of its fantastic speed, but there are many other differences between microwave cooking and conventional cooking. Microwave cooking is probably the best thing to happen in cookery since the invention of the range.

Your new microwave will help you save time and money. You will use only a fraction of the energy consumed in conventional cooking. Your kitchen will stay cooler, since there is no warm-up or cool-down time for your microwave oven. You'll waste less and have fewer utensils to scour, while cooking and serving in the same dish.

You'll enjoy your microwave-cooked meals with more retained natural flavor and color. A bonus: the nutrients usually poured down the drain after extended cooking remain in your microwave-cooked meal.

Not only is your new microwave fast, convenient, and a good cook — it's safe. It's impossible to get a microwave burn as automatic switches and other protective devices immediately cut the power when the door is opened. Since the oven stays cool, spills and splatters aren't baked on and wipe clean in an instant.

All these benefits are nice, but the real advantage is yet to be realized. With your days becoming more hurried, you'll find the speed, convenience and fun of the microwave will return the joy of creating your own masterpieces. Gormet meals needn't be an all day project. Your family and friends can share in the creation of your favorite meals, but remember, you are the chef. So let's get on with it.

MICROWAVE COOKING TIPS

The skills and techniques which have made you a good cook still apply to microwave cooking. You still test meat for doneness the way you've always done, by sight, touch or with a food sensing device. A cake's stiffness still tells you when the center is cooked. A microwave, however, will require some adjustment. Food cooks at an amazing rate, and you can use utensils you've never used before.

Indicated cooking times are approximate and may vary according to electrical currents, portion sizes, and altitudes. A vegetable which is just right for one person may seem hard for another and mushy for a third. The cooking dish's shape and composition can make a difference, too. A deep casserole takes longer to heat than a large shallow one of the same capacity. Many cooking hints apply to conventional cooking as well as microwave, but because of the microwave's speed, they take on new importance.

FOOD SHAPES AND SIZES: When you cook on a conventional range, you understand that large pieces take longer than small or thin slices, and that the peas need to be added to the stew late in the cooking process. Small pieces on the other hand, cook quickly and uniformly. Microwave cooking is the same. When several foods are cooked together, they should be of similar size and shape so they reach the same doneness at the same time. The same is true of the quantity of food placed in the oven. Twice the quantity will take less than twice as long to cook. The principle is constant: Variations in size and quantities can make a real difference in cooking times — this is where the microwave is most sensitive, and where your attention will be most richly rewarded. When in doubt, consider the technique used for conventional cooking, then exaggerate it for the microwave.

STIRRING in a microwave need not be constant, but only occasional. Foods cook from the outside in, so stirring should be from the outside in, instead of from the bottom up as in conventional cooking.

For those foods which cannot be stirred, turning or rearranging in the oven is recommended if cooking times are more than a few minutes. Roasts or poultry can be turned over while cooking and cake and bread should be rotated occassionally.

STANDING TIME is more critical in microwave cooking. Conventional cookbooks recommend standing time to finish cooking, retain juices, and facilitate carving. The same is true for microwave cooking. Vegetables and fast cook items made need no additional time, but the larger and longer cooked items will need a few minutes. Remember, you can always cook your food a little more. It is difficult to make it "more rare." Small parts of food such as poultry wings or legs may be SHIELDED with a little tin foil to give the bulkier parts a head start. After the foil is removed the smaller parts will be cooked so that the whole piece is done at once. One important area where microwave cooking and conventional cooking are different is in BROWNING. The high outside heat which browns in conventional cooking is not present in the microwave oven. Browning will be attained in those meat products that stay in the microwave for at least 15 minutes. For smaller pieces of meat browning can be achieved in three ways:

1) Brush meat with a commercial browning sauce or sprinkle with gravy mix or browning powder.
2) Sear meat on a conventional range-top before completing the cooking in your microwave.
3) Use a microwave browning dish.

The microwave browning dish was developed especially for microwave cooking where foods cook too fast to brown. It is usually ceramic with a special bottom coating which becomes hot enough to brown foods. Be sure to follow manufacturer's instructions carefully.

ROASTING is improved through the use of a roasting rack, as in conventional cooking. Your roasting rack will also be useful in cooking bacon, as it will allow the fat to drain. If the recipe calls for you to cover food while microwaving, a sheet of waxed paper or plastic wrap may be used.

HOW THE HEAT CONTROL WORKS

Many microwave ovens have heat control selectors as well as timers to assist in the control of microwave cooking. When you set the heat control on your conventional oven, the oven heats until it reaches a selected temperature then turns on and off to maintain that temperature. If you turn the temperature down, the oven "coasts" until it cools to the desired temperature. Heat controlled microwave ovens are never preheated and respond to heat control changes instantly.

Many foods require different amounts of "on off" time to taste their best, or alternatively, require that the microwave be set at different heat levels. The more settings available on your microwave, the more control you'll have over food quality PROVIDED you learn what settings to use.

Many of the recipes in this book indicate a suggested power setting to be used. Understand that power settings and cooking times are approximate and may vary from oven to oven and from instalation to instalation. Carefully read the manual that accompanies your particular microwave, and familiarize yourself with its power-setting alternatives.

IS IT REALLY MAGIC?

Although it does seem like a science-fiction movie prop, there is really no magic to microwave cooking.

In conventional cooking wood, charcoal, gas, or electricity is converted to intense heat which is either applied to the bottom of the food or surrounds the food in an oven. If food comes in direct contact with these heat sources, the outside burns before it cooks through. The inside of the food is heated by conduction from the food's surface.

Microwave cooking relies on a tube called a magnetron, which converts electrical energy into microwave energy, a type of high frequency radio wave. Microwaves are sent directly into the food and may penetrate from all sides as much as 1½ to 2 inches. The cooking process begins as soon as the oven is turned on, with no need to heat the air or cooking utensils.

Microwaves move directly into the food because they are attracted to the moisture, fat, and sugar molecules. They cause these molecules to vibrate at a fantastic rate, bumping and rubbing against each other causing heat. As one group of molecules begins to vibrate, it causes the neighboring molecules to move, creating heat within the food. The vibration of molecules cannot be seen or felt by you, never-the-less, it is happening, and is the cause of the amazing speed, tastiness, and nutrition of microwave cooked food.

THE BASICS

WHAT YOU NEED TO KNOW ABOUT FOOD BEING COOKED

Successful microwave cooking is dependent mostly on time (and in the case of multi-power ovens, on energy level). The amount of time (and energy) is directly related to the starting temperature, volume and density of food items that go into the oven.

Starting temperature: The colder the food, the longer it takes to cook or heat.

Volume: As the amount or volume of food increases, the heating, defrosting and cooking times increases.

Density: Dense food takes longer to cook, heat or defrost.

KEY USES FOR THE MICROWAVE OVEN

Defrost frozen cooked or uncooked foods quickly and efficiently using an automatic defroster so microwaves will penetrate the food to thaw it without cooking or drying the outer edges. All automatic defrosters cycle the power on and off to allow surface heat to conduct towards food's center and defrost it evenly.

Heat previously cooked foods in a very short time — without excessive drying or flavor loss.

Cook individual portions or large mixtures of uncooked foods. Varible power ovens have a number of different power settings that take into account the fact that all foods do not cook equally well at the same energy level.

Browning: Large meat items will brown in a microwave oven after 15 minutes of microwave cooking because the fat attracts micrdwaves and reaches a high surface temperature during prolonged cooking. Small food items such as steaks and chops brown and sear well in the oven on the microwave browning dish accessory. Cakes and breads will cook but not brown because a microwave oven cooks with moist heat.

High altitude cooking: The usual high altitude adjustments in ingredients are not necessary in microwave cooking. The only change may be a slight increase in cooking time — about 1 to 2 minutes for every 10 minutes of cooking time.

OVEN CARE — KEY TO GOOD COOKING AND SAFETY

- Always read and follow the oven manufacturer's instruction manual.
- Examine the oven for evidence of shipping damage.
- Never shut the oven door with anything between it and the oven face or the door seal will be broken.
- Never try to insert objects through the door grill.
- Do not try to modify the oven.
- Never tamper with oven safety switches or built-in inter-locks.
- Do not use the door of the bottom-hinged oven as a shelf.
- Keep the oven clean. Frequently wash oven cavity, door and seals with a soft cloth, water and mild detergent. Do not use abrasive. See the microwave browning dish use and care manual for special instructions for cleaning.
- If odors from foods such as fish or broccoli linger in the oven, combine equal amounts of lemon juice or vinegar and water in a cup. Boil in the oven for one minute. Remove cup of liquid and wipe oven with warm, soapy water.
- Refer to the use and care manual if your oven does not seem to be working properly.
- If the oven will not "turn on" check these things: Is the oven plugged in? Is the door shut securely? Has the timer been engaged? Has the cook button been pressed?
- If the oven should operate while the door is open, have it checked by an authorized microwave oven service representative.
- A damaged oven should be inspected and repaired only by the manufacturer's authorized service personnel. State or city health inspectors will check microwave ovens for safety by taking measurements around the door closure while the oven is in operation. In Arizona, these technicians can be found at the Arizona State Atomic Energy Commission.

MICROWAVE OVENS COME IN ASSORTED SHAPES AND SIZES

Essentially there are four different groups of microwave ovens and ranges with microwave ovens —plus several microwave cooking accessories. All ovens offer a time savings of one-fourth to one-half and more when compared to conventional cooking. Most countertop models use up to 75 percent less electricity than is used by conventional ranges. Oven categories include:

Countertop basic or single-power microwave ovens, that cook, heat and defrost. Time is the only variable or changing factor. Microwave power remains constant. Countertop models have from .4 to 1.4 cubic feet of usable oven interior.

Countertop variable power microwave ovens, feature a number of different power settings for cooking, defrosting and warming. Variable or multi-power is available on many larger, full-featured countertop models.

Double-oven microwave ranges, pack all the popular cooking conveniences into one appliance. The 1.2 to 1.4-cubic-foot microwave oven is at eye level. This microwave unit plus a 30 to 36-inch lower conventional oven and conventional cooktop allows great flexibility.

Combination microwave ranges features a single oven with microwave speed, plus the browning and crisping of conventional baking or broiling. Time savings range from one-fourth to one-half the cooking time needed for conventional cooking alone. Microwave and conventional baking or broiling can be used together, separately or in sequence. Combination ovens have 3.5 cubic feet of usable interior, which accommodates large portions of food.

UTENSILS

Microwave cooking will open a whole new world of cooking utensils and containers to you. Since microwaves are attracted to fat, sugar, and water molecules, food can be cooked before many utensils or containers are damaged by heat. You'll find you can use paper, plastic, and china in place of the usually messy and inconvenient metal cookware. There are some simple rules that should be followed, however, to assure best performance from your oven, and protect utensils and containers from damage.

Many utensils now in the stores have microwave information on them. Look for it, and follow the manufacturers instructions and precautions. In the absence of a label, you can TEST cooking dishes or utensils by placing them in the microwave on its highest setting for about fifteen seconds. If the utensil or container becomes heated, don't use it in the microwave! All dishes containing food will eventually become warm in your microwave, just from the natural transfer of heat from the food being cooked; this is a common and non-destructive occurance.

GLASS, CERAMIC AND CHINA

As long as they have no metalic trim, these items are generally not affected by microwaves. You can warm dessert in a glass dish, heat coffee in a cup, cook foods in their serving dishes — and without the usual scouring required after conventional cooking. Be careful with delicate glassware, since the heat of food inside may eventually crack the glass.

Most manufacturers are now identifying their products with microwave-safety labels. Any of the pottery or glass products suitable for conventional cooking are certainly suitable for microwave cookery.

Utensils or dishes with metalic trim or metal parts such as screws, bands, handles, etc., should be avoided. Pottery with high metal content glazes should also be avoided. When in doubt, use the simple test described earlier.

PAPER GOODS

For low heat or short time cooking, paper products such as napkins, towels, plates, cups, cartons, and cooking pouches are good for microwave cooking since they present no barrier to the microwaves and aid in the ease of clean-up.

PLASTICS

There are an extraordinary variety of plastics on the market, but those that say "dishwasher safe" on them should be acceptable for microwave use. Some plastics may change shape with the heat of the food or produce an odor when heated. Again, if in doubt, test the dish or utensil first.

WICKER, WOOD, AND STRAW

Wicker, wood and straw may be used in the microwave although they should not be used for high sugar or fat content foods, or for long cooking periods, since the heat of the food may char the utensil.

BROWNING DISHES

Browning dishes are usually ceramic with a special ferric coating on the bottom. Microwaves heat the bottom of the browning dish cooking the food conventionally and with microwaves simultaneously. For this reason, browning dishes require preheating in the microwave. Preheat time varies with the type of food you wish to cook. Follow the directions that come with your particular browning dish. The browning dish should not be used on conventional cooking surfaces.

METAL CONTAINERS AND UTENSILS

In general, metal containers should not be used in your microwave. They not only reflect the microwaves and slow cooking, but there is also the possibility of "arcing." Arcing is a static discharge or spark between two metal pieces in the oven or between the oven and a metal utensil. If arcing occurs, simply turn the oven off and transfer the food to a non-metalic container.

NEVER use a conventional meat thermometer in a microwave. You may use it after cooking, however, to determine the internal doneness of meats. Remove the thermometer before returning food to the oven.

DISHES — KINDS AND SIZES THAT WORK BEST

In general, heatproof glass, glass ceramic and pottery without metal trim are best for microwave cookery — metal should not be used except as listed below. Between these two extremes are paper, plastic and straw utensils which can be used in particular situations.

Ovenproof glass and glass ceramic baking dishes are the most-used microwave cooking utensils. These dishes allow microwaves to pass through them directly to food. Dishes will remain cool unless cooking is prolonged causing hot food to heat the dish.

Fine china is not ovenproof. Do not use it at all if it has metal trim. Fine china without metal trim may be used to heat precooked foods for short periods of time.

Some paints or glazes used on glass dishes do contain metallic substances and should not be used in a microwave oven.

Corning products can be used in the oven, except for the following items: Centura dinnerware, Cook-n-Serve covers and closed-handle cups of Corelle Livingware. Other Corelle dishes can be used.

Heat from boiling liquid can soften epoxy glues. So cups, pitchers or beverage servers which have handles attached with a sealant like epoxy may loosen when picked up after use in a microwave oven.

Dishwasher-safe plastics, usually quite rigid material, can be used for cooking or heating.

Hard plastic trays, picnic ware, thermal cups, mugs and bowls (including the sturdy bowls in which a number of dairy toppings and other products are packaged) may be used in the oven. Melamine ware has a tendency to absorb energy, so you should give it a 15 to 20 second test on high or cook to be certain your particular brand is safe.

Plastic foam cups and dishes can be used for heating. When covering, do it loosely to avoid dish distortion. *Plastic baby bottles and liners* are safe for heating milk for formulas.

Plastic spatulas and spoons designed for non-stick pans can be left in the oven for short time periods.

Plastic cooking pouches can be used to heat and/or cook contents, but should be slit before cooking so excess steam can escape.

Other facts about plastics: Use plastic in a microwave oven only for heating cooked food to serving temperature. Prolonged cooking causes food to reach a higher temperature and can distort plastic.

Paper cups, plates, towels, wax paper and paper cartons can be used for heating. Prolonged time in the oven can cause paper to burn if it is close to foods with very little moisture content. Wax paper can be used as a covering during cooking to keep oven bottom free of spatters, and for baking cookies. Paper napkins and towels can be used to absorb moisture when heating sandwiches or grease from bacon.

Straw baskets can be used in the oven for the very short time it takes to heat rolls.

Small pieces of aluminum foil can be used to cover spots on large pieces of meat which appear to be overcooking.

Foil TV-type trays can be used in some micro-ovens (check your cookbook) if not more than ¾ inch deep. Although cooking in metal foil TV trays occurs from the top surface only, food in these containers is shallow enough so that it heats adequately. Make certain that no part of the metal tray is touching the metal walls of the oven because arcing may occur.

Metal skewers and clamps are usable when the proportion of food is much greater than the metal. A shish-kabob skewer covered with food will microwave well without arcing. Metal clamps and clips on turkeys may be left on during cooking.

Moisture in *wooden utensils* evaporates during microwave cooking and will cause wood to crack. Small items such as a wooden spoon or wood-handled rubber spatula can be left in the oven for short periods of time.

Plastic wrap creates a tight seal when stretched tautly across the top of a cooking dish. Cut a small slit in it to allow steam to escape before removing cover after cooking.

Wax paper does not give a really tight seal, but is used in preference to plastic wrap when cooking comes in prolonged contact with the covering.

Ovenproof glass or pottery plates without metal trim may be used to cover dishes during cooking.

Dish size is important: Food volume (size) should match the size of the dish — with some leeway for bubbling. Fill dishes ½ to ⅔ full. If the dish is too small, food will bubble over the edges. If the dish is too large, the saucy portions will spread out and over-cook, leaving the center uncooked.

APPETIZERS

With your Microwave Oven, you can now serve piping hot appetizers, snacks and hors d'oeuvres as needed. You can save time by preparing these dishes in advance and just heating them in the microwave oven when your guests arrive.

Heat-resistant, non-metallic platters can go directly from your Microwave Oven to your table in just minutes. The recipes in this chapter are able to be prepared ahead of time or be whipped up when unexpected company arrives. Many of these recipes can be frozen successfully, enabling you to combine the advantages of your freezer and Microwave Oven.

When preparing appetizers for baking, arrange in a single layer on a glass or paper plate. Appetizers may be covered with paper toweling to prevent spatters.

Breads and bread-based foods may be made more crisp by placing them on paper towels to absorb excess moisture.

CRAB AND CLAM DIP

1 (8-oz.) package cream cheese
5 tablespoons soft butter or margarine
4 tablespoons French dressing
1 (8-oz.) can minced clams, drained
1 (6-oz.) package frozen crabmeat, thawed and drained
Few drops Tabasco sauce
Melba toast rounds

— In a medium-sized glass mixing bowl, blend together cream cheese, butter and French dressing until smooth.
— Add drained clams and crabmeat. Stir to combine.
— Add Tabasco sauce to taste. Mix well.
— Spread on Melba toast rounds.
— Place on serving paper towel lined plate and heat, uncovered, on medium for 45 seconds.
— Serve immediately.

(2 cups)

MEXICAN BEAN DIP

4 slices bacon, cut into pieces
1 can (31-oz.) pork and beans
½ cup sharp Chedar cheese
1 teaspoon garlic salt
1 teaspoon chili powder
½ teaspoon salt
2 teaspoons Worcestershire sauce
Cayenne pepper

— Place bacon pieces in 1 ½-quart glass casserole.
— Cover with paper toweling and Microwave on high for 3 to 4 minutes or until crisp.
— Remove bacon pieces, set aside.
— Place pork and beans in blender and blend until smooth.
— Pour into bacon drippings in 1 ½-quart glass casserole.
— Stir in remaining ingredients, except bacon.
— Cover with glass lid or plastic wrap.
— Microwave on high for 7 to 8 minutes or until mixture is hot in center.
— Sprinkle top with bacon pieces.

(3 ½ cups dip)

MUSHROOMS BOURGUIGNON

¼ cup butter or margarine
1 lb. fresh mushrooms, cleaned
1 cup dry red wine or beef broth
1 tablespoon finely chopped green onion
½ teaspoon garlic salt
½ teaspoon dillweed
¼ teaspoon salt
Dash pepper

— Place butter in shallow 3-quart glass baking dish.
— Microwave, uncovered, on medium for about 1 ½ minutes or until melted.
— Stir in remaining ingredients, except for mushrooms.
— Arrange mushrooms, caps down, in sauce.
— Cover with glass lid or plastic wrap.
— Microwave on medium for 8 to 10 minutes or until hot.

(About 3 dozen mushrooms)

ACAPULCO BEAN DIP

1 can (1-lb.) kidney beans
1 jar (8-oz.) pasteurized cheese spread
¼ cup catsup
1 teaspoon chili powder
Dash of hot-pepper sauce

— Pour beans into a glass 1½-quart casserole.
— Mash beans with a fork.
— Add remaining ingredients and blend well.
— Microwave, covered, for about 2 minutes on high.
— Stir well.
— Microwave again, covered, for about 2 minutes on high, or until piping hot.
— Keep hot on a heated tray or a candle warmer.

(3 cups)

FRUITY CHEESE DIP

1 can (6-oz.) evaporated milk
1 cup shredded Cheddar cheese
1 cup shredded Swiss cheese
1 tablespoon prepared mustard
1 teaspoon Worcestershire sauce
Dash bottled hot pepper sauce
¼ cup finely chopped pimiento
6 to 8 firm fresh apples or pears, cut in wedges

— Mix milk, cheeses, mustard, Worcestershire sauce and pepper sauce in deep 2-quart glass mixing bowl.
— Microwave, uncovered, 6 minutes on medium or until cheese melts.
— Stir once after 3 minutes, and again when removed from oven.
— Stir in pimiento and serve hot, as a dip for apple or pear wedges.
— Dip can be reheated.

(3-4 cups)

HAM AND PINEAPPLE KABOBS

¼ cup honey
¼ cup firmly packed brown sugar
¼ cup barbecue sauce
24 1-inch cubes cooked ham
1 can (8-oz.) pineapple chunks, drained

— Combine honey and brown sugar in 2-cup glass measure.
— Microwave 1 minute on high, uncovered, or
— Stir to soften sugar.
— Microwave, uncovered, 30 seconds on high,
— Add barbecue sauce.
or until boiling.
— Alternate ham cubes and pineapple chunks on wooden picks.
— Dip in sauce.
— Arrange on paper towel-lined plate.
— Microwave, uncovered, 1 minute on high, or until hot.

(24 kabobs)

SHRIMP AND OLIVE DIP

1 can (10½-oz.) cream of shrimp soup, undiluted
1 package (8-oz.) cream cheese, cut into chunks
1 can (8-oz.) chopped ripe olives, drained
2 tablespoons lemon juice
1 teaspoon Worcestershire sauce

— Combine soup and cream cheese in deep glass 1-quart casserole.
— Microwave, covered, for 3 minutes on high.
— Remove and stir until cheese is well blended. Stir in remaining ingredients.
— Microwave, covered, for 1½ minutes, on high, or until hot.
— Serve as a dip with corn chips or potato chips.

(2½ cups)

CURRIED SHRIMP DIP

3 tablespoons butter
3 tablespoons flour
¼ teaspoon curry powder
¼ teaspoon salt
⅓ cup milk
⅓ cup dry white wine
1 package (8 oz.) frozen shrimp

— Place butter in 1½-quart glass casserole.
— Microwave, uncovered, on medium about 1 minute or until melted.
— Blend in flour, curry powder, salt.
— Stir in milk and wine; add shrimp.
— Cover with glass lid or plastic wrap.
— Microwave on high for 5 minutes.
— Stir; recover, and continue cooking on high for 4 to 5 minutes or until hot.

(Makes 1½ cups dip)

CREAMY FRENCH CHEESE FONDUE

1 ½ cups dry sherry
5 cups shredded process American Cheese
2 tablespoons cornstarch
¼ teaspoon dry mustard
⅛ teaspoon garlic salt
1 loaf French bread

— Pour sherry into 2-cup glass measure.
— Microwave, uncovered, on high for 4 to 5 minutes or until very hot but not boiling.
— Toss remaining ingredients together, except bread, in 3-quart glass mixing bowl.
— Pour hot sherry over cheese mixture; stir to blend well.
— Microwave on low for 3 minutes, uncovered.
— Stir and continue cooking for 3 to 4 minutes, uncovered, on low or until hot.
— Beat mixture until smooth.
— Serve hot with chunks of French bread.

(4 cups Fondue)

SHRIMP IN BACON

18 large shrimp, fresh or frozen
6 slices raw bacon cut in thirds
1 bottle Italian dressing

— Wrap each shrimp in a piece of bacon securing it with a toothpick.
— Place on paper towel-lined plate.
— Microwave, uncovered, 5 to 6 minutes on high, or until bacon is crisp and shrimp pink.

(18 servings)

ESCARGOTS

½ cup butter
1 tablespoon chopped parsley
1 tablespoon chopped shallots
½ teaspoon chopped garlic
½ tablespoon white wine
½ teaspoon lemon juice
1 can (4 ½ oz.) snails
Snail shells

— Mix butter, parsley, shallots, garlic, white wine and lemon juice in a small glass bowl.
— Microwave, uncovered, 1 minute.
— Arrange snails in 4 small deep dishes. Add buttered mixture to a quarter depth of the dish
— Microwave each dish, covered with waxed paper, 45 seconds on high, or until butter begins to bubble.
— Serve in snail shells.

(4 servings)

ITALIAN SHRIMP

½ cup butter
12 oz. frozen raw, peeled and deveined shrimp, defrosted
Garlic salt
Paprika
Parsley

— Place butter in 9-inch glass cake dish.
— Microwave on high, until butter melts.
— Add remaining ingredients. Stir to coat shrimp.
— Cover with plastic wrap.
— Microwave 3 to 5 minutes on high, or until shrimp are pink, stirring once.
— Serve with cocktail picks.
— NOTE: Small shrimp cook faster than large ones. Over cooking will toughen the shrimp.

(6 servings)

SPANISH OLIVES IN BACON BLANKETS

18 large suffed olives, drained
6 slices bacon, cut in thirds

— Wrap each olive in a piece of bacon and fasten with a toothpick. Place on paper towel-lined plate.
— Microwave, uncovered, 5 to 6 minutes on high, or until bacon is crisp.

(18 olives)

MUSHROOM AND EGG CANAPES

2 tablespoons butter or margarine
1 tablespoon finely minced onion
½ cup finely chopped mushrooms
2 hard-cooked eggs, finely chopped
1 tablespoon chopped parsley
½ teaspoon salt
18 toast rounds or crackers
¼ cup grated Cheddar cheese

— Put butter, onion, and mushrooms in a small glass mixing bowl.
— Microwave, uncovered, for 2 to 3 minutes on high, or just until mushrooms are soft.
— Stir in eggs, parsley, and salt.
— Spread 1 rounded teaspoon of mixture on each toast round.
— Sprinkle with grated Cheddar cheese.
— Arrange on a glass plate lined with paper towels.
— Microwave for about 30 seconds, on high, uncovered, long enough to melt the cheese.
— Serve warm.

(18 canapes)

CHEESY CANAPES

¼ cup grated Cheddar cheese
2 tablespoons light cream
2 tablespoons grated Parmeasan cheese
⅛ teaspoon Worcestershire sauce
⅛ teaspoon hot-pepper sauce
1 tablespoon sesame seeds
24 rounds of toast or crisp crackers
Chopped parsley

— Combine all ingredients except crackers and parsley in a small glass bowl. Blend with an electric mixer until smooth.
— Spread 1 teaspoon of the mixture on each of the toast rounds or crackers.
— Arrange on a platter lined with paper towels.
— Microwave for 15 to 20 seconds, uncovered, on high, or just until mixture is warm and cheese is melted.
— Top with parsley; serve warm.

(24 canapes)

ORIENTAL RUMAKI

1 lb. extra thin slices bacon, cut in half
2 (5-oz.) cans water chestnuts, drained and cut in half
1 lb. chicken livers, cut in half
1 cup soy sauce
½ cup dark brown sugar, firmly packed
⅛ teaspoon ginger

— Wrap a piece of bacon around a half piece of water chestnut and chicken liver half.
— Fasten with toothpick, set aside.
— Combine soy sauce, dark brown sugar and ginger in a shallow 2-quart glass baking dish.
— Mix well.
— Marinate bacon wrapped chicken livers for 2 hours.

— Drain excess liquid.
— Place 17 Rumaki on a double layer of paper toweling in a shallow, heat-resistant, non-metallic baking dish.
— Microwave on medium, uncovered, for 15 to 16 minutes, covered with a paper towel.
— Repeat until all cooked.

(50 Rumaki)

SWISS FONDUE

4 cups shredded Swiss cheese
¼ cup flour
¼ teaspoon salt
¼ teaspoon nutmeg
Dash of pepper
2 cups dry white wine
2 tablespoons Kirsch
1 loaf French bread, cut into cubes

— In a 1½-quart glass dish combine cheese, flour, salt, nutmeg, and pepper. Toss lightly to coat cheese with flour. Stir in wine.
— Microwave, covered, for 3 to 4 minutes on high, stirring during last 2 minutes of cooking. Stir well after removing from oven to finish melting cheese.
— Stir in Kirsch.
— Serve with cubes of French bread.
— If fondue cools during eating time, return to oven for 1 minute to reheat on high.

(6 servings)

SHRIMP COCKTAIL

½ lb. raw shrimp
2 tablespoons butter
½ clove garlic, chopped fine
3 tablespoons white wine
Salt
Chopped parsley
¼ teaspoon paprika

— Remove shells and veins from shrimp.
— For small shrimp, take off head. For large shrimp, cut into 1-inch pieces.
— Rinse in cold water and set aside.
— In a shallow 2-qt. glass baking dish, put butter, garlic and white wine.
— Microwave, uncovered, for 8 minutes on high.
— Stir mixture and place shrimp in dish without stirring.
— Cover with wax paper and Microwave for 2 minutes on high.

— Stir shrimp, and Microwave, covered, for 2 minutes or until shrimp are pink in color and just tender.
— Pour shrimp and sauce into cocktail glasses.
— Season with salt, parsley and paprika.
— Chill and serve.

(3 servings)

CRAB CANAPES

1 cup fresh cooked or canned crab meat
1 tablespoon chopped celery
⅓ cup mayonnaise
½ teaspoon prepared mustard
½ teaspoon Worcestershire sauce
1 teaspoon grated horseradish
¼ cup whipped cream
6 slices toast
½ cup grated Parmesan cheese

— Flake crab into a bowl.
— In another bowl mix in celery, mayonnaise, mustard, Worcestershire sauce, horseradish and whipped cream.
— Cut toast into quarters.
— Spread paper napkin on a plate and arrange 2 quarters of bread on it.
— Place 1 teaspoon crab mixture on each slice.
— Sprinkle with Parmesan cheese and Microwave, uncovered, 1 minute, on high.

TUNA BALLS

1 can (6 oz.) tuna
1 egg, beaten
1 cup bread crumbs
¼ cup chopped onion
½ can (10½ oz.) consomme (concentrated)
¼ cup mayonnaise
2 tablespoons chopped parsley
1 tablespoon mustard (paste)
1 teaspoon mixed spice (for meat)
1 cup crushed crackers

— In a 2-quart mixing bowl flake tuna and combine with beaten egg, bread crumbs, chopped onion, consomme, mayonnaise, chopped parsley, mustard paste and mixed spice.
— Refrigerate the mixture 15 minutes.
— Shape the mixture into ½-inch balls and roll in cracker crumbs.
— Place the balls on a wax paper lined plate.
— Microwave 3 minutes, uncovered, on high.

(6 servings)

BAKED CHERRYSTONE CLAMS

1 dozen cherrystone clams
2 tablespoons butter or margarine
¼ cup finely chopped onion
1 clove crushed garlic
1 egg, slightly beaten
¼ cup seasoned bread crumbs
⅛ teaspoon dried oregano leaves
⅓ cup seasoned dry bread crumbs
2 tablespoons butter or margarine

— Remove clams from half shell and chop coarsely.
— Set clams and shells aside.
— In a medium-sized, glass mixing bowl place 2 tablespoons butter.
— Microwave, uncovered on high for 30 seconds or until melted.
— Add onion and garlic.
— Microwave, uncovered, on high 3 minutes or until onion is tender.
— Add egg, the ¼ cup bread crumbs, chopped clams and oregano to onion mixture.
— Spoon mixture into reserved shells.
— Place shells on a heat-resistant, non-metallic serving platter.
— In a small bowl, heat the 2 tablespoons butter on high for 15 seconds.
— Stir in the ⅓ cup dry bread crumbs. Sprinkle buttered bread crumbs on top of clam mixture.
— Microwave, uncovered, on high for 5 minutes or until heated through.

(4 servings)

CRAB MEAT SUPREME

¾ lb. fresh cooked or canned crab meat
½ cup chopped celery
3½ tablespoons mayonnaise
½ teaspoon curry powder
Salt and pepper
6 corn toaster muffins
½ cup potato chip crumbs
6 slices Swiss cheese

— Mix crab meat with celery in a small bowl; set aside.
— Stir together mayonnaise and curry powder; mix with crab.
— Season to taste with salt and pepper.
— Place each toaster muffin on a paper plate.
— Pile crab mixture onto muffins.
— Sprinkle with potato chip crumbs; top with a slice of cheese.
— Microwave, uncovered, one at a time, for 1 to 1½ minutes, or until cheese is melted.

(6 servings)

SCALLOP EN COQUILLE

1 lb. scallops
1 lb. mushrooms
5 tablespoons butter
2 tablespoons lemon juice
1 cup white wine
¼ teaspoon savory
1 bay leaf
Dash of salt and pepper
3 tablespoons flour
1 cup cream
½ cup toasted bread crumbs
Dash of paprika

— Cut scallops into quarters and set aside.
— Wash mushrooms in cold water and drain.
— Cut into thin slices and place on a glass plate.
— Mix 2 tablespoons butter and lemon juice with sliced mushrooms.
— Microwave 1 minute, uncovered, on high, stir and cook again to evaporate moisture for 1 minute, uncovered, on high.
— Put white wine, savory, bay leaf, salt and pepper in a shallow 2-quart glass baking dish and mix.
— Place scallops in the mixture and Microwave, uncovered, on high for 3 minutes.

(8 servings)

VARIATIONS ON A STUFFED MUSHROOM BASIC RECIPE

8 oz. fresh, uniform size mushrooms, cleaned
1 small onion, finely chopped
2 tablespoons butter or margarine
¼ cup seasoned bread crumbs

— Remove stems from mushrooms and chop finely.
— Combine chopped stems, onion, and butter in small bowl.
— Microwave, uncovered, 1 to 2 minutes on high, or until onions are transparent and mixture is hot, stirring once.
— Spoon mixture into caps with teaspoon. Place 10 or 12 on plate.
— Depending on size of mushrooms, Microwave, uncovered, 1 to 2 minutes, 30 seconds on high, watching carefully not to over cook.

(6-8 servings)

CRAB OR LOBSTER

1 can (6½-oz.) crab or lobster, drained and flaked
1 tablespoon mayonnaise
1 package (3-oz.) cream cheese, softened
½ teaspoon lemon juice
Dash prepared mustard

— Mix above ingredients well and fill caps.
— Garnish with parsley.
—Heat as above.

(6-8 servings)

BLEU CHEESE

¼ cup crumbled bleu cheese
Basic filling

— Mix 1 tablespoon cheese into basic filling.
— Fill caps and top with remaining cheese.
— Heat as above.

(6-8 servings)

MEXICAN FIESTA

¼ pound crumbled ground beef, cooked and drained
1 tablespoon taco sauce
1 small tomato, chopped
Grated cheddar cheese

— Combine hamburger and taco sauce in a small bowl with basic filling with crumbs.
— Fill mushroom caps.
— Spread chopped tomatos on filling, top with grated cheese.
— Heat as above, or until mushrooms are hot and cheese melts.

(6-8 servings)

CHESTNUT AND CELERY

½ teaspoon cream sherry
Basic filling
16 slices celery, ⅛-inch thick
5 chestnuts, cut in triangles

— Add sherry to basic filling after heating.
— Fill caps.
—Garnish with celery slices and chestnut triangles.
— Heat as above.

(6-8 servings)

POLYNESIAN

1 can (8-oz.) pineapple chunks, drained
1 can (5-oz.) chicken
2 tablespoons mayonnaise
½ teaspoon lemon juice
16 walnut halves

— Combine pineapple, chicken, mayonnaise and lemon juice. Fill caps.
— Garnish with walnut halves.
— Heat as above.

(6-8 servings)

FLORENTINE

1 package (3-oz.) cream cheese
1 can (8-oz.) spinach, drained and chopped
2 slices bacon, cooked and crumbled

— In a small bowl, Microwave, uncovered, on high for 30 seconds to soften cream cheese.
— Mix in spinach.
— Fill mushroom caps.
— Garnish with small bacon pieces.
— Heat as above.

(6-8 servings)

BACON

1 package (3-oz.) cream cheese
½ teaspoon finely chopped onion
6 slices bacon, cooked and crumbled

— In a small bowl, Microwave, uncovered, on high for 30 seconds to soften cream cheese.
— Mix in onion.
— Form into ½-inch balls.
— Roll balls in crumbled bacon.
— Fill caps and heat as above.

(6-8 servings)

ITALIANO

½ lb. ground sausage, cooked and drained
2 tablespoons catsup
⅛ teaspoon oregano
Dash garlic powder
2 tablespoons fresh parsley, torn in small pieces
Grated mozzarella cheese

— Mix cooked sausage, catsup, oregano and garlic powder in glass measure or small bowl.
— Microwave, uncovered, 1 minute on high.
— Fill caps.
— Sprinkle parsley on filling.
— Top with grated cheese.
— Heat as above, or until mushrooms are hot and cheese melts.

(6-8 servings)

STROGANOFF

¼ lb. crumbled ground beef, cooked and drained
1 packet (18-oz.) single serving instant beef broth, diluted with 1 ½ teaspoons water
2 tablespoons dairy sour cream

— Combine ground beef and beef broth in a small glass bowl.
— Microwave, uncovered, 1 minute on high.
— Stir in sour cream.
— Fill caps.
— Heat as above.

(6-8 servings)

HOT BEVERAGES

*Microwave beverages on high.

Beverage	Serving Size	Cooking Time
Water or Milk for tea or instant beverages	1 (6 oz.) cup	2 to 2½ minutes
	2 (6 oz.) cups	3 to 3½ minutes
	4 (6 oz.) cups	5 to 6½ minutes
	1 (8 oz.) mug	3 to 3½ minutes
	2 (8 oz.) mugs	4 to 5½ minutes
	4 (8 oz.) mugs	8 to 9½ minutes
Reheating beverages like coffee and tea	1 (6 oz.) cup	1½ to 2 minutes
	2 (6 oz.) cups	2 to 2½ minutes
	4 (6 oz.) cups	4 to 5 minutes
	1 (8 oz.) mug	2 to 2½ minutes
	2 (8 oz.) mugs	3 to 3½ minutes
	4 (8 oz.) mugs	6 to 7 minutes
Milk, hot chocolate or hot eggnog	1-quart glass pitcher	7 to 8 minutes

***high — 100% power : medium — 60% power : low — 30% power.

BEVERAGES

COOKING HINTS

You may mix, heat and serve beverages in the same container. Heat items that tend to boil over in a deep uncovered container. If a boilover does occur, open the oven door and it will stop instantly. Use a larger than needed container when preparing beverages containing milk, since milk does boil over rather quickly.

This chapter does not include recipes for everyday beverages such as tea and coffee (times for these beverages are included in following chart), but presents festive drinks like Irish Coffee and Hot Buttered Rum. The chart below lists heating times and number of servings for all types of hot beverages. Heating time may vary from oven to oven.

AVERAGE COOKING TIME FOR DRINKS

Number of cups	Cooking time
1 cup	1 minute to 1 minute, 30 seconds
2 cups	2 minutes to 2 minutes, 40 seconds
3 cups	3 minutes, 30 seconds to 4 minutes
4 cups	4 minutes, 30 seconds to 5 minutes
5 cups	5 minutes, 40 seconds to 6 minutes, 40 seconds
6 cups	6 minutes, 40 seconds to 7 minutes, 40 seconds
7 cups	8 minutes to 9 minutes
8 cups	9 minutes to 10 minutes
9 cups	10 minutes to 12 minutes
10 cups	12 minutes to 14 minutes

ANDRE'S MULLED WINE

1 cup sugar
2 pieces (1 inch each) stick cinnamon
1 lemon, sliced
24 whole cloves
½ cup water
4 cups orange juice
1 quart Burgundy wine
lemon or pineapple slices

— Combine sugar, cinnamon, lemon, and cloves with ½ cup water in a deep 3-quart glass casserole.
— Microwave for 2 minutes, uncovered, on high.
— Add orange juice and Burgundy.
— Microwave, uncovered, for 5 minutes on high.
— Garnish with lemon or pineapple slices, if desired.

(8-10 servings)

TOM AND JERRY

2 egg whites
1 cup powdered sugar
2 egg yolks
½ teaspoon vanilla
3 cups water
½ cup rum
½ cup brandy
Nutmeg

— Place egg whites in small mixing bowl.
— Beat with rotary beater until soft peaks form.
— Fold in ½ cup powdered sugar.
— Beat egg yolks with remaining sugar until thickened.
— Fold in beaten egg white mixture and vanilla.
— Cover and refrigerate until serving time.
— Fill four 8-oz. glass mugs ¾ full of water.
— Microwave on high for 8 to 9 minutes, uncovered, or until hot and bubbly.
— Stir 1 heaping tablespoon batter, 1½ tablespoons rum and 1½ tablespoons brandy into each mug of water.
— Sprinkle with nutmeg; serve.

(About four 1-mug servings)

HOT TODDY

1 teaspoon sugar
1 piece (1-inch) stick cinnamon
1 slice lemon, studded with 2 cloves
½ cup water
2 ounces bourbon

— Combine sugar, cinnamon, and lemon slice with ½ cup water in a 1-cup glass measuring cup.
— Microwave for 5 minutes on high, uncovered.
— Meantime, place bourbon in a serving cup or mug.
— Remove hot mixture from oven and pour over bourbon. Stir and serve.

(1 serving)

NEW ENGLAND TODDY

1 tablespoon brown sugar
¾ cup water
¼ teaspoon lemon juice
1 jigger (1½-oz.) light rum
1 teaspoon butter
Nutmeg

— Dissolve sugar in water and lemon juice in mug or cup.
— Microwave 1 to 2 minutes on high, uncovered, or until piping hot.
— Add rum.
— Float butter on top.
— Sprinkle with nutmeg.

(1 serving)

HOT BUTTERED RUM

1 tablespoon brown sugar
1 tablespoon water
⅔ cup apple cider
1 1-inch piece cinnamon stick
1½ oz. rum
1 teaspoon butter or margarine
Ground nutmeg

— Dissolve sugar in water and apple cider in a heat-resistant, non-metallic mug or cup. Add cinnamon stick.
— Microwave, uncovered, on high for 1½ to 2 minutes or until it comes to a boil.
— Stir in rum.
— Top with butter and a sprinkling of ground nutmeg.

(1 serving)

GREAT LAKES CRANBERRY PUNCH

1½ cups cranberry juice cocktail
4 whole cloves
1 piece (2-inch) stick cinnamon
3 tablespoons sugar
1 can (6 oz.) frozen lemonade concentrate, thawed; or frozen orangeade plus 1 tablespoon lemon juice
3 orange slices, cut in half
6 maraschino cherries

— In a 1-quart glass measuring cup, combine cranberry juice, cloves and cinnamon stick.
— Microwave 5 minutes, uncovered, on high.
— Cover and let stand for 1 minute.
— Take out spices.
— Add sugar, stirring until dissolved, and add lemonade.
— Microwave 3 minutes, covered, on high.
— Serve hot, garnished with half an orange slice and a maraschino cherry on a toothpick.

(6 servings)

SPICED CIDER

1 cup water
¼ cup firmly packed brown sugar
2 sticks cinnamon
1 teaspoon whole cloves
½ teaspoon mace
¼ teaspoon nutmeg
1 quart cider

— Combine water, sugar and spices in 2-cup glass measure. Microwave, uncovered, 10 to 12 minutes on high, until mixture is reduced to ½ cup.
— Strain into a deep 1½-quart bowl or pitcher.
— Stir in cider.
— Microwave 4 to 5 minutes on high, or until cider is hot.

(6-8 servings)

RUM AND EGG NOG

4 egg whites
3 tablespoons sugar
4 egg yolks
½ cup sugar
¼ teaspoon salt
3 cups milk
1 teaspoon rum or vanilla
Grated chocolate
Nutmeg

— Beat egg whites until foamy in quart glass bowl.
— Slowly beat in 3 tablespoon sugar.
— Continue beating until stiff and glossy. Set aside.
— Combine egg yolks, ½ cup sugar and salt in a deep 2-quart bowl.
— Beat until thick and lemon-colored.
— Stir in milk and rum or vanilla.
— Microwave, uncovered, 4 minutes on high, or until mixture is hot but not boiling.
— Carefully fold egg whites into milk mixture until well blended.
— Fill serving cups ½ to ¾ full.
— Top with grated chocolate and nutmeg.

(Egg nog cannot be reheated, as egg white will cook.)

(8-12 servings)

WASHINGTON APPLE NOG

2 egg yolks
¼ cup sugar
½ teaspoon salt
½ teaspoon ground cinnamon
Dash of ground nutmeg
⅔ cup apple juice
3 cups milk
2 egg whites
½ cup whipped cream

— Place egg yolks in a deep 2-quart bowl. Beat lightly with a fork.
— Stir in sugar, salt, cinnamon, nutmeg, and apple juice until well blended. Stir in milk.
— Microwave, uncovered, for 5 minutes on high.
— Meantime, beat egg whites in a 2-quart mixing bowl or pitcher.
— Remove milk mixture from oven and pour quickly over egg whites, stirring rapidly.
— Top each serving with a mound of whipped cream.

(5-6 servings)

O'BRIEN'S IRISH COFFEE

1 teaspoon packed brown sugar
4 to 6-oz. strong black coffee, brewed
1 ½ oz. Irish whiskey
1 rounded tablespoon whipped cream

— Dissolve sugar in black coffee in coffee mug or Irish coffee goblet.
— Microwave, uncovered, 1 to 2 minutes on high, or until hot.
— Add Irish whiskey.
— Top with whipped cream.

(1 serving)

COFFEE CREAM PUNCH

6 tablespoons instant coffee, or 4 cups brewed coffee
4 cups water
1 ½ pints vanilla ice cream
Ground nutmeg
Cinnamon stick, if desired

— In a deep 2-qt. glass bowl or pitcher, combine coffee and 4 cups water. (Omit water if using brewed coffee.)
— Microwave for 4 minutes, uncovered on high.
— Put ice cream in a deep 3-qt. glass bowl, and pour hot coffee over.
— Stir until ice cream melts.
— Pour into cups and sprinkle nutmeg on each serving.
— Add cinnamon stick if desired.

(8 servings)

HOT SPICED CRANBERRY PUNCH

1 ½ cups cranberry juice cocktail
4 whole cloves
1 piece (2 inches) stick cinnamon
1 ½ cups water
3 tablespoons sugar
1 can (6-oz.) frozen lemonade concentrate, thawed
3 orange slices, cut in half
6 maraschino cherries

— Combine cranberry juice, cloves, and cinnamon stick with 1 ½ cups water in 1-quart glass measuring cup.
— Microwave, uncovered, for 5 minutes on high.
— Cover and let stand 1 minute.
— Remove spices.
— Stir in sugar until dissolved. Blend in lemonade.
— Microwave, uncovered, for 3 minutes on high.
— Serve hot, garnished with half an orange slice and a maraschino cherry on a toothpick

(6 servings)

DEHYDRATED AND CANNED SOUPS

Soup	Amount	Setting	Cooking Time
Cup O' Soup			
any kind	1 envelope	high	2 to 2½ minutes
1½-oz. pkg.	2 envelopes	high	3 to 3½ minutes
with 4 envelopes	4 envelopes	high	6 to 7 minutes
Soup mix			
without rice or			
noodles	1 envelope	high	12 to 15 minutes
2¾-oz. pkg.			
with 2 envelopes			
with rice or noodles			
3½-oz. pkg.	1 envelope	high	7 to 8 minutes
with 2 envelopes		medium	5 to 6 minutes
5-oz. pkg.		high	9 to 10 minutes
		medium	10 to 12 minutes
Canned Soup,			
Diluted, Broth	10¾-oz.	high	2½ to 3 minutes
Tomato, Cream			
Noodle or	10¾-oz.	high	4 to 5½ minutes
Vegetable	26-oz.	high	7 to 8 minutes
Mushroom	10¾-oz.	medium	7 to 8 minutes
Canned Soup,			
undiluted,			
Chunky Vegetable,			
Noodle or	10¾-oz.	high	2 to 3 minutes
Split Pea and Ham	19-oz.	high	5 to 7 minutes

***high — 100% power : medium — 60% power : low — 30% power.

SOUPS

COOKING HINTS

An individual serving or a whole recipe can be made quickly and easily in your new Microwave Oven. Soups can be made and served in the same container so there are fewer dishes to wash. There are recipes in this section that all members of the family will enjoy and they are so easy to make that any family member can become the chef. Try a hot soup on a cold winter's evening or an unusual cold soup on a warm summer's day — all of these recipes are included in the following pages.

Hearty homemade soups containing beef should be cooked slowly to develop flavor and tenderize the meat, while many other soups are quick and do not require such long cooking times. Your own favorite soups containing meats should be cooked on low.

Milk-based soups or sauces should be prepared in a dish twice as deep as your ingredients because of possible over-boiling.

Soups are generally heated uncovered.

HOW TO COOK DEHYDRATED SOUP

- Pour specified amount of water noted on package into glass casserole or large mug.
- Cover containers with glass lids, saucers or plastic wrap.
- Microwave on high until liquid is hot and bubbly.
- Stir in dry mix and continue cooking if package specified that mix is added after water boils.
- Microwave most soups on high until hot.
- Microwave soups with dehydrated rice or noodles on medium until rice or noodles are tender.
- Let stand, covered, 5 minutes before serving.

HOW TO HEAT CANNED SOUP

- Pour soup into a deep 1½-quart glass casserole.
- Add milk or water as directed on can.
- Cover with glass lid or plastic wrap.
- Microwave on high until hot — except mushroom soup whch heats on medium.
- Stir when taken from oven.
- Let stand, covered, 3 minutes before serving.

SOUP	SETTING	MINUTES
DILUTED		
Broth		
10¾-oz.	High	3 to 4
Tomato, Cream Noodle or Vegetable		
10¾-oz.	High	5 to 6
26-oz.	High	8 to 9
Mushroom		
10¾-oz.	Medium	7 to 8
UNDILUTED		
Chunky Vegetable, Noodle or Split Pea and Ham		
10¾-oz.	High	2½ to 3½
19-oz.	High	5 to 7

CREAM OF MUSHROOM SOUP

2 cups chopped fresh mushrooms
½ teaspoon onion powder
⅛ teaspoon garlic powder
⅛ teaspoon white pepper
¼ teaspoon salt
2½ cups chicken broth
1 cup heavy cream

— Combine mushrooms, seasonings, and broth in a deep 2-quart glass casserole.
— Microwave for about 4 minutes, uncovered, on high, stirring after 2 minutes.
— Stir in cream.
— Microwave for 1 minute, uncovered, on high, or until piping hot.

(6 servings)

MEXICAN CHILI CHOWDER

¾ lb. ground beef
1 medium onion, chopped
1 clove garlic, chopped
2 tablespoons chopped green pepper
1 can (1-lb.) peeled plum tomatoes
2 cups tomato juice
1 teaspoon salt
⅛ teaspoon sugar
2 teaspoons chili powder, or to taste

— Place beef, onion, garic, and green pepper in a deep 2-quart glass ovenproof casserole.
— Microwave, covered, for about 4 minutes on high.
— Remove casserole and stir to break up beef.
— Add tomatoes, including liquid from can, stirring to break up tomatoes.
— Add remaining ingredients and mix well.
— Microwave, covered, for about 3 minutes, on high or until piping hot.

(6 servings)

TROPICAL FRUIT SOUP

2 (10-oz.) pckages frozen raspberries, in pouches
2 cups chicken broth
1 ¼ cups boiling water
½ cup pineapple juice
2 tablespoons sugar
½ cup sour cream

— To thaw raspberries, slit pouches and place in Microwave Oven on medium for 9 to 10 minutes or until completely defrosted.
— Pour thawed berries and juice ino the container of a blender and blend until smooth. Berries may also be pressed through a sieve or food mill.
— In a large glass mixing bowl, combine chicken broth, water, pineapple juice and sugar; stir until dissolved.
— Microwave, uncovered, on high 2 minutes.
— Stir in raspberries.
— Chill several hours or overnight.
— Serve garnished with a spoonful of sour cream.

(4-6 servings)

CANADIAN CHEESE SOUP

1 cup water
1 large potato, finely chopped
1 large onion, finely chopped
¼ cup carrots, thinly sliced
¼ cup celery, finely chopped
2 cups chicken broth
1 cup grated sharp Cheddar cheese
½ cup cream
2 tablespoons chopped parsley

— In a deep, 3-quart casserole place 1 cup water, potatoes, onion, carrots and celery.
— Microwave, covered, on high for 8 minutes or until vegetables are tender.
— Add remaining ingredients, except parsley, and heat on medium, covered, 7 minutes or until soup bubbles and cheese has melted. Stir occasionally.
— Serve garnished with chopped parsley.

(4-6 servings)

FRENCH ONION SOUP

2 tablespoons butter
3 medium onions, thinly sliced
3 cans (10½-oz.) condensed beef broth
2¼ cups water
Salt
6-8 French bread slices, toasted
Grated Parmesan cheese

— Combine butter and onion in a 3-quart glass casserole.
— Cover.
— Microwave 8 minutes on high, or until onions are transparent, stirring after 4 minutes.
— Stir in broth and water.
— Cover and Microwave 8 to 10 minutes on high.
— Salt to taste.
— Place bread slices on top and cover with Parmesan cheese.
— Serve immediately.

(6-8 servings)

VICHYSSOISE

4 servings prepared instant mashed potatoes
1 teaspoon instant chicken bouillon
1 cup hot water
1 cup heavy cream
1 ½ teaspoons Worcestershire sauce
1 teaspon onion powder
⅛ teaspoon white pepper
½ to 1 teaspoon chopped chives

— Prepare potatoes according to package directions using a deep 2-quart glass mixing bowl.
— In another glass mixing bowl, mix instant bouillon with hot water and blend with cream, Worcestershire sauce, onion powder and pepper.
— Blend into instant mashed potatoes with wire whip to make a smooth soup.
— Microwave, uncovered, 4 to 5 minutes on high, or until hot and bubbly, stirring after 2 minutes.
— Garnish with chives.
— Serve hot or cold

(4 servings)

OYSTER STEW

1 quart light cream
1 pint fresh oysters, drained, reserve liquid
½ teaspoon onion salt
½ teaspoon Worcestershire sauce
⅛ teaspoon pepper
6 tablespoons butter or margarine

— Combine light cream and reserved oyster liquid in deep glass 2-quart casserole.
— Cover.
— Microwave 10 to 12 minutes on high, or until mixture is almost boiling.
— Add oysters, salt, Worcestershire sauce and pepper.
— Do not cover.
— Microwave 2 minutes on high, or until oysters swell and edges begin to curl.
—Place 1 tablespoon of butter in each soup bowl.
— Ladle stew into bowls.
— Serve immediately.

(6 servings)

SEAFOOD BISQUE

4 cups water
1 can (8 oz.) tomato sauce
½ cup finely chopped onion
1 clove garlic, finely chopped
2 tablespoons dried parsley flakes
2½ teaspoons salt
1 teaspoon lemon juice
¼ teaspoon curry powder
¼ teaspoon pepper
1 lb. fish fillets, cut into 2 inch pieces
1 package (12 oz.) frozen shrimp, thawed
6 ounces frozen crab or lobster meat, thawed
1 pint oysters or clams

— Pour water into deep 4-quart glass casserole.
— Cover with glass lid or pastic wrap.
— Microwave on high for 10 to 12 minutes or until bubbly.
— Stir in remaining ingredients in order given. Recover and continue cooking on high for about 12 minutes.
— Stir and continue cooking on high for 8 to 10 minutes or until seafood is done.
— Let stand, covered, 5 minutes before serving.

(10-12 servings)

BOUILLABAISSE

1 tablespoon butter
1 small onion, finely chopped
1 stem celery, finely chopped
1 carrot finely grated
1 can (13¾-oz.) chicken broth
2 cans (6-oz. each) shrimp, lobster or crab, drained and mashed fine with a fork
⅛ teaspoon thyme
1 cup heavy cream
¼ cup dry sherry
½ teaspoon salt
¼ teaspoon pepper

— Combine butter, onion, celery and carrot in a deep glass 2-quart casserole.
— Microwave 4 to 5 minutes, on high, uncovered, or until onion is transparent, stirring once.
— Stir in chicken broth, seafood and thyme.
— Microwave 4 to 6 minutes, on high, uncovered, or until mixture boils.
— Strain mixture, pressing as much of the seafood as possible through sieve.
— Return soup to the casserole.
— Stir in cream, sherry, salt and pepper.
— Microwave on low 5 to 6 minutes.

(4-6 servings)

CLAM CHOWDER

2 slices bacon
1 can (7-oz.) minced clams, with liquid
1 large potato, peeled and cubed
½ cup water
¼ cup minced onion
1 can (13-oz.) evaporated milk
Salt and pepper
1 tablespoon butter
Crumbled crackers

— Put bacon slices in a deep glass 2-quart casserole.
— Cover with a piece of paper towel.
— Microwave for 1½ to 2 minutes on high, or until bacon is crisp.
— Remove paper towel and bacon, leaving drippings in casserole.
— Crumble bacon into bits and reserve.
— Add clams, clam liquid, potato, onion, and ½ cup water to casserole.
— Microwave, covered, for 8 minutes on high, or until potatoes are tender.
— Stir every 3 minutes.
— Add milk, crumbled bacon, salt and pepper to taste, and butter.
— Microwave, covered, for 2 to 3 minutes, on high, or just until mixture comes to a boil.
— Let stand 2 minutes. Serve with crumbled crackers if desired.

(3-4 servings)

RUSSIAN BORSCHT

½ lb. beef stew meat, cut in ½-inch cubes
1 onion, thinly sliced
1 clove garlic, pressed or finely chopped
7 cups water
1 bay leaf
1 teaspoon dried thyme
½ teaspoon pepper
2 cups finely shredded cabbage
1 carrot, thinly sliced
1 turnip, thinly sliced
2 medium tomatoes, peeled and chopped
1 tablespoon salt
2 large beets, cooked, peeled, cut in julienne strips
1 carton (8-oz.) dairy sour cream

— Combine meat, onion, garlic, water, bay leaf, thyme and pepper in a deep 3-quart glass casserole.
— Cover.
— Microwave 10 minutes on high.
— Reduce setting. Microwave 30 minutes on medium.
— Stir in cabbage, carrot, turnips, tomatoes and salt. Cover.
— Microwave 10 minutes on medium.
— Add beets. Cover.
— Microwave 5 minutes on medium, or until beets are heated through and vegetables tender crisp.
— Let stand 5 minutes, covered.
— Remove bay leaf before serving.
— Top each serving with sour cream.

NOTE: Beets lose their color if allowed to stand in soup. To make ahead, remove soup from oven before adding beets. Cool and refrigerate. Before serving, reheat, add beets and finish cooking.

(4-6 servings)

EGG DROP SOUP

2 cans (13¾-oz.) chicken broth
1 tablespoon cornstarch
2 tablespoons water
1 can (4-oz.) water chestnuts, diced
2 scallions, chopped, including green tops
2 eggs, slightly beaten
Salt to taste

— Put chicken broth in a deep 1½-quart glass casserole or mixing bowl.
— Microwave, covered, for 4 minutes, on high.
— Combine cornstarch with 2 tablespoons water.
— Stir in hot broth.
— Stir in water chestnuts and scallions.
— Microwave, covered, for about 2 minutes, on high, or until mixture is clear and piping hot.
— Remove and quickly stir in beaten eggs.
— Taste and season with salt, if necessary.

(4 servings)

SHRIMP VERACRUZ

1 lb. jumbo fresh shrimp, shelled and deveined
1 large onion, coarsely chopped
1 green pepper, oarsely chopped
2 cloves crushed garlic
3 tablespoons oil
1 can (8-oz.) tomato sauce
½ teaspoon oregano
¼ teaspoon cumin
½ teaspoon salt
¼ cup dry white wine or water
Dash hot sauce
2 tablespoons parsley, chopped

— In a deep glass 2-quart casserole dish, stir together onion, pepper, garlic and oil.
— Microwave 3 minutes, uncovered, on high, stirring once.
— Add tomato sauce, oregano, cumin, salt, white wine or water.
— Microwave, uncovered, 5 minutes on high, stirring once.
— Season to taste with hot sauce and add shrimp, spooning sauce to cover shrimp.
— Microwave, uncovered, 5 minutes on high, or just until shrimp are pink.
— Garnish with parsley and serve with hot rice or noodles.

(4 servings)

CREAM OF CHICKEN SOUP

1 can (10½-oz.) condensed cream of chicken soup, undiluted
1 soup can milk
1 pimiento, diced
¼ cup chopped ripe olives
½ teaspoon turmeric

— Combine all ingredients in a glass 1-quart ovenproof bowl or measuring cup.
— Microwave for about 3 minutes, on high or until piping hot.
— Stir well before serving.

(4 servings)

CREAME SUDANESE

1 can (10 ½-oz. condensed cream of tomato soup, undiluted
1 can (10 ½-oz.) condensed pea soup, undiluted
½ cup heavy cream
3 tablespoons sherry

— Place both soups and 1 ½ soup cans of water in a deep glass 1 ½-quart ovenproof bowl. Stir to blend well.
— Microwave for 2 minutes, on high, uncovered.
— Stir in cream and sherry.
— Microwave, uncovered, for 1 ½ minutes, or until piping hot.

(6 servings)

GAZPACHO

3 cups tomato juice or vegetable juice cocktail
2 beef bouillon cubes, crumbled or 2 envelopes instant beef broth
2 medium-sized ripe tomatoes, peeled and chopped
¼ cup chopped green pepper
¼ cup chopped onion
¼ cup wine or cider vinegar
2 tablespoons olive oil
1 teaspoon salt
1 teaspoon Worcestershire sauce
Few drops Tabasco sauce, to taste
1 clove garlic, peeled and crushed
Croutons
Chopped tomato
Chopped cucumber
Chopped onion
Chopped green pepper

— Place tomato juice in a non-metallic soup tureen or deep, 2 ½-quart, heat-resistant, non-metallic casserole and heat, uncovered, on high 6 minutes or until boiling.
— Stir in bouillon cubes until dissolved.
— Add the 2 chopped tomatoes, the green pepper, onion, vinegar, oil, salt, Worcestershire sauce, Tabasco sauce and garlic.
— Microwave, uncovered, on high 2 minutes.
— Serve accompanied by croutons and chopped tomato, cucumber, onion and green pepper.
— Serve either hot or cold.

(8 servings)

SPLIT PEA SOUP

2 quarts boiling water
1 pound split peas
1 ham bone or hock
1 small onion, sliced
5 peppercorns
1 cup diced cooked ham
½ cup diced potato
⅓ cup sliced carrot
Salt and pepper

— Combine ham bone, peas, water, onion and peppercorns in a deep glass 4-quart casserole.
— Cover and Microwave 25 minutes, on high, or until peas are tender, stirring after 15 minutes.
— Remove ham bone. Cut away meat and add to soup.
— Add diced ham, potatoes and carrots.
— Cover and Microwave 15 to 20 minutes, on high, or until vegetables are tender-crisp.
— Taste for seasoning and correct for salt and pepper.

(8 servings)

HOT SANDWICHES

Sandwich	Amount	Setting	Cooking Time
Meat Filling Type; made with cooked ingredients	1 sandwich	high	1 to 1½ minutes
	2 sandwiches	high	2 to 2½ minutes
	4 sandwiches	high	3½ to 4 minutes
Cheese Fillings	1 sandwich	medium	45 to 60 seconds
	2 sandwiches	medium	1 to 1½ minutes
	4 sandwiches	medium	2½ to 3 minutes
Reuben Sandwiches	1 sandwich	high	1 to 1½ minutes
	2 sandwiches	high	1½ to 2 minutes
	4 sandwiches	high	3 to 3½ minutes
Hamburger, cooked pattie in bun	1 hamburger	high	15 to 20 seconds
	2 hamburgers	high	25 to 30 seconds
	4 hamburgers	high	45 to 50 seconds
	6 hamburgers	high	1 to 1½ minutes
Hot Dog in bun	1 hot dog	high	30 to 35 seconds
	2 hot dogs	high	45 to 50 seconds
	4 hot dogs	high	1 to 1½ minutes
	6 hot dogs	high	1½ to 2 minutes

***high — 100% power : medium — 60% power : low — 30% power.

SANDWICHES

SANDWICH BASICS

Sandwiches heat very quickly. Be careful not to over cook. Heat bread until warm, not hot, cheese just until it begins to melt.

The best sandwiches are made with day-old or toasted bread; breads rich in eggs or shortening; full-bodied breads such as rye or whole wheat.

Several thin slices of meat heat better than one thick slice.

Always heat sandwiches on paper napkins or towels to absorb steam which can make the bread soggy, except when grilling cheese or Reuben sandwiches on the micro-browner.

DELECTABLE DELI SANDWICHES

I

- Three decker on rye bread, turkey, tongue, pastrami, with mayonnaise on the top and bottom slices.
- Wrap in waxed paper and cook 45 seconds on high.
- Serve with cole slaw and dill pickle wedge.

II

- Two slices rye bread with pastrami and corned beef, a slice of Swiss cheese and salad dressing on the top and bottom bread slices.
- Wrap in waxed paper and cook 45 seconds on high.
- Serve with potato salad and a dill pickle wedge.

III

- Two slices rye or pumpernickle bread, chopped chicken liver, pastrami and salad dressing on the slice next to the liver.
- Wrap in waxed paper and cook 45 seconds on high.
- Serve with sliced tomatoes or cole slaw.

IV

- Three decker on rye bread, turkey, tongue, and Swiss cheese, with salad dressing on the top and bottom bread slices.
- Wrap in waxed paper and cook 45 seconds on high.
- Serve with potato salad and dill pickled tomato.

V

- Two slices pumpernickle bread, roast beef, turkey and Swiss cheese, with salad dressing on the bread slice next to the turkey.
- Wrap in waxed paper and cook 45 seconds on high.
- Serve with dill pickle wedge.

VI

- Two slices rye bread, sliced smoked sturgeon, sliced onion and tomato, with salad dressing on the bread slice next to the sturgeon.
- Wrap in waxed paper and cook 45 seconds on high.
- Serve with black olives and cole slaw.

VII

- Three decker on rye bread, chopped chicken liver, Swiss cheese and salami, with salad dressing on top and bottom bread slices.
- Wrap in waxed paper and cook 45 seconds on high.
- Serve with cole slaw and dill pickle wedge.

VIII

- Three decker on rye or pumpernickle bread, corned beef, Swiss cheese, tongue and salami, with salad dressing on top and bottom bread slices.
- Wrap in waxed paper and cook 45 seconds on high.
- Serve with potato salad and dill pickle wedge

IX

— Three decker on rye bread, tongue, liverwurst, salami and cream cheese, with salad dressing on the top and bottom bread slices (the cream cheese is spread on the center slice).
— Wrap in waxed paper and cook 45 seconds on high.
— Serve with cole slaw and black olives.

X

— Two slices rye bread, salami, bologna and Swiss cheese with salad dressing on the bread slice next to the Swiss cheese.
— Wrap in waxed paper and cook 45 seconds on high.
— Serve with dill pickle wedge.

XI

— Two slices rye or pumpernickle bread, tongue, bologna, Swiss cheese and sauerkraut (drained). Lay sauerkraut on bottom bread slice and build sandwich up, spreading top bread slice with salad dressing.
— Wrap in waxed paper and cook 45 seconds on high.
— Serve with tomato wedges and potato salad.

XII

— Kaiser roll or onion roll, with lox, cream cheese and salad dressing. Spread one half of the roll with dressing, the other with cheese. Sandwich lox in the middle.
— Wrap in waxed paper and cook 45 seconds on high.
— Serve with olives and cole slaw.

XIII

— Two slices of pumpernickle bread, Swiss cheese and bologna, with salad dressing on the bread slice next to the cheese.
— Wrap in waxed paper and cook 45 seconds on high.
— Serve with dill pickle wedge.

BROWNING DISH HAMBURGERS

— Form 1 pound ground beef into 4 patties, ½ inch thick.
— Place empty browning dish in oven.
— Microwave 5 minutes to preheat on high.
— Without removing dish from oven, place hamburgers on browner.
— Microwave ½ to 1 minute on high.
— Turn hamburgers over. Microwave on high ½ to 1 minute or depending on doneness preferred.

BARBECUED CRAB SANDWICHES

3 tablespoons butter or margarine
½ cup finely chopped celery
¼ cup finely chopped onion
1 teaspoon instant chicken bouillon
½ cup tomato sauce
2 teaspoons Worcestershire sauce
2 teaspoons soy sauce
2 whole cloves
2 bay leaves
¼ teaspoon salt
⅛ teaspoon pepper
1 can (6½-oz.) crab meat, broken up with fork
1 teaspoon parsley flakes
6 large rolls, split and buttered

— Combine butter, celery and onion, in 1-quart glass casserole. Microwave, uncovered, 3 minutes on high, or until onion is transparent.
— Add instant bouillon, tomato sauce, Worcestershire sauce, soy sauce, cloves, bay leaves, salt and pepper.
— Mix well.
— Microwave 2 minutes on high, or until bubbly.
— Remove bay leaves and cloves.
— Stir in crab meat and parsley.
— Microwave, uncovered, 3 minutes on medium to heat crab meat.
— Spoon hot mixture into rolls.

NOTE: For party sandwiches, spoon mixture on warm biscuits. Garnish with stuffed olives.

(6 servings)

CHEESEBURGER

1 tablespoon butter
1 medium onion silced into rings
4 hamburger patties, cooked
4 sesame buns split
4 slices American process cheese

— Place butter in 2-cup glass measure and microwave until melted for 30 seconds on high.
— Stir onion rings in hot butter until coated.
— Place hamburger patties on bottom half of buns.
— Top with cheese slices and onion rings. Arrange on paper towel.
— Microwave 30 seconds to 1 minute on high, or until cheese starts to melt.
— Cover with bun tops.

(4 servings)

FISHWICHES

1 package (8 oz.) frozen precooked breaded fish sticks
4 hot dog buns, split and buttered
Tartar sauce

— Place fish sticks on glass plate in spoke fashion.
— Microwave, uncovered, on low for 3 minutes.
— Spread buns with tartar sauce.
— Place 2 fish sticks on each bun.
—Arrange on paper towel in oven.
— Microwave, uncovered, on low until heated through:
1 fishwich — 45 to 60 seconds
2 fishwiches — 1 to 1 ½ minutes
4 fishwiches — 2 ½ to 3 minutes
— Garnish with sliced dill pickle or pickle relish.

TUNA SALAD SANDWICHES

1 can (6 ½-oz) flaked tuna, drained
1 cup cubed process American cheese
2 tablespoons chopped onion
2 tablespoons chopped green pepper
2 tablespoons pickle relish
¼ cup sliced pimento stuffed olives
⅓ cup mayonnaise
6 hot dog buns, split and toasted

— Combine all ingredients, except buns, in medium mixing bowl; mix well.
— Spread equal amounts of tuna mixture on bottom half of toasted buns.
— Place other half of bun on top.
— Wrap loosely in paper towel or napkin.
— Microwave on medium for 3 to 5 minutes or until hot and cheese is melted.

(6 sandwiches)

TUNA 'N CHEESE BUNS

1 can (6 ½ oz.) tuna drained and flaked
1 cup grated sharp cheddar cheese
½ cup mayonnaise
3 hard cooked eggs, finely chopped
¼ cup finely chopped onion
¼ cup chopped stuffed green olives
¼ cup sweet pickle relish
8 hamburger buns splt

— Combine tuna, cheese, mayonnaise, eggs, onion, olives and relish in a bowl.
— Mix well.
— Spoon mixture onto buns.
— Wrap each bun in a paper towel.
— Place 2 at a time in microwave
— Microwave 1 to 2 minutes on high, or until cheese has softened into mixture.

(8 servings)

SARDINE BUNS

¼ lb. process American cheese, cubed
5 hard-cooked eggs, chopped
½ cup drained mashed sardines
1 tablespoon minced green pepper
2 tablespoons minced onion
3 tablespoons chopped stuffed olives
2 tablespoons pickle relish, drained
½ cup mayonnaise
6 hamburger buns, split and buttered

— Combine all ingredients except buns.
— Fill each bun with cheese mixture.
— Wrap each sandwich in waxed paper and twist ends of paper.
— Cook one at a time, for 1 to 1 ½ minutes, on high, or until rolls are hot.

Note: These may be prepared in advance and refrigerated in their waxed paper wrapping. Cook before serving.

(6 servings)

HOT DOGS

4 wieners
4 wiener buns split

— Place weiners on open buns. Arrange on paper towel.
— Microwave 1 ½ minutes on high or until wieners feel warm.
— For 1 wiener cook 30 seconds on high.
— Let stand 1 minute before serving.

(2-4 servings)

HOT TURKEY SANDWICHES

1 cup chopped cooked turkey
¼ cup chopped onion
⅓ cup mayonnaise or salad dressing
2 teaspoons prepared mustard
6 slices bread, toasted
6 slices (¾ oz. each) process American cheese

— Combine turkey, onion, mayonnaise and mustard in medum mixing bowl; mix well.
— Spread equal amounts of turkey mixture on each toasted bread slice.
— Top with cheese.
— Arrange on paper towel in oven.
— Microwave, uncovered, on medium for 1 ½ to 2 minutes or until cheese is melted.

(6 sandwiches)

SAUSAGE AND PEPPER HERO

4 Italian sausages
½ cup prepared barbecue sauce
1 green pepper, seeded and cut in strips
4 hero rolls

— Place a layer of paper towels in an (8-inch) square dish.
— Place sausage on towels.
— Cover with paper towels.
— Microwave for 8 minutes on high, uncovered, Drain off fat and reserve.
— Cook barbecue sauce with pepper strips in a 2-cup glass measure for 1 to 2 minutes on high, uncovered.
— Split hero rolls almost in half.
— Place 1 cooked sausage in each roll. Top with one-quarter of this sauce and peppers.
— Wrap each roll in waxed paper and twist ends of paper.
— Microwave, one at a time, for 1 to 1½ minutes on high, or until rolls are piping hot.

(4 servings)

CHICKEN TACOS

½ cup chopped onions
2 tablespoons butter or margarine
2 cups coarsely diced cooked chicken
1 can (7½-oz.) taco sauce
¼ teaspoon salt
¼ teaspoon garlic salt
10 to 12 fully cooked taco shells
Grated Cheddar cheese
Shredded lettuce
Chopped fresh tomatoes

— Microwave, uncovered, onion and butter in a 1-quart glass casserole for about 3 minutes on high.
— Add chicken, taco sauce, salt, and garlic salt
— Cover wth paper towel.
— Microwave for about 5 minutes on high, or until mixture thickens and is hot.
— Spoon filling into taco shells. Place tacos in a straight-side glass dish so that they will stand upright.
— Serve with grated cheese, shredded lettuce and chopped tomatoes.

(10-12 servings)

DIEGO'S SOUTH OF THE BORDER BUNS

1 lb. lean ground beef
1 medium onion, chopped
1 small green pepper, chopped
1 clove garlic, pressed or finely chopped
1 can (8-oz.) tomato sauce
1 teaspoon Worcestershire sauce
½ teaspoon salt
¼ teaspoon chili powder
Dash hot pepper sauce
8 hamburger buns
Tomato slices
Shredded lettuce
Grated cheddar cheese

— Crumble ground beef into 2-quart glass casserole.
— Add onion, pepper and garlic.
— Microwave, uncovered, 4 to 5 minutes on high, or until beef loses its pink color.
— Stir in tomato sauce, Worcestershire sauce, salt, chili powder and pepper sauce. Cover.
— Microwave 5 to 6 minutes on high, or until sauce is thickened and very hot.
— Serve on hamburger buns.
— Garnish with tomato slices, shredded lettuce and grated cheese.

(8 sandwiches)

CONEY ISLANDS

1 can (15-oz.) chili without beans
1 package (1-lb). wieners
6 wiener buns, split
½ cup chopped onion
Grated cheddar cheese

— Place chili in 1-quart glass casserole
— Microwave, uncovered, 2 minutes on high, or until hot and bubbly, stirring once after 1 minute.
— Set aside.
— Place wieners on open buns.
— Arrange on paper towel. Microwave 2 minutes on high or until wiener feels warm
— Spoon chili over wieners.
— Sprinkle with raw onions.
— Top with grated cheddar cheese.
— Microwave, uncovered, 10 seconds on high, or until cheese begins to melt.

(10-12 servings)

OLD MYSTIC

1 can (7 ½-oz.) crab meat, drained
1 can (5-oz.) shrimp, drained
2 packages (3-oz. each) cream cheese, at room temperature
½ cup chopped almonds
2 tablespoons dry white wine
2 teaspoons lemon juice
1 teaspoon minced onion
1 teaspoon prepared horseradish
1 teaspoon prepared mustard
½ teaspoon salt
¼ teaspon white pepper
⅛ teaspoon cayenne pepper.
6 French rolls
⅓ cup shredded Gruyere cheese

— Pick over crab meat and remove any bits of shells or cartilege. Combine with shrimp and cream cheese and blend well.
— Add almonds, white wine, lemon juice, onion, horseradish, mustard, salt, pepper and cayenne.
— Remove top third from each roll and scoop out inside, being careful not to puncture shell
— Spoon mixture evenly into 6 shells.
— Sprinkle cheese over top of filling.
— Place tops on rolls.
— Place 2 rolls at a time on paper towels or paper plates in oven.
— Microwave, uncovered, for 1 to 1 ½ minutes on high, or until filling is piping hot and cheese has melted.

(6 servings)

HOT TUNA OLIVE SANDWICHES

1 cup canned pitted ripe olives, chopped coarsely
1 can (6-7 oz.) tuna, drained
1 cup shredded cheddar cheese
¼ cup mayonnaise
¼ teaspoon Worcestershire sauce
½ cup minced celery
1 green onion, chopped
1 tablespoon sweet pickle relish
½ teaspoon mustard
4 rolls, split

— Mix olives, tuna, cheese, mayonnaise and Worcestershire sauce.
— Add celery, green onion, relish and mustard.
— Spread on split rolls, and wrap each in a paper towel. Microwave 30-45 seconds, on high, or until hot.

(4 servings)

FRENCH RIVIERAS

¼ cup butter, softened
1 tablespoon prepared mustard
6 large hard rolls, split
6 slices bologna
6 slices cooked ham
6 slices salami
6 slices cheese, Swiss, cheddar or American process

— Blend butter with mustard in small bowl.
— Spread inside rolls.
— For each sandwich, layer 1 slice bologna, 1 slice ham, 1 slice salami and 1 slice cheese on half of roll and cover with other half.
— Secure top with toothpick and place on paper napkin. Microwave 30 seconds on high, or until cheese melts.

NOTE: Long loaf sandwiches are easy for entertaining. Cut French bread in half lengthwise, layer with your favorite cold cuts and cheese. Garnish with fresh tomatoes and cucumbers. Follow above directions for heating.

(6 sandwiches)

TODD'S TERRIFIC PIZZA

Half English muffin, toasted
Pepperoni slices
Canned pizza sauce
Grated Mozzarella cheese
Chopped onions
Garnish with ripe olives

— Place pepperoni, cheese and other ingredients on muffin.
— Sandwich should cook within 20 seconds on high.
— Watch through oven door for cheese to melt and bubble.

(1 serving)

CHICKEN CRUMPETS

4 tablespoons butter or margarine
¼ cup all-purpose flour
1 teaspoon salt
⅛ teaspoon pepper
2 cups mlik
3 tablespoons sherry
2 cups diced cooked chicken
Paprika
4 crumpets
8 baked ham slices

— Place butter in a 1-quart glass casserole.
— Microwave, uncovered, for 30 seconds on high, or until butter is melted.
— Stir in flour, salt, and pepper. Microwave for 30 seconds on high.
— Stir in milk. Microwave for 3 to 4 minutes, on high, stirring at 1 ½ minutes.
— Remove from oven and stir in sherry, chicken and a dash of paprika.
— Split, toast, and butter crumpets.
— Place each crumpet on a paper plate.
— Place 1 slice of ham on each crumpet half.
— Divide chicken mixture over ham slices and sprinkle lightly with paprika
— Microwave 4 at a time, for about 2 minutes, on high or until heated through.

(8 servings)

SKIP'S SECOND-ACT HAM

¾ cup hollandaise sauce
4 slices bread, toasted
Ham slices from leftover baked ham
1 can (8-oz.) asparagus, drained, or 9 to 12 fresh asparagus, cooked
2 hard-cooked eggs, sliced (optional)

— Prepare hollandaise sauce, using your favorite recipe.
— Cover with waxed paper and set aside.
— Arrange toast, cut in quarters, in 4 small individual casseroles.
— Put desired amount of ham on top of toast.
— Arrange 3 or 4 asparagus spears on top of ham. Add ½ egg, sliced, on top if desired.
— Microwave, covered with waxed paper, 1 casserole at a time, for 1 to 2 minutes on high, or until heated.
— Top with hollandaise sauce.
— Cover with waxed paper and heat for 30 seconds on high.
— If hollandaise sauce is cold, double the heating time.

(3-4 servings)

BARBECUE BURGERS

½ lb. lean ground beef
½ cup chopped onion
½ cup catsup
2 tablespoons vinegar
1 tablespoon brown sugar
½ teaspoon salt
¼ teaspoon dry mustard
4 hamburger buns

— Combine ground beef crumbled and onion in a glass 1-quart casserole.
— Microwave 2 to 3 minutes, uncovered, on high.
— Add catsup, vinegar, brown sugar, salt and mustard.
— Cover and microwave 4 minutes on high. Stirring after 2 minutes.
— Serve on hamburger buns.

(4 servings)

SLOPPY JOE SANDWICH

1 lb. ground beef
½ cup chopped onions
½ cup chopped green pepper
½ teaspoon paprika
1 can tomato sauce
1 teaspoon salt
Pinch of sugar
Freshly ground pepper to taste
Toasted hamburger buns

— Crumble beef in a 2-quart glass casserole. Add onion, pepper, and paprika.
— Microwave, uncovered, for 5 to 6 minutes, on high, or until meat loses its red color. Stir once during cooking time.
— Break up meat with a fork. Add remaining ingredients except buns and blend well.
— Cook, covered, for about 10 minutes, on high, stirring occasionally.
— Spoon onto bottom half of toasted hamburger buns; cover with top half.

Note: The Sloppy Joe mixture can be made up well in advance and kept in the refrigerator. To serve, remove any congealed fat on top of mixture. Spoon desired amount of meat on hamburger buns or hard rolls, speading mixture out to edges. Place single serving on a small plate. Heat for 1 to 1 ½ minutes on high, until mixture is piping hot.

(6 servings)

MUFFIN PIZZA

1 package (14 oz.) English muffins
1 1/4 cups chili sauce
Italian seasoning

PIZZA GARNISHES:
Green pepper, sliced
Pepperoni, sliced
Green onion, bias cut
Mushrooms, sliced
Olives, sliced
Mozzarella cheese, shredded

— Split English muffins in half.
— Top each muffin half with 1 1/2 tablespoons chili sauce, a sprinkle of Italian seasoning and some Pizza Garnishes.
— Arrange 2 pizzas on paper towel in oven.
— Microwave, uncovered, on high for 1 1/2 to 2 minutes or until cheese is melted.

(Makes 12 Pizzas)

PEANUT BUTTER KIDWICHES

The children's favorite sandwich filling forms the base for hot and bubbly sandwiches they can microwave themselves.

1 slice toast
Peanut butter

— Spread toast with peanut butter.
— Top with one of the following combinations:
Jelly
Marshmallow
Cheese
Bacon Bits
Tomato slice
Cheese
— Place sandwich on napkin.
— Microwave, uncovered, 15 seconds to 30 seconds on high, or until melted.

GRILLED CHEESE SANDWICH

2 slices American process cheese
2 slices bread
Butter

— Place cheese slices between bread slices.
— Spread butter on outsides of sandwich.
— To preheat microwave browner, Microwave 4 minutes on high.
— With oven door open, place sandwich on browner and microwave for 30 seconds on high. Turn to brown other side and microwave for 30 seconds on high, if necessary, to melt cheese.

REUBEN SANDWICH

8 slices dark rye or pumpernickel bread
Butter
1/2 lb. sliced corned beef
1 can (8-oz.) sauerkraut, drained
Thousand Island dressing
4 slices Swiss cheese

— Toast bread. Butter lightly.
— Arrange sliced corned beef on 4 slices of toast.
— Divide sauerkraut among sandwiches.
— Top with Thousand Island dressing. Top each with a slice of Swiss cheese. Top with other slices of toast, buttered side down.
— Place each sandwich on a paper plate.
— Microwave, uncovered, one at a time, for about 1 minute, on high, or just until cheese is melted.

(4 servings)

RANCHBURGERS

6 slices bacon
1 1/2 cups grated process American cheese
2 tablespoons finely chopped onon
1/4 cup catsup
1 tablespoon prepared mustard
6 sandwich buns

— Microwave bacon by putting slices in between paper toweling on top of a paper plate and cooking for 4 1/2 minutes on high. Remove bacon and discard paper plate. Crumble bacon and combine with remaining ingredients except buns.
— Spread 3 tablespoons cheese mixture on bottom half of each bun and cover with bun top.
— Wrap each sandwich in waxed paper and twist ends of paper.
— Microwave each sandwich separately, for 1 to 1 1/2 minutes on high, or until heated through.

(6 servings)

EGGS

Egg Dish	Amount	Setting	Cooking Time
Baked Eggs	1 egg	medium	35 to 40 seconds
	2 eggs	medium	1 to 1¼ minutes
	4 eggs	medium	2 to 2½ minutes
Fried Eggs, on a microwave browning dish	1 egg	medium	45 to 55 seconds
	2 eggs	medium	1½ to 2 minutes
	4 eggs	medium	2 to 2½ minutes
Scrambled Eggs	1 egg	medium	50 seconds to 1 minute
	2 eggs	medium	2 to 2½ minutes
	4 eggs	medium	4½ to 5 minutes
	6 eggs	medium	4 minutes, stir and 2½ minutes more

***high — 100% power : medium — 60% power : low — 30% power.

CHEESE & EGGS

HAM 'N EGGS AU GRATIN

4 tablespoons butter or margarine
¼ cup flour
2 cups milk
1 teaspoons prepared mustard
2 teaspoons Worcestershire sauce
1 ½ cup shredded sharp cheddar cheese
1 cup cubed, cooked ham
6 hard cooked eggs, halved

— Place butter in 1 ½-quart casserole.
— Microwave on high until butter melts.
— Blend in flour.
— Stir in milk.
— Microwave 4 to 6 minutes on high, or until thickened.
— Beat with wire whip.
— Add mustard, Worcestershire sauce and cheese. Microwave 1 minute on high, or until cheese melts.
— Mix in ham and eggs.
— Microwave 1 minute, 30 seconds to 2 minutes on high, or until bubbly.
— Serve over toast.

(4-6 servings)

POACHED EGG

1 egg

— Bring ⅓ cup water to a boil in a small custard cup, for 1 to 1 ½ minutes on high.
— Carefully break egg into a small dish or saucer.
— Slide egg into boiling water.
— Microwave tightly covered, for 30 seconds.
— Keep covered and let stand for 1 minute before serving.

(1 serving)

WELSH RAREBIT ON TOAST

4 teaspoons butter or margarine
4 cups, shredded, sharp Cheddar cheese
¾ teaspoon Worchestershire sauce
½ teaspoon salt
½ teaspoon paprika
¼ teaspoon dry mustard
¼ teaspoon cayenne
2 eggs, lightly beaten
1 cup flat beer, at room temperature

— Melt butter in a 2-quart casserole or bowl, 1 minute on high.
— Add cheese, Worchestershire, salt, paprika, dry mustard, and cayenne.
— Mix thoroughly.
— Cook, covered, for 3 minutes on high, stirring at 1 ½ minutes.
— Stir some of the hot cheese into beaten eggs
— Return slowly to hot mixture and stir briskly.
— Gradually stir in beer and blend well.
— Cook, covered, for 6 to 7 minutes on high, stirring at 2-minute intervals.
— Remove from oven and beat briskly with a whisk to blend thoroughly.
— Serve over crisp toasted French bread slices.

(4-6 servings)

CREAMED EGGS WITH CHIPPED BEEF

6 hard cooked eggs, shelled and quartered
1 can (10¾ oz.) condensed cream of mushroom soup
1 package (3 oz.) corned beef, cut into pieces
¼ teaspoon dried parsley flakes

— Combine all ingredients in 1 ½-quart glass casserole.
— Cover.
— Microwave on medium for 8 to 10 minutes or until hot.

(3-4 servings)

SHIRRED EGGS

1 teaspoon butter
2 eggs

— Melt butter in a small cereal bowl for about 30 seconds on high.
— Break eggs carefully into bowl. Cover tightly with plactic wrap.
— Microwave, covered, for 1 minute 20 seconds on high.
— Remove and let stand 1 minue before serving
— Serve with crisp bacon and buttered toast.

(1 serving)

BROWNING DISH FRIED EGGS

1 tablespoon butter
2 eggs

— Preheat browning dish on high for 2 minutes.
— Add butter to hot browning dish, stirring to melt. Place eggs in browning dish.
— Cook, covered, on medium for 2 minutes, 15 seconds.
(Do not overcook as eggs will continue cooking while standing.)

(1 serving)

SHRIMP AND ASPARAGUS QUICHE

Bake quiche shell or 10-inch pastry shell
½ cup cooked shrimp.
1 can (8-oz.) asparagus, drained and cut in 1-inch lengths
1 egg
¾ cup light cream
¼ teaspoon salt
Pinch white pepper
2 tablespoons grated Parmesan cheese

— Flake shrimp and mix with asparagus.
— Spread over bottom of baked quiche shell.
— Beat egg lightly with wire whip.
— Stir in evaporated milk, salt and pepper.
— Sprinkle with Parmesan cheese.
— Microwave 8 minutes, 30 second on medium

(5-6 servings)

BRUNCH SPECIAL

1 package (12 oz.) frozen hash brown potatoes
⅓ cup sour cream
⅓ cup cream
½ teaspoon salt
1 tablespoon chives
4 slices Canadian bacon
4 eggs

— Place potatoes in 2-quart (8x8-inch) glass baking dish.
— Cover.
— Microwave on high for 6 to 7 minutes or until partly cooked.
— Blend in sour cream, cream, salt and chives.
— Place bacon slices down center of dish.
— Make two hollows in potatoes on each side of bacon.
— Break 1 egg into each indentation; recover.
— Microwave on medium for 6 to 8 minutes or until eggs are cooked to desired doneness.
— Let stand, covered, 2 minutes before serving.

(2-4 servings

CURRIED EGGS

1 can (10¾-oz.) condensed cream of celery soup, undiluted
1 tablespoon milk
1 teaspoon curry powder
4 eggs, hard cooked and sliced

— Combine soup, milk and curry powder in 1-quart casserole.
— Mix well.
— Cover.
— Microwave 3 minutes on high, or until hot.
— Add eggs.
— Cover.
— Microwave 3 minutes on high or until hot.
— Serve as a side dish over green beans, broccoli or cooked noodles.

(2-3 servings)

SPINACH QUICHE

Baked quiche shell or 10-inch pastry shell
1 cup cooked, drained spinach
2 eggs, beaten
½ cup evaporated milk or light cream
½ teaspoon nutmeg
¼ teaspoon salt
Pinch pepper
1½ tablespoons grated Parmesan cheese

— Combine spinach, eggs, evaporated milk, nutmeg, salt and pepper.
— Pour into baked quiche shell.
— Sprinkle with Parmesan cheese.
— Microwave 30 minutes on low.

(5-6 servings)

EGGS A LA GOLDENROD

6 eggs, hard cooked

2 cups white sauce

Toast

— Cook eggs on conventional range. Reserve two yolks, and cut whites and remaining yolks in ½-inch dice.

— Prepare white sauce and pour into 1-quart casserole.

— Stir in diced eggs.

— Microwave 2 minutes on high.

— Serve on toast with reserved egg yolks sieved over the top

— *Variation:*

Substitute cheese sauce for white sauce. Dice 6 hard cooked eggs and stir into sauce.

SCRAMBLED EGGS

1 tablespoon butter

2 eggs

2 tablespoons light cream or milk

⅛ teaspoon salt

Few grains pepper

— Melt butter in a bowl on high 15 seconds.

— Beat remaining ingredients until well-blended.

— Pour egg mixture into bowl.

— Cook, covered with plastic wrap or a saucer, on medium for 1 minute.

— Stir.

— Cook, covered on medium an additional 45 seconds to 1 minute.

— Stir.

— Stop cooking eggs when they are slightly softer than desired, as they will continue to cook after they are removed from the Microwave oven.

— Allow to stand 1 to 2 minutes before serving.

(1 serving)

FOR FOUR SCRAMBLED EGGS:

2 tablespoons butter

4 eggs

4 tablespoons light cream or milk

¼ teaspoon salt

Few grains pepper

— Melt butter in a bowl on high for 30 seconds.

— Beat remaining ingredients until well-blended.

— Pour egg mixture into bowl.

— Cook, covered with plastic wrap or a saucer, on medium for 1½ to 2 minutes.

— Stir.

— Cook, covered, on medium an additional 1½ to 2 minutes.

— Allow to stand 1 to 2 minutes before serving.

(2 servings)

EGGS BENEDICT

¼ cup butter or margarine

¼ cup cream

2 egg yolks, beaten

1 tablespoon cider vinegar

¼ teaspoon salt

Cayenne pepper to taste

½ teaspoon dry mustard

1 (17-oz.) can asparagus spears, drained

4 English muffins, split and toasted conventionally

4 slices ham

4 poached eggs ((see recipe page 39)

— In a 2 cup, non-metallic measuring cup melt butter on high 1 minute.

— Add cream, egg yolks, vinegar, salt, cayenne and mustard; stir to blend.

— Heat, uncovered, on medium for 2 minutes or until tickened. Stir frequently.

— Beat sauce until light and fluffy; set aside.

— Place asparagus in a shallow, heat-resistant, non-metallic baking dish and heat, uncovered, on high 1 to 2 minutes or until heated through.

— Arrange toasted English muffin halves on serving platter.

— Place 1 slice of ham over each English muffin.

— Divide asparagus among the 4 muffins.

— Heat, uncovered, on high 2½ to 3 minutes or until muffins and ham are heated through.

— Carefully place poached eggs on asparagus. Top with sauce and heat, uncovered, on medium for 1 minute or until hot.

(4 servings)

CHEESE AND EGG PUFF

1 tablespoon butter
4 eggs, well beaten
¼ cup unsifted flour
1 cup milk
1 cup shredded Swiss cheese
¼ teaspoon salt
¼ teaspoon pepper
2 tablespoons snipped chives

— Place butter in 9-inch glass pie plate.
— Microwave on medium for about ½ minute or until melted.
— Beat eggs in medium mixing bowl; then gradullay beat in flour until smooth.
— Stir in remaining ingredients; mix well.
— Pour into buttered pie pan.
— Cover with plastic wrap.
— Microwave on medium for 5 minutes.
— Gently fold over omelet; recover, and continue cooking on medium for 3 to 4 minutes.
— Let stand, covered, 5 minutes before serving.

(3-4 servings)

BAKED EGGS

2 eggs
butter

— Lightly grease two glass custard cups with butter. Break one egg into each prepared cup and puncture yolk with the tines of a fork
— Cook, covered with plastic wrap, on low for 2 minutes, 15 seconds or until eggs appear almost done.
— Allow to stand for 1 minute to complete cooking.

(Baked eggs can be chopped and used as a garnish or in salads that call for chopped boiled eggs.)

(1 serving)

CHEESE SOUFFLE

¼ cup all-purpose flour
½ teaspoon salt
½ teaspoon dry mustard
⅛ teaspoon paprika
1 ⅔ cup evaporated milk, undiluted
¼ teaspoon hot pepper sauce
6 ounces sharp cheddar cheese, grated
6 eggs, separated
1 teaspoon cream of tartar

— Blend flour, salt, mustard and paprika in 1 ½-quart casserole. Add evaporated milk and pepper sauce. Stir.
— Microwave 3 to 4 minutes on high, or until thickened, stirring after 2 minutes, then every 30 seconds.
— Add cheese.
— Stir until melted.
— If necessary, Microwave 1 to 2 minutes on high until cheese melts, stirring every minute.
— Beat egg whites with cream of tartar until stiff but not dry; set aside.
— Beat egg yolk until thick with lemon coloring.
— Slowly pour cheese mixture over beaten egg yolks, beating constantly until well combined.
— Spoon mixture over egg whites.
— Fold in gently until just blended.
— Turn into ungreased 2-quart souffle dish.
— Microwave 20 to 30 minutes on low, or until top is dry, rotating dish every 10 minutes.
— Serve immediately.

(6 servings)

HERB OMELET

1 tablespoon butter
3 eggs
3 tablespoons water
¼ teaspoon salt
⅛ teaspoon pepper
¼ teaspoon leaf basil

— Place butter in 9-inch glass pie plate.
— Microwave on medium for about ½ minute or until melted.
— Beat remaining ingredients into melted butter. Cover with plastic wrap.
— Microwave on medium for 2 minutes.
— Stir lightly; recover, and continue cooking on medium for 1 to 1 ½ minutes or until also set in center. Let stand, covered, 2 minutes before serving.

(1-2 servings)

HAM QUICHE

3 eggs
1 cup cream
¼ teaspoon ground nutmeg
½ teaspoon salt
⅛ teaspoon pepper
⅛ teaspoon cayenne pepper
½ pound cooked ham, cut into thin strips
2 cups shredded Swiss cheese
1 baked 10-inch pastry shell

— In a medium-sized bowl beat eggs, cream, nutmeg, salt, pepper and cayenne pepper until well mixed.
— Stir in ham and cheese.
— Pour mixture into baked pastry shell.
— Cook, uncovered, on low for 10 minutes.
— Move cooked edges toward center and continue to heat on low for 20 minutes or until a knife inserted in center comes out clean.
— Let stand at room temperature 3 to 4 minutes to finish cooking.

(6-8 servings)

DENVER BRUNCH SANDWICH

8 slices bacon
6 eggs
⅓ cup milk
⅓ cup mayonnaise or salad dressing
¼ cup chopped pimento
3 tablespoons chopped green pepper
¼ teaspoon salt
Tomato slices

— Place bacon slices between paper napkin or in 1½-quart (10x8) glass baking dish.
— Microwave on high for 7 to 9 minutes or until bacon is crisp.
— Remove bacon; drain drippings; crumble bacon; set aside.
— Combine eggs, milk and mayonnaise in medium mixing bowl; beat well with rotary beater.
— Stir in bacon and remaining ingredients.
— Pour into baking dish.
— Cover with plastic wrap.
— Microwave on medium for 6 to 7 minutes or until center is almost set.
— Garnish with tomato slices.
— Let stand, covered, 5 minutes before serving.

(4-6 servings)

CHEESE AND SHRIMP BAKE

8 slices bread
2 cans (4½ oz. each) shrimp, drained
¼ cup chopped celery
2 tablespoons chopped onion
1 can (10½ oz.) condensed cream of mushroom soup
½ teaspoons lemon juice
½ teaspoon Worcestershire sauce
8 oz. (1 cup) grated Chedar cheese
¾ cup milk
3 eggs
¼ cup butter

— Place 4 slices of bread in a baking dish. Top with shrimp, celery and onion.
— Blend soup with lemon juice and Worcestershire sauce.
— Pour over shrimp.
— Top with cheese and remaining 4 slices of bread.
— Beat milk and eggs; pour over sandwich mixture.
— Arrange pieces of butter on top.
— Chill in the refrigerator overnight, covered with wrap.
— Cook 15 minutes on high after loosening plastic wrap slightly.
— Let stand, covered, 5 minutes before serving.

(4 servings)

FRIED EGG

1 teaspoon butter
1 egg

— Place butter in a small custard cup or sauce dish.
— Microwave for 30 seconds on high, or just until melted.
— Carefully break egg into dish.
— Microwave tightly covered, for 30 to 35 seconds on high.
— Keep covered and let stand 1 minute before serving.

(1 serving)

MEATS

Cut and Weight	Setting #1	Setting #2	Approximate Cooking Time — minutes per lb. Rare	Medium	Well Done
BEEF					
Rib Roast, rolled 3 to 4 lbs.	high	medium	8 to 9	10 to 11	12 to 13
Rib Roast, standing 5 to 6 lbs.	high	medium	7 to 8	8 to 9	10 to 11
Sirloin Tip Roast 4 to 5 lbs.	high	medium	8 to 9	10 to 11	12 to 13
PORK					
Loin Roast, Boneless 4 to 5 lbs.	high	medium			10 to 11
Loin Roast, Center rib cut 4 to 5 lbs.	high	medium			10 to 11
Ham, boneless, ready to eat					
2 to 3 lbs.	medium	medium			12 to 13
4 to 5 lbs.	medium	medium			11 to 12
6 to 8 lbs.	medium	medium			9 to 10
Ham, canned					
3 lbs.	medium	medium			10 to 11
5 lbs.	medium	medium			8 to 9
LAMB					
Leg Roast 4 to 4½ lbs.	medium	medium			10 to 11
Shoulder Roast, rolled 3 to 4 lbs.	medium	medium			9 to 10
VEAL					
Rump Roast, bone in 2½ to 3 lbs.	medium	low			20 to 21
VENISON					
Rump Roast, bone in 3 to 3½ lbs.	medium	medium			12 to 13

***high — 100% power : medium — 60% power : low — 30% power.

MEATS

COOKING HINTS

The cooking times of meats may vary slightly when cooked in your Microwave Oven, depending upon the shape and size of the meat, the amount of fat present, the degree of aging, and the type of cut. Because it is often difficult to judge the doneness of meat by external appearance, you will find that a meat thermometer is a tremendous help in cooking meats. Meat should be roasted in a shallow, heat-resistant, non-metallic baking dish. Place the meat on an inverted saucer in the center of the dish so that it does not sit in the drippings. Plastic trivets or racks designed for microwave cooking may be used in your Microwave Oven. Wax paper or paper towelling may be placed loosely over the top of the meat to control spattering and help in basting. Meats may be cooked in roasting bags, provided that string is used instead of the metal tie to secure bag. Follow package directions, making sure to slit the bag.

When cooking meat with your Microwave Oven, we suggest that you do not salt the meat before cooking. Salt draws the moisture out of meat and toughens the outer layer. Add salt after the meat is cooked. Pepper and other seasonings may be added prior to cooking.

Microwave cooked foods continue to cook somewhat even after being removed from the oven. Meats should be allowed to stand, covered in aluminum foil, at room temperature 10 to 15 minutes before making a final temperature reading to determine doneness. The internal temperature of meats will increase by 10° to 15°F. during this standing time following microwave cooking.

Small portions of meat may be as brown as you desire when cooked by microwaves. Larger roasts and other meats, cooked longer than 10 minutes, will become acceptably brown. The amount of browning varies with the amount of fat on the surface of the meat. To add to the brown appearance of smaller portions, try basting the meat with a diluted brown gravy mix such as Kitchen Bouquet®.

A browning dish may be used to brown meats in your microwave oven. See information in this chapter for directions and individual recipes.

Best results are achieved when meats, particularly roasts and larger cuts, are completely defrosted before cooking.

Thinner sections of meats may be shielded with aluminum foil to prevent overcooking before thicker portions are done. For example, corners or thinner areas of meat can be covered with small, smooth pieces of foil before cooking, or the wing and leg tips of a turkey may be wrapped in a small amount of foil to reflect microwaves away from these thin areas. Foil should be removed during part of the cooking time in order to cook covered portions.

MEAT THERMOMETERS

Conventional meat thermometers should not be used in the Microwave Oven during operation. Specially designed Microwave Cooking Thermometers may be used in your Microwave Oven during operation, but these are the only thermometers which should be used during cooking.

If using a conventional meat thermometer, insert into meat at the end of the suggested cooking time, after removing meat from oven. Insert thermometer in the center and fleshy portion of the meat, away from boney or fatty sections. For poultry, insert between the inner thigh and body of the bird.

STANDING RIB ROAST

1 rib roast of beef with at least 2 bones
1 clove garlic, slivered
Salt to taste

— Place an inverted saucer or Microwave roasting rack in the bottom of an oblong 2-quart glass baking dish.
— Make slits in beef with a sharp knife and insert a thin sliver of garlic in each slit. Sprinkle roast with salt
— Place roast, fat side down.
— Cover bones with a small piece of aluminum foil.
— Microwave, uncovered, on high for about 2½ minutes per pound for rare, 3¼ minutes for medium, and 5 minutes for well-done.
— Remove pieces of foil. Turn ribs fat side up.
— Cover roast with a piece of paper towel to prevent fat from splattering oven walls.
— Microwave, covered, on high for about 2½ minutes per pound for rare, 3¼ minutes for medium and 5 minutes for well-done.
— Remove roast, insert a thermometer into heavy part of meat, making sure that it does not touch the bone.
— If reading is correct, 120° for rare, 140° for medium, and 160° for well-done, cover roast tightly with aluminum foil and let stand at least 15 minutes to bring meat up to desired temperature and to make it easier to carve. If desired temperature has not been reached, remove thermometer and return meat to the oven for 1 to 2 minutes.
— Season with salt and pepper.

(6-8 servings)

MEXICAN BEEF

2 lbs. beef tenderloin
4 tablespoons butter
1 teaspoon salt
½ teaspoon chili powder
Dash of ground sage
1½ lb. sliced mushrooms
1 onion
2 green peppers
2 cloves garlic, minced
½ cup soy sauce
1½ tablespoons vinegar
3 tablespoons tomato paste

— Slice beef into ¼-inch wide strips.
— Heat a baking dish 30 seconds.
— Place butter in the dish to brown the meat.
— Saute half of the meat in butter 4 minutes, on high, stirring halfway through cooking.
— Remove meat with slotted spoon to a casserole.
— Saute other half of meat in same way.
— Sprinkle beef with salt, chili and sage.
— Toss lightly to mix.
— Saute mushrooms in a baking dish. for about 2 minutes on high.
— Stir in meat.
— Cut onion into eighths.
— Cut peppers into 1-inch pieces.
— Mix garlic, onion and green pepper into drippings in a baking dish.
— Saute 2 minutes and stir into meat.
— Cut each tomato into 8 wedges and stir into meat.
— Combine soy sauce, vinegar and tomato paste in a dish and heat 2 minutes on high.
— Pour over meat and toss lightly together.
— Microwave, covered, 15 minutes, on high, or until vegetables are barely tender, stirring every 5 minutes.
— Let stand few minutes before serving.

STUFFED CABBAGE

1 large head cabbage, cored
½ cup water
1½ lbs. ground beef
½ cup finely chopped onion
½ cup quick-cooking rice
1 egg
1 teaspoon salt
¼ teaspoon pepper
1 can (8 oz.) tomato sauce

— Place cabbage in deep 2-quart glass casserole.
— Pour water in bottom of dish.
— Cover with plastic wrap.
— Microwave on high for 8 to 10 minutes or until cabbage is partly cooked; set aside.
— Crumble ground beef in medium mixing bowl
— Stir in remaining ingredients, except tomato sauce.
— Remove 12 cabbage leaves from partly cooked cabbage.
— Place an equal amount of meat mixture in each leaf of cabbage.
— Roll up leaves and secure with toothpick.
— Place in 2-quart (12 x 7-inch) glass baking dish
— Cover with plastic wrap.
— Microwave on high for 13 to 15 minutes.
— Pour tomato sauce over cabbage rolls.
— Recover and continue cooking on high for 2 to 3 minutes or until hot.
— Let stand, covered, 5 minutes before serving.

(6 servings)

ONION STEAK

¼ cup flour
¼ teaspoon salt
¼ teaspoon pepper
1½ lbs. round steak
½ pkg. onion soup mix
1 onion, sliced
Chopped parsley

— Mix flour, salt and pepper.
— Pound the steak with the back of a heavy knife working in half of the flour mixture per side.
— Cut meat into 4 and put in baking dish.
— Sprinkle any remaining flour over top of meat.
— Add 1 cup water to onion soup mix and pour over meat.
— Microwave, covered, 14 minutes on high.
— Stir and rearrange meat in sauce occasionally.
— Place sliced onion on top and sprinkle with chopped parsley.
— Cook, covered, 10 minutes more on high.

(4 servings)

SHORT RIBS

2 pounds meaty short ribs of beef
1 clove garlic, minced
½ teaspoon salt
½ cup dry red wine
1 tablespoon liquid gravy seasoning
Chopped parsley

— Arrange short ribs in a 2 or 3 quart casserole.
— Sprinkle with garlic and salt.
— Combine wine and liquid gravy seasoning.
— Pour over short ribs.
— Microwave, covered, for 15 to 18 minutes, on high, or until meat is tender, stirring once or twice during cooking period.
— Remove and let stand 5 minutes.

(4 servings)

WESTERN POT ROAST

3 tablespoons butter or margarine
½ cup soy sauce
½ cup Worcestershire sauce
½ cup water
1 large onion, chopped
4 to 5 pound beef rump roast or 2-inch thick chuck pot roast

— Place butter in 1-quart measure.
— Microwave on high for 30 seconds, or until melted.
— Add soy sauce, Worcestershire sauce, water and onion.
— Place roast in plastic storage bag.
— Pour in marinade.
— Seal bag tightly with twist tie.
— Let stand overnight at refrigerator temperature.
— Place roast on Microwave roasting rack in (12x8-inch) utility dish. (If roast has layer of fat, place fat side down.)
— Microwave 60 to 65 minutes on medium, or until fork tender, turning roast over after 30 minutes.
— Let stand 15 minutes, covered with tent of aluminum foil.

CORNED BEEF 'N CABBAGE

2¾ to 3-lb. corned beef brisket with seasonings
1½ cups water
2 medium onions, quartered
3 carrots, sliced
3 potatoes, quartered
1 cabbage, cut into wedges

— Place corned beef brisket in 3-quart glass casserole; add water, and sprinkle with seasonings included with meat.
— Cover with glass lid or plastic wrap.
— Microwave on high for 10 to 12 minutes or until water is boiling.
— Turn meat over.
— Microwave on low for about 1½ hours or until fork tender.
— Turn meat over; add remaining ingredients; recover.
— Microwave on low for 30 to 45 minutes or until vegetables are tender.
— Let stand, covered, 5 minutes before serving.

ROLLED RIBS OF BEEF

4 to 5-pound rolled rib of beef roast
1 clove garlic, cut in slivers
Seasoned salt (optional)

— Place an inverted saucer in the bottom of a baking dish or use a Microwave roasting rack in a glass 2-quart dish.
— Poke holes in meat with a sharp knife and insert a thin sliver of garlic in each slit.
— Sprinkle roast with seasoned salt.
— Place roast fat side down on saucer.
— Cook, uncovered, on high, for about 2½ minutes per pound for rare, 3¼ minutes for medium.
— Remove roast, insert a thermometer halfway into meat, check for doneness.
— If reading is correct (120° rare, 140° medium or 160° well done), cover roast tightly and let stand about 15 minutes before serving.

(8-10 servings)

FLANK STEAK

1 ½ to 2-lb. beef flank steak
Salt
Pepper
2 tablespoons butter
2 tablespoons chopped onion
¼ cup chopped celery
2 cups bread cubes
¼ teaspoon ground sage
Water, if necessary
1 can (10¾ oz.) condensed tomato soup
Parsley

— Pound flank steak well. Season with salt and pepper; set aside.
— Combine butter, onion and celery in medium glass mixing bowl.
— Microwave on medium for about 3 minutes or until onion and celery are partly cooked.
— Stir in bread cubes and sage, moisten with water if necessary.
— Spread stuffing lengthwise down center of flank steak.
— Roll up lengthwise.
— Tie with strings in 3 or 4 places.
— Place in 1 ½-quart (10x6) glass baking dish.
— Cover with plastic wrap.
— Microwave on low for 20 minutes.
— Pour soup over meat. Sprinkle with snipped parsley and continue cooking on low for 4 to 5 minutes or until fork tender.
— Let stand, covered, 5 minutes before serving.

(4-6 servings)

BEEF RAGOUT

2 lbs. cubed beef stew meat
2 medium potatoes, cubed
2 medium carrots, sliced
2 medium onions, cut into 6 pieces each
1 can (16 oz.) stewed tomatoes
½ cup cold coffee or ½ cup bouillon
1 teaspoon salt
¼ teaspoon pepper
1 can (16 oz.) peas, undrained
¼ cup unsifted all-purpose flour

— Place meat in 3-quart glass casserole.
— Cover with glass lid or plastic wrap.
— Microwave on high for about 8 minutes or until meat is no longer pink.
— Stir in remaining ingredients, except peas and flour; recover.
— Microwave on low for 45 minutes; stir. Recover and continue cooking on low for 45 to 50 minutes.
— Blend juice from peas with flour to make a smooth paste.
— Stir into meat mixture along with peas; mix well.
— Recover and continue cooking on low for 3 to 4 minutes or until hot.
— Let stand, covered, 5 minutes before serving.

(6-8 servings)

EASY SWISS STEAK

¼ cup all-purpose flour
1 teaspoon salt
¼ teaspoon pepper
2 pounds round steak
1 large onion, chopped
1 can (10½ oz.) condensed tomato soup, undiluted

— Combine flour, salt and pepper.
— Place steak on a board and pound half of the flour mixture into each side of steak with the back of a heavy knife.
— Cut meat in 4 pieces and place in an (8 x 8-inch) square glass baking dish.
— Sprinkle any remaining flour over top of meat.
— Combine tomato soup with ½ cup water.
— Pour over steak.
— Microwave, covered, for 30 to 35 minutes, on high, or until meat is tender.
— Stir meat and sauce several times during cooking period and add a little additional water if necessary.

(4 servings)

BEEF ORIENTAL

1 lb. beef (½-inch thick)
¼ cup sliced onion
1 can (10½ oz.) cream of mushroom soup
1 can (16 oz.) Chinese vegetables
3 tablespoons chopped mushrooms
3 tablespoons chopped carrots
2 teaspoons soy sauce
1 teaspoon salt
Dash of pepper
4 cups hot cooked chow mein noodles

— Combine beef and onion in a casserole.
— Microwave, covered, 3 minutes on high.
— Stir and Microwave 3 more minutes on high.
— Mix in mushroom soup, Chinese vegetables, mushrooms, carrots, soy sauce, salt and pepper.
— Cook 5 minutes, stirring every 2 minutes.
— Pour over chow mein noodles and serve.

(4 servings)

PEPPER STEAK

1 tablespoon salad oil
1 ½ lbs. top round steak sliced and cut into strips
1 clove garlic, pressed or finely chopped
½ teaspoon sliced ginger, or ¼ teaspoon ginger.
½ cup water
1 teaspoon instant beef bouillon
2 cups green pepper, cubed
1 medium onion, thinly sliced
2 large stems celery, sliced diagonally
1 jar (2 oz.) chopped pimento
1 teaspoon salt
¼ teaspoon pepper
2 teaspoons corn starch dissolved
1 tablespoon soy sauce

— Place browning dish in oven (if available).
— Microwave 5 minutes on high.
— Add oil and beef strips to dish.
— Microwave 2 to 3 minutes on high, or until meat is brown, stirring after 1 minute.
— Add garlic and ginger. Cover. Microwave 7 to 10 minutes on medium.
— Stir in remaining ingredients.
— Cover.
— Microwave 7 to 10 minutes on medium or until vegetables are tender-crisp. (Meat may be browned on conventional range in 2-quart glass-ceramic casserole).

(4 servings)

FRESH BEEF BRISKET

3-3 ½ lb. fresh beef brisket
2 teaspoons garlic salt
1 envelope (1 ¼ oz.) onion soup mix

— Sprinkle both sides of meat with garlic salt.
— Place in 3 quart (13x9) glass baking dish.
— Cover with plastic wrap.
— Microwave for 45 minutes on high.
— Turn meat over; recover and Microwave for an additional 30 minutes on high or until fork tender.
— Remove meat to platter; cover, and chill for several hours.
— Dissolve onion soup mix in hot meat juices; set aside.
— When ready to serve, slice meat and place in reserved seasoned juices in 3-quart (13x9) glass baking dish.
— Cover.
— Microwave for 8-10 minutes on high or until heated through.
— Let stand, covered, for 5 minutes before serving.

(8 servings)

BEEF BOURGUIGNONNE

4 slices bacon, quartered
2 lbs. lean beef sirloin or top round steak, cut in ¾-inch cubes
¼ cup flour
1 package (8-oz.) fresh mushrooms, sliced
1 medium onion, sliced
1 clove garlic, finely chopped
1 bay leaf
1 tablespoon parsley
½ teaspoon thyme
1 ½ cups burgundy wine
2 teaspoons instant beef bouillon
1 teaspoon salt
¼ teaspoon pepper

— Place bacon in 2-quart casserole, cover with paper towel.
— Microwave 2 minutes on high.
— (Do not drain).
— Coat beef cubes with flour.
— Add to bacon and drippings.
— Toss to coat with fat.
— Sprinkle any remaining flour over meat.
— Add mushrooms, onion, garlic, bay leaf, parsley and thyme.
— Stir in wine and bouillon.
— Cover.
— Microwave 5 minutes on high.
— Reduce setting. Microwave 30 minutes on medium, or until beef is fork tender, stirring once.
— Season with salt and pepper.
— Let stand 10 minutes, covered.
— Remove bay leaf.
— Serve over noodles.

(6 servings)

STROGANOFF SUPREME

3 tablespoons margarine or butter
1 lb. round steak, cut into thin strips
½ cup chopped onion
1 (4 oz.) can sliced mushrooms, drained
¼ teaspoon dry mustard
½ teaspoon salt
¼ teaspoon pepper
1 (8 oz.) package cream cheese, cubed
⅔ cup beer
Hot parsleyed noodles

— Place 3 tablespoons butter or margarine in a deep, 2-quart, heat-resistant, non-meallic casserole.
— Melt on high 30 seconds, uncovered.
— Add steak strips to butter and Microwave, uncovered, on high for 10 minutes or until meat is browned.
— Add onion, mushrooms and seasoning to meat.
— Microwave, uncovered, on high for 4 minutes.
— Add cubed cream cheese and beer to meat mixture and heat, uncovered, on high for 6 minutes or unil cheese melts.
— Stir occasionally.
— Serve over hot parsleyed noodles.

(4 servings)

SUKIYAKI

1 ½ to 2-lbs. beef sirloin steak, cut into thin strips
¾ cup soy sauce
½ cup water
3 tablespoons sugar
1 can (4 oz.) mushroom stems and piecs, drained and sliced
½ cup sliced green onion
1 can (5 oz.) water chestnuts, drained and sliced
1 can (5 oz.) bamboo shoots, drained
1 can (16 oz.) bean sprouts, drained

— Combine steak, soy sauce, water and sugar in 2-quart (12x7-inch) glass baking dish.
— Cover with plastic wrap. Marinate 3 to 4 hours at room temperature.
— Place remaining ingredients in rows across meat and sauce with mushrooms and onions in center rows; recover.
— Microwave on high for 10 to 12 minutes. Let stand, covered, 2 minutes before serving.

(4-6 servings)

GROUND BEEF KEY

Microwave ground beef into juicy patties on high. Meatball, meatloaf and stuffed vegetable dishes on even-cooking medium.

Meat should be completely thawed before cooking.

Cook ground beef patties, uncovered, on a microwave browning grill, a glass pie plate, dinner plate or serving platter (without silver or other metal trim).

Microwave most other ground beef dishes in glass casseroles or baking dishes with fitted glass lids, tight coverings of pastic wrap or wax paper.

Drain off excess fat and moisture as directed in a recipe, to preserve flavor and sauce consistency.

Rearrange or stir ground beef dishes thoroughtly when called for in a recipe so the entire mixture cooks evenly.

(Food continues to cook after it comes from a microwave oven.)

SWEDISH MEATBALLS

¼ cup butter or margarine
1 cup finely chopped onion
3 eggs
1 ⅓ cups milk
1 ½ teaspoons ground allspice
½ teaspoon nutmeg
1 tablespoon salt
2 cups soft bread crumbs
2 lbs. lean ground beef round
1 lb. lean ground lamb
1 cub beef bouillon, crumbled
1 cup boiling water
4 tablespoons flour
2 cups light cream or milk

— Melt butter in a shalow, 2-quart, heat-resistant, non-metallic dish on high 30 seconds, uncovered.
— Add onions and heat, uncovered, on high 3 minutes or until onions are lightly browned.
— Set aside.
— In a small bowl, mix eggs and milk until well blended.
— Add egg mixture, allspice, nutmeg, salt and bread crumbs to cooked onions.
— Stir to combine.
— Crumble meat into mixture.
— Mix with hands or kitchen fork until thoroughly combined.
— Form meat mixture into 1-inch balls.
— Microwave half of the meatballs in a single layer in a shallow, 1-quart, heat-resistant, non-metallic casserole on medium for 7 to 8 minutes, uncovered, or until almost done.
— Turn meatballs every 2 minutes.

— While meatballs are cooking, combine beef bouillon and water in a small bowl and set aside.

— Repeat the cooking process with the remaining meatballs. Set meatballs on serving plate.

— Reserve any meat juices that collect in the bottom of the baking dish.

— Skim off excess fat and discard.

— Pour meat juices into a deep, 2 ½-quart, non-metallic casserole and stir in flour. Stir in reserved beef broth.

— Microwave, uncovered, on high 2 minutes or until slightly thickened.

— Gradually stir in cream.

— Microwave, uncovered, on medium for 8 minutes or until thickened and smooth.

—Stir occasionally.

— Pour sauce over meatballs and serve warm.

(8 servings)

MEAT LOAF PARMESAN

2 slices white bread, trim crust
2 slices rye bread, trim crust
1 cup wine
1 ½ lbs. of lean ground beef
1 medium onion, chopped
2 tablespoons parsley, chopped
3 tablespoons parmesan cheese, grated
1 egg
1 teaspoon salt
⅛ teaspoon pepper
1 (8-oz.) can tomato sauce

— Soak bread in wine 5 minutes, then squeeze out as much liquid as possible.

— Break up the bread, and mix with beef, onion, parsley, cheese, egg, salt and pepper.

— Form into a loaf and place into a 1 ½-quart glass loaf dish.

— Microwave, covered, with wax paper, 10 to 12 minutes on high.

— Pour tomato sauce over meat loaf.

— Return to microwave and cook, uncovered, until sauce is hot, about 2 minutes on high.

— Let stand 5 minutes before slicing.

(4-6 servings)

BEEF TACOS

1 lb. ground beef
½ cup chopped onions
1 can (8-oz.) tomato sauce
¼ teaspoon chili powder
¼ teaspoon salt
¼ teaspoon garlic salt
10 to 12 cooked taco shells
Graded Cheddar cheese
Shredded lettuce
Chopped fresh tomato
Finely diced avocado

— Crumble beef into a deep 1-quart glass casserole.

— Add onion.

— Microwave, uncovered, for about 5 minutes on high or until meat loses its pink color, stirring after 3 minutes.

— Add onions, tomato sauce, chili powder, salt, and garlic salt.

— Cover casserole with a paper towel.

— Cook for about 5 minutes on high, or until sauce is blended and thickened.

— Spoon filling into taco shells.

— Place tacos in a straight-side glass dish so they will stand upright.

— Microwave, covered with waxed paper, for 1 ½ minutes on high, or until tacos are piping hot.

— Serve with cheese, lettuce, tomato, and avocado in side dishes or sprinkle as desired over top of hot filling.

WESTERN MEAT LOAF

1 ½ lbs. ground beef
2 cups soft bread cubes
½ cup chopped celery
¾ cup catsup
¼ cup finely chopped green pepper
1 ½ teaspoons salt
1 egg, beaten

— Combine all ingredients in medium mixing bowl; mix well.

— Pat into (8 x 4-inch) glass loaf dish.

— Microwave, uncovered, on medium for 25 to 30 minutes or until well done in center.

— Let stand, covered, 5 minutes before serving.

Variation: Top meat loaf with chili sauce after cooking is completed.

(5-6 servings)

SESAME MEATBALL DINNER

1 lb. ground beef
1 cup shredded raw potatoes
2 tablespoons parsley
½ teaspoon salt
¼ teaspoon pepper
1 small onion, finely chopped
2 tablespoons sesame seeds
1 egg, beaten
2 cups water
1½ tablespoons beef bouillon
2 tablespoons cornstarch
2 tablespoons water

— Mix all ingredients except water, beef bouillon and cornstarch in medium mixing bowl.
— Shape into 12 (1½-inch) meatballs; set aside.
— Combine 2 cups water and instant beef bouillon in a deep 2-quart glass casserole.
— Cover with glass lid or plastic wrap.
— Microwave on high for 6 to 7 minutes or until boiling.
— Add meatballs; recover.
— Microwave on medium for 8 minutes.
— Stir in a mixture of cornstarch and 2 tablespoons water; recover.
— Microwave on medium for 3 to 4 minutes or until sauce is thickened.
— Let stand, covered, 5 minutes before serving.

(4 servings)

MEAT LOAF

1 egg slightly beaten
1 tablespoon Worcestershire sauce
1½ lbs. lean ground beef
1 cup cracker crumbs
½ cup chopped onion
½ teaspoon salt
Dash of pepper
Cherry tomato slices
Parsley sprigs

— Mix all ingredients thoroughly together.
— Spread mixture evenly in a (9x5-inch) loaf dish.
— Microwave, uncovered, 10 to 12 minutes on high or until done.
— Allow to stand a few minutes before serving.
— Garnish with slices of cherry tomato and parsley sprigs if desired.

(4 servings)

BROCCOLI AND BEEF

1 large stalk broccoli
2 tablespoons cooking oil
½ cup coarsely chopped onions
1 clove garlic, minced
½ lb. ground beef
½ cup sliced celery
2 teaspoons soy sauce
1 tablespoon dry sherry

— Cut off flowerets from top of broccoli and cut large flowers in halves or quarters.
— Peel broccoli stalks and cut in diagonal slices about ½ inch thick. Set aside.
— In a deep, 1½-quart glass casserole place oil, onion and garlic.
— Add beef, broken into pieces.
— Microwave, covered, for 4 minutes on high.
— Remove casserole and break up pieces of beef with a fork.
— Add celery, soy sauce, sherry, and broccoli.
— Stir.
— Microwave, covered, for 4 minutes on high, or just until broccoli is crisply tender.
— Serve over hot cooked rice with additional soy sauce.

(2 servings)

STUFFED GREEN PEPPERS

4 large green peppers
1 lb. ground beef
1 medium onion, finely chopped
1 teaspoon salt
¼ teaspoon pepper
1½ cups cooked rice
1 can tomato soup

— Wash peppers. Remove tops, seeds and membrane. Set aside.
— Crumble beef in a 1½-quart glass casserole.
— Add onion.
— Microwave, uncovered, for about 5 minutes on high, stirring after 3 minutes to break up meat. Microwave until meat loses its red color.
— Stir in salt, pepper, rice, and half of the tomato soup.
— Fill green peppers with mixture, mounding mixture on top. Place in a shallow, 2-quart glass baking dish.
— Top each pepper with a dribble of remaining tomato soup.
— Cook, covered, for 8 to 10 minutes on high, or just until peppers are tender.

(4 servings)

BEEF STROGANOFF WITH AVOCADO

1 ½ lb. lean ground beef
1 medium sized onion, chopped
½ teaspoon salt
½ teaspoon garlic salt
1 teaspoon seasoned pepper
1 can (10¾-oz.) cream of mushroom soup
½ teaspoon oregano
1 cup plain yogurt
1 medium sized avocado, cubed
3 cups hot steamed rice
Paprika

— Crumble ground beef into bottom of a deep 3-quart glass casserole.
— Microwave, uncovered, 4 minutes on high.
— Stir.
— Add onion, salt, garlic salt and pepper to beef.
— Microwave, uncovered, 4 minutes on high and stir.
— Drain off excess fat.
— Blend in soup, oregano, yogurt and avocado
— Cover and microwave 10 to 12 minutes on high or until bubbly hot.
— Garnish top of casserole with paprika.
— Serve immediately with rice.

(4-6 servings)

SOUTH SEAS BEEF

1 lb. lean ground beef
½ cup flaked coconut
1 teaspoon salt
¼ teaspoon nutmeg
¾ cup pineapple tidbits, drained
1 cup pineapple juice
2 teaspoons lemon juice
2 tablespoons cornstarch
1 can (6-oz.) chow mein noodles
3 tablespoons salted almonds

— Crumble ground beef into bottom of a deep 2-quart glass casserole.
— Microwave, uncovered, 3 minutes on high and stir.
— Microwave 3 minutes more on high and stir.
— In small bowl combine coconut, salt, nutmeg, pineapple tidbits, pineapple juice, lemon juice, and cornstarch.
— Mix well.
— Add to meat mixture and stir.
— Cover and microwave 5 minutes on high or until sauce thickens slightly.
— Arrange chow mein noodles on platter and top with coconut beef mixture and garnish with salted almonds.

(4 servings)

SHISH KABOB

½ cup wine vinegar
½ cup cooking oil
1 teaspoon onion salt
1 clove garlic, split in half
¼ cup soy sauce
2 teaspoons Italian seasoning
½ cup water
2 lbs. boneless lamb or steak
½ lb. small fresh mushrooms
1 dozen tomato wedges
1 green pepper, cut in 1-inch squares

— Combine vinegar, oil, onion salt, garlic, soy sauce, Italian seasoning, and ½ cup water in a large mixing bowl. Set aside.
— Cut steak in 1-inch cubes.
— Add to marinade and let stand, covered with plastic wrap, at room temperature 5 to 6 hours.
— Place meat cubes and desired vegetables noted above alternately on long wooden skewers.
— Place 2 or 3 skewers on a dinner plate.
— Microwave, uncovered, for about 3 minutes, on high, for medium rare.
— Microwave slightly longer for well-done meat

(The marinade turns the meat brown while standing, for attracive color in the finished kabobs.)

(6-8 servings)

CHILI CON CARNE

1 tablespoon butter or margarine
1 lb. ground beef
1 onion, sliced
Dash of garlic powder
2 teaspoons chili powder
½ teaspoon mustard
Dash of pepper
½ teaspoon salt
2 cups undrained tomatoes
1 lb. kidney beans

— Put butter, beef, sliced onion and garlic powder in a shallow, 2-quart glass dish. Microwave 3 minutes on high, uncovered.
— Add chili powder, mustard, pepper, salt, tomatoes and beans. Mix.
— Microwave, covered, 5 minutes on high.
— Stir and cook 5 more minutes, on high, covered.

(4 servings)

CURRIED LAMB MEATBALLS

1 lb. ground lamb
1 clove gagrlic, finely chopped
1 medium onion, sliced
1 stalk celery, sliced
2 tablespoons flour
1 1/2 teaspoon curry powder
1 teaspoon salt
2 teaspoons instant chicken bouillon
1/4 cup chutney
1 teaspoon prepared mustard
3/4 cup water

— Combine ground lamb and garlic in medium mixing bowl; mix well.
— Shape into 16 to 18 (1-inch) lamb balls.
— Place in 2-quart (12 x 7-inch) glass baking dish.
— Add onion and celery.
— Cover with plastic wrap.
— Microwave on medium for 5 minutes.
— Combine remaining ingredients in 4-cup glass measure; mix well. Set aside
— Drain and rearrange lamb balls; pour on sauce.
— Recover and continue cooking on medium for 8 to 10 minutes or until hot.
— Let stand, covered, 5 minutes before serving.

(4 servings)

RACK OF LAMB WITH ORANGE-HONEY SAUCE

1 2 to 2 1/2 lb. lamb rack (5 to 6 ribs)
Salt
Pepper
1 tablespoon Kitchen Bouquet or soy sauce
3 tablespoons honey
3 tablespoons concentrated orange juice

— Trim excess fat from meat, leaving only a thin covering.
— Score fat side paralleling bones, cutting just into the meat.
— Rub with salt, pepper and Kitchen Bouquet.
— Place fat side down in a baking dish and microwave 6 minutes on high, uncovered.
— Remove meat and baste with orange mixture.
— Microwave fat side up 4 minutes on high, uncovered, baste again.
— Microwave on high 2 minutes longer for medium.
— Let lamb sit about 5 minutes before carving.
— Mix any remaining marinade with pan juices for a table sauce.

(4 servings)

CURRIED LAMB

1 lb. boneless lamb, cut in 1-inch cubes
2 tablespoons all-purpose flour
1 clove garlic, minced
1 large onion, sliced
1/4 cup butter or margarine
1 1/2 tablespoons curry powder
2 apples, peeled, cored, and chopped in coarse pieces
2 tablespoons seedless raisins
1 1/2 teaspoons salt
1/2 cup water

— Toss lamb cubes lightly with flour. set aside.
— Place garlic, onion, and butter in a 2-quart (12 x 7-inch) glass casserole. Microwave, uncovered, for 3 minutes on high.
— Add lamb and curry powder and toss lighly.
— Microwave, uncovered, for 10 minutes on high, stirring after 5 minutes.
— Add apples, raisins, and salt. Stir in 1/2 cup water.
— Microwave, covered, for about 20 minutes, on high, or until meat is tender. Stir occasionally during cooking time.
— Let stand 3 minutes.
— Serve with hot cooked rice and accompaniments such as flaked coconut, chopped peanuts or walnuts, and chutney.

(4 servings)

LAMB SHANKS

2 tablespoons flour
1 teaspoon salt
1/2 teaspoon pepper
1/4 teaspoon garlic salt
4 lamb shanks (2 1/2 to 3 lbs.)
1/2 cup chopped onion
1 cup thinly sliced carrots
1 tablespoon dried parsley flakes
1/2 teaspoon leaf rosemary
1 teaspoon salt
1 can (10 1/2 oz.) condensed beef consomme

— Combine flour, salt, pepper and garlic salt in 9-inch glass pie dish.
— Roll lamb shanks in seasoned flour; place in shallow 2-quart glass baking dish. Cover with plastic wrap.
— Microwave on medium for 20 minutes.
— Turn meat over. Stir in remaining ingredients.
— Recover and continue cooking on medium for 20 to 25 minutes or until fork tender.

(4 servings)

LAMB CHOPS A L'ORANGE

4 shoulder lamp chops (about 2 lbs.)
Garlic salt
4 fresh orange slices, ½-inch thick
½ cup orange marmalade

— Place chops in a 10-inch, heat-resistant, non-metallic baking dish.
— Sprinkle chops with garlic salt
— Place fresh orange slice and spread orange marmalade over each chop.
— Microwave, covered,, on medium for 25 minutes or until chops are tender.

(3-4 servings)

FRUIT GLAZED LAMB CHOPS

1½ lbs. lamb chops — 4 or 5
2 tablespoon soy sauce
½ cup apricot-pineapple jam
1 tablespoon prepared mustard
Salt and pepper

— Rub chops with soy sauce and coat both sides with mixture of jam and mustard.
— Place in a shallow, 2-quart glass baking dish and cover with plastic wrap.
— Puncture one or two holes in plastic and microwave 5 minutes on high.
— Turn chops and baste with sauce.
— Recover and microwave 4 to 5 minutes on high, or longer depending on doneness desired.

(4-5 servings)

VEAL AND NOODLES

1½ lbs. veal, cut up for stewing
2 teaspoons butter
2 tablespoons flour
1½ cups beef bouillon
1 large tomato, sliced
1 cup thinly sliced fresh mushrooms
1 onion, minced
1 bay leaf
1 tablespoon tomato paste
Salt and pepper, to taste

— Microwave butter and veal in a 2-quart glass baking dish, 3 minutes on high.
— Remove veal.
— Blend in flour.
— Gradually stir in beef bouillon.
— Add tomato, mushrooms, onion, bay leaf and tomato paste to beef bouillon mixture.
— Microwave, uncovered, for 10 minutes on high, or until mixture begins to bubble.
— Season with salt and pepper to taste.
— Add veal.
— Microwave, uncovered, for 20 minutes on high, or until veal is fork tender.
— Serve with rice or noodles.

(4 servings)

SWEET AND SOUR LAMB CHOPS

2 tablespoons butter
2 lbs. shoulder lamb chops
Salt and pepper
1 (8-oz.) can pineapple chunks in unsweetened juice
¼ cup firmly packed dark brown sugar
¼ cup white vinegar
1 tablespoon cornstarch
½ teaspoon brown bouquet sauce
2 carrots, peeled and thinly sliced
1 large green pepper, cut into 1-inch squares

— Melt butter in a heat resistant, non-metallic baking dish on a conventional surface unit.
— When butter is hot, sear lamb chops on both sides until lightly browned.
— Sprinkle with salt and pepper to taste.
— While the chops are browning, drain pineapple juice into a small heat-resistant, non-metallic bowl.
— Reserve pineapple chunks; add brown sugar, vinegar, cornstarch and brown bouquet sauce to pineapple juice. Stir to combine.
— Microwave pineapple juice mixture, uncovered, on high 2 minutes or until thickened and clear.
— Pour thickened sauce over browned lamb chops.
— Add carrot slices and cook, covered, on medium for 7 minutes.
— Add pineapple chunks and cook, covered, on medium for 3 minutes.
— Add green pepper squares and heat, uncovered, on medium for 4 to 5 minutes, or until lamb and vegetables are tender.

(3-4 servings)

VEAL CUTLETS IN WHITE WINE

¼ cup butter
1 clove garlic, finely chopped
5 veal cutlets
Salt
Pepper
1 tablespoon instant beef bouillon
1 medium onion, thinly sliced
¼ cup dry white wine
1 tablespoon dried parsley flakes

— Place butter and garlic in 2-quart glass baking dish.
— Microwave on medium for about 2 minutes or until butter melts.
— Coat veal in garlic butter and arrange in dish
— Add remaining ingredients.
— Cover with plastic wrap.
— Microwave on low for 25 to 30 minutes or until meat is fork tender.
— Let stand, covered, 5 minutes before serving.

(4-5 servings)

VEAL SCALLOPPINE

1 ½ lbs. veal cutlets, pounded until ¼-inch thick
Salt and pepper
¼ cup flour
3 tablespoons butter
1 can (4-oz.) sliced mushrooms, drained
1 cup beef bouillon
1 can (6-oz.) tomato paste
1 teaspoon lemon juice
1 tomato, sliced

— Season cutlets with salt and pepper.
— Coat with flour and shake off excess.
— Place butter in a shallow 2-quart glass casserole.
— Microwave on high 30 seconds, uncovered, until butter melts.
— Place veal in casserole and turn to coat with butter. Cover.
— Microwave 4 mintues on high, turning cutlets over after 2 minutes. Add mushrooms
— Stir bouillon, tomato paste and lemon juice together in 1-quart measure. Pour over cutlets.
— Microwave 12 to 15 minutes on medium, or until veal is fork tender.
— Arrange cutlets and sauce on platter. Garnish with tomato slices.
— Microwave 2½ minutes on medium, uncovered, or until heated through.

(4 servings)

VEAL A LA PALKO

3 tablespoons vegetable oil
1 clove garlic, peeled and crushed
¼ cup flour
½ teaspoon salt
¼ teaspoon pepper
2 pounds boneless veal, cut into bite-sized pieces
1 cup boiling water
2 (1-inch strips) lemon peels
½ teaspoon sage
Dash of cayenne pepper
1 cup heavy cream
2 tablespoons finely chopped parsley

— In a 10-inch heat resistant, non-metallic baking dish, heat 3 tablespoons oil on top of a conventional surface unit.
— While oil is heating, combine flour, salt and pepper in a paper or plastic bag.
— Coat veal pieces with seasoned flour.
— Add crushed garlic to hot oil.
— Brown coated veal pieces in hot oil.
— When veal pieces are browned, add boiling water, lemon peel, sage and cayenne pepper. Stir to combine.
—Microwave, covered, on medium for 15 minutes or until veal is tender.
— Remove lemon peel and stir cream into veal mixture gradually.
— Microwave, covered, on medium, an additional 8 minutes. Stir once, after 4 minutes.
— Garnish with chopped parsley before serving

(4 servings)

APRICOT LOIN OF PORK

1 (12-oz.) package dried apricots
1 (3-inch) stick cinnamon
½ lemon
½ cup water
1 cup apricot nectar
3 tablespoons orange juice
4 tablespoons honey
1 (6-lbs.) loin of pork roast

— Remove twice as many dried apricot halves from the package as there are bones on the roast and set aside.
— Place remaining dried apricots, cinnamon, the juice from the lemon half, the remainder of the lemon half cut into quarters, and the water in a medium sized heat-resistant, non-metallic bowl.
— Microwave mixture, uncovered, on medium for 10 minutes or until apricots are tender.
— Remove cinnamon stick and lemon peel chunks.
— Add apricot nectar, orange juice, and honey.
— Microwave, uncovered, on medium for 3 minutes.
— Spread glaze over pork loin and heat, uncovered, in a shallow, 2-quart heat-resistant, non-metallic baking dish in Microwave Oven on medium for 12 minutes per pound, or until meat thermometer inserted in the thickest part of the meat registers 170° to 175°F.
— While roast cooks, baste meat with glaze.
— Allow roast to stand wrapped in aluminum foil 15 minutes.
— Before serving, place two of the reserved apricot halves on each bone tip.
— Press apricot halves firmly together so they stay in place.
— Pork should be cooked to well-done.
— After standing time, pork should register 180° to 185°F.

(6-8 servings)

VEAL PARMIGIANA

1 1 egg, lightly beaten
¼ teaspoon salt
4 tablespoons cracker crumbs
½ cup grated Parmesan cheese
1 lb. veal cutlets
2 tablespoons cooking oil
¼ cup dry vermouth
1 medium onion, chopped
1 cup shredded mozzarella cheese
1 can (8-oz.) tomato sauce
Fresh pepper
⅛ teaspoon oregano

— Beat egg with salt in a shallow 2-quart glass baking dish.
— Combine cracker crumbs and Parmesan cheese.
— Cut veal into 4 serving pieces.
— Place each piece between two pieces of waxed paper and pound to about ¼ inch thick with the side of a cleaver.
— Dip veal in egg and then in cracker crumbs. Heat oil in a skillet on top of the range.
— Cook veal in hot oil until golden brown on both sides.
— Place veal in a (10 x 6-inch) baking dish
— Add vermouth to skillet and heat about 1 minute, scraping up browned bits from bottom of skillet.
— Pour over veal cutlets.
— Sprinkle onion over meat.
— Top with mozzarella cheese.
— Spoon tomato sauce over top, and season with pepper and oregano.
— Microwave, covered, for 7 minutes, or until sauce is bubbly and cheese is melted.

(4 servings)

HAM SAUTE

1 small cauliflower
5 tablespoons salad oil
2 tablespoons vinegar
Dash of salt and pepper
12 ham slices
2 tablespoons white wine

— Wash cauliflower.
— Microwave 5 minutes, 30 seconds on high in covered casserole.
— Blend salad oil, vinegar, salt and pepper in a cup to make French dressing.
— Separate cauliflower into small branches.
— Toss with French dressing.
— Arrange ham on a serving plate (not cooking dish).
— Pour white wine over it.
— Microwave 1 minute on high, uncovered
— Arrange cauliflower on the plate.

(4 servings)

WINE-STUFFED PORK CHOPS

2 tablespoons butter or margarine
1 medium onion, finely chopped
¼ cup celery, finely chopped
1 cup bread crumbs
2 tablespoons parsley, chopped
⅛ teaspoon sage
4 pork chops, 1½ inches thick, cut with pocket
2 tablespoons flour
1 can (10½-oz.) chicken broth
¼ cup dry white wine

— Combine butter, onion and celery in small 1-quart glass mixing bowl.
— Microwave 3 to 5 minutes on high, or until onion is transparent.
— Stir in bread crumbs, parsley, sage.
— Fill pockets of pork chops with stuffing.
— Secure openings with toothpicks.
— Arrange chops in (12 x 8-inch) baking dish, meatiest portions of outside.
— Sprinkle with flour.
— Pour chicken broth and wine over chops.
— Cover with plastic wrap and cook on high 20 minutes, or until chops are fork tender, turning dish once during cooking.

(4 servings)

GERMAN STYLE SPARERIBS

2 tablespoons butter
½ cup finely chopped onion
3 tablespoons dark brown sugar
⅛ teaspoon pepper
½ teaspoon salt
2 tablespoons prepared mustard
½ cup catsup
3 cups sauerkraut, drained
1 large apple, chopped
2 teaspoons caraway seeds
3 lbs. spareribs, cut into ribs

— In a medium-sized glass bowl, heat butter on high 30 seconds, uncovered.
— Add onion, brown sugar, pepper, salt, mustard, and catsup.
— Microwave, uncovered, on high 3 minutes.
— In a 3-quart, heat-resistant, non-metallic casserole, place sauerkraut, apple and caraway seeds.
— Stir to combine thoroughly.
— Dip each sparerib into sauce and place on top of sauerkraut.
— Pour remaining barbecue sauce over the top.
—Microwave, covered, on low for 40 to 50 minutes.
(Pork should always be cooked to well-done.)

(6 servings)

BAKED HAM

Fully cooked ham (any size)
Ham glaze
Whole cloves
Score ham, if desired

— Place ham fat side down on an inverted saucer or on a microwave roasting rack in (12 x 8-inch) utility dish. (Do not cover).
— Microwave on medium for half the roasting time.
— Turn ham fat side up.
— Brush with glaze and stud with cloves, if desired. (See below for recipe of Ham Glaze).
— Microwave on medium for remaining time, or until internal temperature registers 140°F to 150°F.
— Let stand 15 minutes, tented with aluminum foil, shiny side in. (Temperature will rise 10 degrees during standing.)
(Refer to meat cooking chart for cooking times in relation to the weight of ham at beginning of the chapter.)

HAM GLAZES

¼ cup honey
½ cup firmly packed brown sugar
— Measure honey in 1-cup measure.
— Microwave 1 to 2 minutes on high, uncovered, or until hot.
— Stir in brown sugar.
— Glaze ham after turning

½ cup firmly packed brown sugar
2 teaspoons prepared mustard
1 can (8-oz.) pineapple rings
Maraschino cherries
— Blend sugar and mustard together.
— Add enough pineapple juice to make smooth paste.
— After turning ham, arrange pineapple rings on top.
— Spoon on glaze.
— Garnish with maraschino cherries, if desired.

BRATWURST IN BEER

6 uncooked bratwurst
½ cup finely chopped onion
2 tablespoons butter
1 can beer, room temperature
— Place bratwurst in a (8-inch) round glass baking dish.
— Add remaining ingredients.
— Cover with plastic wrap.
— Microwave on medium for 5 to 6 minutes or until done.
— Let stand, covered, 5 minutes before serving.

(3 servings)

SWEET AND SOUR PORK

1 ½ lbs. lean pork, cut in ½-inch cubes
1 small onion, sliced
1 teaspoon salt
1 can (8-oz.) pineapple slices
1 package (2-oz.) sweet and sour mix
2 green peppers, seeded and cut in squares
2 carrots, peeled and sliced in thin strips
— Place pork, onion, and salt in a 2- to 3-quart shallow, glass baking dish or casserole.
— Microwave, covered, for 10 to 11 minutes on high.
— Stir meat once or twice.
— Drain off fat.
— Drain pineapple slices, reserving juice.
— Add enough water to pineapple juice to make 1 ¼ cups liquid.
— Add to pork mixture.
— Microwave, covered, for 8 mintues on high, stirring once or twice during cooking period.
— Stir in sweet and sour mix.
— Microwave, covered, for 8 minutes, on high, stirring occasionally during cooking period.
— Cut pineapple slices in small pieces.
— Add to pork mixture with green pepper and carrots.
— Microwave, covered, for 4 minutes on high, stirring once or twice during cooking period.
— Remove from oven and let stand 5 minutes.
— Serve with hot cooked rice or chow mein noodles.

(6 servings)

PORK TENDERLOIN IN ORANGE SAUCE

¼ cup butter or margarine
1 medium onion, chopped
1 ½ tablespoons sugar
1 tablespoon cornstarch
2 teaspoons salt
1 teaspoon grated orange peel
⅛ teaspoon pepper
¼ cup orange juice
⅓ cup dry sherry
2 pork tenderloins (about 1 lb. each)
— Place butter and onion in 2-quart (12 x 7-inch) glass baking dish.
— Microwave on medium for 3 minutes, uncovered.
— Stir in remaining ingredients, except pork.
— Coat pork tenderloin in sauce.
— Cover with plastic wrap.
— Microwave on medium for 25 to 30 minutes or until meat is fork tender.
— Let stand, covered, 5 minutes.
— Slice diagonally to serve.

(6-8 servings)

POLISH SAUSAGE AND SAUERKRAUT

1 package (32 oz.) refrigerated sauerkraut
2 teaspoons caraway seeds
1 medium apple, cored and finely sliced
1 lb. precooked Polish sausage

— Drain sauerkraut..
— Place in 2-quart glass baking dish.
— Stir in caraway seeds and apples.
— Place sausage on top.
— Cover.
— Microwave on low for 10 minutes.
— Turn sausage over; recover, and continue cooking on low for 5 to 7 minutes
— Let stand, covered, 5 minutes before serving.

(3-4 servings)

CENTER CUT HAM WITH APRICOTS

3 to 3¼-lb. lean center cut ham slice, 2 inches thick
1 can (16 oz.) apricots, undrained
¼ cup packed brown sugar
2 tablespoons cornstarch
2 tablespoons vinegar
¼ teaspoon nutmeg
2 tablespoons butter or margarine

— Score edges of ham slice; place in 2-quart (12 x 7-inch) glass baking dish.
— Combine apricot juice, brown sugar, cornstarch, vinegar and nutmeg in small glass mixing bowl, pour over ham.
— Top with apricots and dot with butter.
— Microwave on medium for 20 to 25 minutes, uncovered, or until ham is hot and sauce thickened.
— Let stand 5 minutes before serving.

(6-8 servings)

BARBECUED SPARERIBS

2 lbs. spareribs
2½ cup catsup
½ cup firmly packed brown sugar
½ tablespoon horseradish
1 tablespoon Worcestershire sauce
1 teaspoon garlic salt

— Place spareribs bone side down in shallow, 2-quart glass dish. Set aside.
— Mix remaining ingredients in 1-quart glass measure.
— Pour sauce over ribs.
— Cover.
— Microwave 5 minutes on high. Recover.
— Reduce setting; Microwave 35 minutes on medium, or until meat is tender, turning ribs over after 15 minutes.
— Let stand 3 minutes.

Variation: Use country style spareribs. Add 5 to 10 minutes to final cooking time.

(4 servings)

HAM STEAK

4 lbs. ham, sliced
1 teaspoon cloves
2 teaspoons brown sugar
2 teaspoons prepared mustard

— Place ham in a shallow, 2-quart glass baking dish.
— Cook, covered, 4 minutes on high.
— Score surface of ham with thin cross-shape cuts and stick cloves in the crosses.
— Stir brown sugar and prepared mustard in the liquid from the ham and brush on the ham.
— Cook from 2 to 4 minutes on high according to taste.

(4 servings)

BAR-B-CUED PORK CHOPS

4 loin pork chops
1 cup barbecued sauce
4 green onion chopped including tops
3 tablespoons brown sugar
3 tablespoons orange juice concentrate
2 tablespoons pineapple juice
½ teaspoon salt
¼ teaspoon pepper

— Place chops in 2-quart glass baking dish.
— Combine remaining ingredients in separate bowl and pour over chops.
— Cover and Microwave 20 mintues on high, turning chops once.

(4 servings)

LOIN OF PORK

4 lbs. loin of pork roast

— Place an inverted saucer or a microwave roasting rack in the bottom of an oblong baking dish.
— Place pork fat side down on baking dish.
— Cover protruding bones with pieces of foil.
— Microwave for 20 minutes on high.
— Remove foil and turn roast fat side up.
— Microwave, covered loosley with waxed paper, for 20 minutes on high, or until meat thermometer registers 170°F.
— Let stand, covered with foil, until meat registers cooking time for pork on meat thermometer.

(Loin of pork should be cooked 10 to 11 minutes per pound. When meat is being cooked, fat side up you may season it very lightly with salt and pepper or brush it very lightly with a barbecue sauce to give it a brown color when served.

(6-8 servings)

SCALLOPED POTATOES AND HAM

1½ cups milk
2 cups baked ham, cubed
4 cups sliced potatoes
⅔ cup chopped onions
1 tablespoon flour
1 teaspoon salt
⅛ teaspoon pepper
2 tablespoons butter
Paprika

— Put milk in a 2-cup measure.
— Microwave, covered with waxed paper or plastic wrap, for 2 to 3 minutes on high, or just long enough to warm milk.
— Put a layer of ham on bottom of a 2- or 3-quart glass casserole.
— Add a layer of potatoes and onion. Sprinkle with flour, salt, and pepper.
— Dot with butter.
— Add another layer of ham, potatoes, and onion.
— Pour hot milk over layers. Sprinkle with paprika.
— Microwave, covered, on high for 12 to 14 minutes, or until potatoes are tender.
— Uncover and cook again for 4 to 6 minutes on high.
— Cover loosely with plastic wrap and let stand 2 minutes before serving.

(4 servings)

HAM LOAF

2 eggs
¾ lb. ground ham
½ lb. ground veal
¼ lb. ground pork
¾ cup bread crumbs
¾ cup milk
2 tablespoon chopped onion
¼ teaspoon pepper
¾ cup packed brown sugar
1 tablespoon prepared mustard
⅓ cup pineapple juice

— Break eggs into mixing bowl and beat slightly.
— Add all meats and mix to combine.
— Add bread crumbs, milk, onion and pepper and mix.
— Spread in a glass loaf pan.
— Mix sugar and mustard in a separate bowl and spread on top of loaf.
— Pour pineapple juice over loaf; cover.
— Microwave for 5 minutes on high.
— Reduce setting; microwave on low for 18 minutes or until firm.
— Let stand 5 minutes uncovered.

LIVER, BACON AND ONIONS

4 slices bacon
2 medium onions, sliced
1 lb. baby beef liver, sliced
Salt
Pepper

— Place bacon between paper napkin or towel in 2-quart glass baking dish.
— Microwave on high for 4 to 4½ minutes or until crisp.
— Remove bacon and drain.
— Coat liver slices with bacon drippings.
— Arrange in baking dish.
— Add onions.
— Cover.
— Microwave on low for 12 to 14 minutes or until meat loses pink color.
— Crumble bacon on top.
— Let stand, covered, 5 minutes before serving.

(4 servings)

LADDIE'S JERKY

— Use lean meats such as beef or game meat.
— Trim all fat.
— Slice lean meat in thin strips (It will slice more easily if partially frozen).
— Lay meat on Microwave roaster rack.
— Lightly sprinkle meat with garlic salt, salt and pepper.
— Microwave on low for 25-35 minutes depending on thickness of meat.
— Turn meat strips and resprinkle with garlic salt, salt and pepper.
— Microwave on low for 25-35 minutes as above.
— Remove from oven when completely dry. Jerky will keep indefinitely.

SAUSAGE WITH BEANS

½ lb. fresh pork sausage links in casing, cut into quarters
1 small onion, finely chopped
¼ cup chopped celery
2 tablespoons packed brown sugar
2 tablespoons prepared mustard
1 tablespoon Worcestershire sauce
1 can (6 oz.) tomato paste
1 can (16 oz.) pork and beans, undrained

— Combine all ingredients in 1½-quart glass casserole.
— Cover with glass lid or plastic wrap.
— Microwave on medium for 12 to 14 minutes or until done.
— Let stand, covered, 5 minutes before serving

(4 servings)

HASENPFEFFER

1 cup water
1 cup vinegar
1 teaspoon sugar
1 teaspoon salt
½ teaspoon whole cloves
⅛ teaspoon pepper
⅛ teaspoon allspice
1 medium onion, sliced
2 to 2½-lb. cut-up rabbit
¼ cup butter
⅓ cup dry bread crumbs
1 teaspoon parsley

— Combine water, vinegar, sugar, seasonings and onion in medium mixing bowl.
— Add rabbit and marinate at room temperature 4 to 6 hours.
— Drain and reserve marinade.
— Put butter in a shallow 2-quart glass baking dish.
— Microwave on medium for about 1½ minutes or until melted.
— Coat drained rabbit pieces in butter, then in bread crumbs.
— Place pieces, thick edges toward outside, in the 2-quart glass baking dish.
— Microwave on high for 10 minutes, uncovered
— Turn pieces over; add ¼ cup marinade.
— Sprinkle with parsely. Recover.
— Continue cooking on high for 10 to 12 minutes or until meat is fork tender.
— Let stand, covered, 5 minutes before serving.

(5 servings)

VENISON CHOPS

6 venison chops (1½ to 2 lbs.), trimmed
1 medium onion, finely chopped
¼ cup choped celery
¼ cup chopped green pepper
¼ cup chili sauce
¼ cup dry sherry
1 teaspoon salt
¼ teaspoon pepper

— Place chops, onion, celery and green pepper in 2-quart glass baking dish.
— Cover.
— Microwave on medium for 10 minutes.
— Drain and turn meat over.
— Combine remaining ingredients in 4-cup measure.
— Pour sauce over chops.
— Recover and continue cooking on medium for 10 to 15 minutes.
— Let stand, covered, 5 minutes before serving.

(3-4 servings)

WILLIE'S WESTERN VENISON STEW

1½ lbs. venison stew meat, cubed
2 tablespoons flour
2 tablespoons butter
1 cup finely chopped carrots
1 medium onion, chopped
1 tablespoon dried parsley flakes
1 teaspoon salt
½ teaspoon garlic salt
½ teaspoon Italian seasoning
¼ teaspoon pepper
1 cup water
1 can (8 oz.) tomato sauce
1 can (10¾ oz.) condensed cream of mushroom soup

— Coat meat with flour.
— Place butter and meat in a shallow 2-quart glass casserole.
— Cover with glass lid or plastic wrap.
— Microwave on high for about 10 minutes or until meat is no longer pink.
— Stir in remaining ingredients; recover.
— Microwave on low for 30 minutes.
— Stir and continue cooking on low for 15 to 20 minutes or until meat is fork tender.
— Let stand, covered, 5 minutes before serving.

(4-6 servings)

LEG OF LAMB

4 to 4½-lb. leg of lamb, bone in
1 large clove garlic, cut in thin slices
Salt and pepper to taste

— Cut small slits in both sides of leg of lamb.
— Insert thin slices of garlic in slits.
— Place a microwave roasting rack or a saucer upside down in an oblong 2-quart glass baking dish.
— Place leg of lamb fat side up on rack.
— Microwave, uncovered, for about 20 minutes on high.
— Turn leg of lamb over so that fat side is down
— Microwave, uncovered, for about 20 minutes on high.
— Sprinkle lightly with salt and pepper.
— Remove from oven and insert thermometer in meat, being sure to not touch the bone. (Thermometer should register 160°).
— Leave thermometer in meat and cover tightly with aluminum foil; let stand about 20 minutes or until thermometer registers 180°.

(The times given are for well-done lamb. For pink lamb, decrease cooking time.)

Cooking Time for Leg of Lamb, Rare: 8 to 9 minutes per pound; Medium: 10 minutes per pound.

(8 servings)

POULTRY

Cut and Weight	Setting #1	Setting #2	Cooking Time in minutes per pound
CHICKEN			
Whole, fryer	high	high	8
2 to 3 lbs.			
3 to 4 lbs.	high	medium	9
Fryer, cut up			
2 to 3 lbs.	high	high	8
TURKEY			
Whole			
8 to 10 lbs.	high	medium	8
10 to 14 lbs.	high	medium	9
Breast, bone-in			
4 to 5 lbs.	medium	medium	11
Parts			
2 to 3 lbs.	medium	medium	15
CAPON			
Whole			
6 to 8 lbs.	high	medium	8
DUCKLING			
Whole			
4 to 5 lbs.	medium	medium	10
GOOSE			
Whole			
9 to 11 lbs.	medium	medium	10

***high — 100% power : medium — 60% power : low — 30% power.

POULTRY

POULTRY BASICS

To prepare whole birds for cooking, remove giblets ,wash thoroughly and pat dry with paper towels. Do not stuff poultry until just before cooking.

You can try microwaving turkeys over 10 pounds but large turkeys require less attention when roasted in a conventional oven. Roasting large birds conventionally frees the microwave oven for cooking side dishes, thus reducing over-all preparation time.

Poultry parts should be washed, cut into serving pieces if necessary, and dried with paper towels unless they are to be coated with crumbs. Arrange them in the dish with meatiest portions to the outside.

Fried chicken is best cooked conventionally. The amount of fat necessary to fry chicken becomes dangerously hot in the microwave oven. The most reliable test for poultry doneness is a meat thermometer. Unless you have a special microwave thermometer, do not use a meat thermometer in the microwave oven while cooking. To test internal temperature of whole birds, insert thermometer in fleshy part of the inside thigh muscle without touching the bone. Remove bird from the oven when temperature registers 175°. Tent with foil and let stand to complete cooking.

Other tests for poultry doneness are:
Pierce inside thigh muscle deeply with fork. If juices run clear without a tinge of pink, poultry is done.

Press thickest part of drumstick meat between fingers, it should be very soft. With whole birds, move drumstick up and down. Joint should move freely or break when bird is done.

HOW TO DEFROST POULTRY

- Thaw poultry in its original wrapping, cut off metal clip. Place in a large flat glass baking dish to catch drippings.
- Whole poultry and parts weighing 4 pounds and over are thawed on medium.
- Whole poultry and parts weighing under 4 pounds are thawed on low. This defrosting technique sends enough heat into meat to warm and defrost center without starting cooking process at outer edges.
- Start whole birds thawing with breast side up.
- Poultry should be icy in center when taken from the microwave oven.
- Finish thawing by immersing poultry in cold water. If not completely thawed, poultry will take longer to cook and will not cook evently.
- Remove loosened giblets from whole birds and set aside for gravy or soup broth.

HOW TO COOK POULTRY

- Poultry should be completely thawed before cooking.
- Place large whole poultry in 3-quart (13x9-inch) glass baking dish; small whole birds and poultry pieces in 2-quart (12x7-inch) glass baking dish.
- Use a microwave roasting rack or inverted saucer in the dish when cooking whole birds.
- Arrange pieces of poultry with skin side up and thick edges toward outside of dish.
- Metal clip holding drumsticks may be left in place on large whole birds during cooking. Pop-out "doneness indicators" may be left in birds but will not indicate doneness in microwave cooking.
- Most whole poultry is cooked uncovered.
- When two different settings are mentioned, use medium during first cooking period; high during the second.
- Stuffing does not increase cooking time.

MICRO-FRIED CHICKEN

1/3 cup butter
1 clove garlic, finely chopped
3/4 cup dry bread crumbs
1 tablespoon dried parsley flakes
1 teaspoon salt
1/4 teaspoon poultry seasoning
1/8 teaspoon pepper
2 1/2 to 3-lb. frying chicken, cut up

— Place butter and garlic in 2-quart glass baking dish.
— Microwave on medium for 2 minutes or until melted.
— Combine remaining ingredients, except chicken, in flat dish.
— Roll chicken in seasoned butter, then in crumb mixture.
— Place chicken pieces, skin side down and thick edges toward outside, in buttered baking dish.
— Sprinkle with remaining bread crumbs.
— Microwave on high for 12 minutes.
— Turn chicken over and continue cooking on high for 10 to 12 minutes or until fork tender.
— Let stand 5 minutes before serving.

(4-6 servings)

CLASSIC DRESSING STUFFINGS

1 cup milk
1 tablespoon cornstarch
2 teaspoons sugar
1 teaspoon dry mustard
1 teaspoon salt
1/4 teaspoon paprika
1/4 teaspoon pepper
1 egg yolk, beaten
2 tablespoons vinegar
1/4 cup cooking oil.

— Pour milk into 4-cup glass measure.
— Blend in cornstarch, sugar, mustard, salt, paprika and pepper; mix well.
— Microwave on high for 3 minutes.
— Beat with rotary beater until smooth and continue cooking on high for 1 to 1 1/2 minutes or until thickened.
— Beat with rotary beater until smooth.
— Add a little warm mixture to beaten egg yolk.
— Stir and combine with remaining hot cream mixture.
— Microwave on medium for 1 to 2 minutes or until slightly thickened.
— Stir in vinegar and oil. Beat with rotary beater until smooth.

(1 1/3 cups dressing)

CRANBERRY STUFFING

1/4 cup butter
1/2 cup chopped onion
1/2 cup chopped celery
2 cups finely chopped tart apple
1 cup whole cranberry sauce
1/3 cup raisins
1 package (8 oz.) seasoned cornbread stuffing mix

— Combine butter, onion and celery in 2-quart glass casserole.
— Microwave on medium for about 4 minutes or until vegetables are partly cooked.
— Stir in remaining ingredients; mix well.
— Stuff poultry.

(Stuffs 5 to 8-lb. bird)

BASIC BREAD STUFFING

2/3 cup butter
1/4 cup finely chopped onion
1/2 teaspoon salt
1/2 teaspoon poultry seasoning
1/4 teaspoon pepper
8 cups dried bread cubes
2-4 tablespoons water, depending on dryness of bread

— Place butter and onion in 2-quart baking dish
— Microwave on medium for 4 to 5 minutes or until butter is melted.
— Stir in remaining ingredients; mix well.
— Stuff poultry.

(Stuffs 4 to 6-lb. bird)

ALMOND STUFFING

3/4 cup butter
1/2 cup chopped celery
1/4 cup chopped onion
1/2 cup chopped almonds
4 cups soft bread cubes
1 tablespoon dried parsely flakes
1/4 teaspoon salt
1 teaspoon instant chicken bouillon
1/3 cup water

— Combine butter, celery and onion in medium mixing bowl.
— Microwave on medium for 4 to 5 minutes or until vegetables are partly cooked.
— Stir in remaining ingredients; mix well.
— Stuff poultry.

(Stuffs 4 Cornish Hens or 4-5-lb. Roasting Chicken)

APRICOT DUCK

1 package (6 oz.) seasoned white and wild rice mix.
2½ cups water
¾ cup chopped mixed dried fruit
1 medium onion, chopped
2 wild Mallard ducks (2 lb. each) or
1 4-5 lb. young duckling
¼ cup apricot preserves

— Combine seasoned rice mix, water, dried fruit and onion in saucepan; cook as directed on rice package.
— Clean ducks; wash, and pat dry.
— Stuff ducks with rice mixture; fasten openings with toothpicks or metal skewers; lace shut with string.
— Place ducks, breast side down on microwave roasting rack, in 2-quart glass baking dish.
— Microwave on medium for 20 minutes.
— Turn ducks over; drain fat from pan.
— Brush ducks with apricot preserves and continue cooking on medium for 18 to 20 minutes or until meat and juices are no longer pink when duck is cut between leg and body.
— Let stand, covered with foil, 5 minutes before serving.

(4 servings)

STUFFED CORNISH HENS

¼ cup butter
1 teaspoon paprika
4 whole Rock Cornish Game Hens (12 oz. each)
1 teaspoon salt
Almond stuffing (see stuffings)

— Place butter and paprika in 2-cup glass measure.
— Microwave on medium for about 1½ minutes or until melted; set aside.
— Salt body cavities of hens.
— Fill each hen with stuffing.
— Tie legs together and wings to body.
— Arrange, breast side up and drumsticks toward center of microwave roasting rack, in 2-quart glass baking dish.
— Brush with seasoned melted butter.
— Microwave on high for 30 to 35 minutes or until microwave meat thermometer registers 170°F. Let stand 5 minutes before serving.

(4 servings)

PINEAPPLE CORNISH HEN

1 Cornish hen
2 teaspoons pineapple preserves
1 tablespoon tomato puree
1 teaspoon sugar
Dash of onion powder
Dash of garlic powder
Dash of Worcestershire sauce
Dash of salt

— Mix pineapple preserves, tomato puree, sugar, onion power, garlic powder, Worcestershire sauce and salt to make a sauce.
— Put chicken in a baking dish, pour sauce over and Microwave 4 minutes on high.
— Turn chicken over and spoon the liquid from the dish over it.
— Microwave 4 more minutes on high.
— Measure the internal temperature of the chicken by inserting a cooking thermometer in the thickest part of the chicken. Microwave until the thermometer reads 185 degrees.

(1 serving)

ITALIAN CHICKEN

1 frying chicken, cut up
¼ cup flour
2 teaspoons salt
½ teaspoon pepper
4 tablespoons salad oil
3 sliced onions
3 sliced green peppers
3 parsley stalks
2 cloves garlic
1 bay leaf
Dash of saffron and basil
1 can (20-oz.) Italian tomatoes

— Using a 2-quart glass baking dish, mix the flour with 1 teaspoon salt and pepper and coat the chicken.
— Cook the chicken 6 minutes on high.
— Pour salad oil into a preheated skillet and fry chicken until it browns.
— In the same baking dish, put onions, green peppers, parsley, garlic, bay leaf, saffron and basil and mix well.
— Microwave 3 minutes, on high, then stir and cook 2 more minutes on high.
— Remove garlic and parsley and add fried chicken.
— Add Italian tomatoes (drained), and remaining 1 teaspoon salt.
— Microwave, covered, 26 minutes on high.
— Stir every 5 minutes.
— Serve hot over hot cooked spaghetti.

(6 servings)

BRUNSWICK STEW

1 (2 to 3 lbs.) broiler-fryer chicken cut into serving pieces
2 cups water
6 whole peppercorns
2 bay leaves
1 teaspoons salt
3 ripe tomatoes, peeled and cut into 8 wedges each
1 medium onion, thinly sliced
1 (10-oz.) package frozen lima beans, thawed
1 (10-oz.) package whole kernel corn, thawed
1 (10-oz.) package frozen okra, thawed and sliced into ½-inch pieces

— Wash chicken and pat dry.
— Place chicken, water, peppercorns, bay leaves and salt in a deep, 3-quart, heat-resistant, non-metallic casserole.
— Stir to combine.
— Microwave, covered, on high 10 minutes.
— Stir. Microwave, covered, on high an additional 8 minutes.
— If desired, remove chicken from bone and cut into 1-inch pieces. Set aside.
— Discard bay leaves and peppercorns.
— Return chicken to broth and add
— Microwave, covered, on high 10 minutes.
— Uncover and heat on high 5 minutes or until chicken and vegetables are tender.
— Serve in soup bowls.

(4-6 servings)

PHEASANT WITH MUSHROOMS

3 lbs. pheasant
½ teaspoon salt
Dash of sage, pepper, allspice, oregano
¼ cup chopped onion
1 tablespoon chopped parsley
2 tablespoons chopped celery
½ cup sliced mushrooms
1 cup concentrated cream of mushroom soup
1 ¼ tablespoons cornstarch
¼ cup white wine
¼ cup sour cream

— Cut pheasant. Do not remove the skin.
— Place in a dish, skin side down.
— Sprinkle with salt, sage, pepper, allspice and oregano.
— Combine onion, parsley, celery, mushrooms and cream of mushroom soup.
— Add cornstarch and white wine and stir well.
— Microwave, covered, 10 minutes on high.
— Turn pheasant over and cook 15 more minutes on high.
— Stir in sour cream before serving.

(6 servings)

ROAST GOOSE

9 lbs. frozen domestic goose, thawed
1 teaspoon salt
3 to 4 medium apples, quartered
8 to 10 dried prunes
1 teaspoon leaf marjoram

— Wash goose; remove giblets.
— Sprinkle inside of cavity with salt.
— Fill cavity with apples and prunes.
— Sprinkle with marjoram.
— Secure openings with toothpicks or metal skewers.
— Tie legs together and wings to body.
— Place goose, breast side down on microwave roasting rack, in 3-quart glass baking dish.
— Microwave on medium for 45 minutes.
— Turn goose breast side up and continue cooking on medium for 45 to 50 minutes or until microwave meat thermometer inserted in thickest part of thigh meat registers 170°
— Let stand, covered with foil, 10 minutes before serving.

(10 servings)

CHICKEN PIE MEXICANA

⅓ cup chopped green pepper
⅓ cup chopped celery
⅓ cup chopped onion
1 clove garlic, crushed
4 tablespoons butter or margarine
1 ½ cups diced cooked chicken
2 ½ cups chicken broth
1 can (8 oz.) tomato sauce
1 can (2 oz.) chopped olives
1 teaspoon chili powder
2 teaspoons salt
Dash of white or black pepper
1 cup yellow cornmeal
1 cup cold water
Paprika

— Put 2 tablespoons butter in a casserole and add green pepper, celery, onion and garlic.
— Saute 3 minutes, on high, stirring occasionally.
— Add chicken, ½ cup chicken broth, tomato sauce, olives, chili powder and 1 teaspoon salt and stir well.
— Boil remaining chicken broth, add 1 teaspoon salt, 1 tablespoon butter, pepper and mix together.
— Mix cornmeal with water and add to chicken broth a little at a time.
— Microwave 5 minutes, on high, stirring every 2 minutes.

— Pour half of the mixture of cornmeal and chicken soup in a casserole greased with 1 tablespoon butter.
— Put chicken with tomato sauce in it and pour on remaining cornmeal.
— Microwave 15 minutes on high.
— Sprinkle with paprika and serve.

(6 servings)

CHICKEN AND SHRIMP IN RED WINE SAUCE

1 (2½ to 3-lb.) broiler-fryer chicken, cut into serving pieces
1 teaspoon salt
¼ teaspoon pepper
¼ cup flour
½ cup butter or margarine
1 large finely chopped onion
2 cloves garlic, peeled and crushed
3 tablespoons chopped parsley
¾ cup red wine
½ teaspoon Italian seasoning
1 (8-oz.) can tomato sauce
1 teaspoon dried sweet basil leaves
1 lb. raw, shelled, deveined shrimp

— Wash chicken and pat dry. Set aside.
— In a plastic bag combine salt, pepper and flour.
— Coat each piece of chicken with seasoned flour.
— In a large shallow, 3-quart heat-resistant, non-metallic skillet, melt butter on top of a conventional surface unit.
— Add chicken pieces and brown on all sides until golden brown.
— Remove chicken pieces and set aside.
— Add onion and garlic to skillet.
— Microwave, uncovered, on high 1½ minutes or until onion is tender.
— Add chopped parsley, wine, Italian seasoning, tomato sauce, and sweet basil to sauteed onion mixture.
— Stir to combine.
— Add reserved chicken pieces and microwave, covered, on medium for 12 to 15 minutes or until chicken is tender.
— Remove chicken pieces and place on serving platter.
— Add shrimp to wine sauce and microwave, uncovered, on high 3 minutes or until sauce bubbles and shrimp turn pink. (Do not overcook shrimp; they will become tough.)
— Skim any fat from surface of sauce.
— Pour shrimp sauce over chicken pieces.

(4-5 servings)

ROAST STUFFED CAPON

1 (6-lb.) capon or roasting chicken
4 tablespoons butter or margarine
½ cup finely chopped onion
½ cup finely chopped celery
½ teaspoon salt
¼ teaspoon pepper
½ teaspoon caraway seeds (optional)
1 envelope instant chicken broth or 1 cube chicken bouillon, crumbled
6 cups cubed day-old rye bread
¼ cup finely chopped parsley
¼ cup boiling water
Salt and pepper, to taste
Seasoned coating for chicken

— Wash capon and pat dry with paper toweling and set aside.
— Melt butter or margarine in a deep, 2-quart, heat-resistant, non-metallic casserole, uncovered, on high 30 seconds.
— Add onion and celery and heat, uncovered, 4 minutes on high or until vegetables are tender.
— Stir salt, pepper, caraway seeds and chicken broth mix into vegetable mixture.
— Add rye bread cubes and parsley; toss until well combined.
— Moisten bread mixture with the ½ cup boiling water. Set aside.
— Rub inside cavity of capon with salt and pepper to taste.
— Stuff capon lightly with stuffing mixture.
— Close body cavity with wooden skewers or sew with string
— Sprinkle capon with seasoned coating for chicken as bottle instructions direct.
— Place capon, breast-side-up in a shallow, 2-quart heat-resistant, non-metallic baking dish.
(Use an inverted saucer or a microwave roasting rack (trivet) to keep capon out of pan drippings.)
— Microwave, uncovered, for 8 minutes per pound on medium (about 48 minutes) or until a meat thermometer inserted in the thickest part of the bird (not touching any bones) registers 170°F.
— Wrap in aluminum foil and allow to stand 15 minutes before carving.

(6 servings)

CHICKEN MARENGO

1 cup all-purpose flour
1 teaspoon salt
¼ teaspoon pepper
1 teaspoon paprika
2½ to 3 pounds frying chicken, cut in serving pieces
1 clove garlic pressed or finely chopped
1 teaspoon sugar
½ teaspoon basil
1 package (8-oz.) fresh mushrooms, sliced
1 can (8-oz.) tomato sauce
8 to 10 stuffed olives
½ cup sherry
1 tablespoon olive brine
¼ cup almonds, toasted
½ pound mozzarella cheese, grated

— Combine flour, salt, pepper and paprika in a shallow dish.
— Coat chicken with flour mixture.
— Place in 2-quart casserole.
— Add garlic, sugar, basil and mushrooms.
— Mix in any remaining seasoned flour.
— Stir in tomato sauce, sherry and olives.
— Sprinkle with almonds and cheese.
— Cover.
— Microwave 25 minutes on high, or until chicken is fork tender, stirring once. Let stand 5 to 10 minutes, covered.

(4-6 servings)

SHERRIED CHICKEN BREASTS

½ pound fresh mushrooms, sliced
3 tablespoons butter
1 tablespoon flour
1 cup whipping cream
2 tablespoons sherry
4 chicken breasts (1½ pounds)

— Combine mushrooms and butter in a 1½ quart bowl.
— Microwave 1 to 2 minutes on high, or until butter melts and mushrooms soften.
— Stir in flour, cream and sherry, mixing until smooth.
— Microwave on low 5 to 6 minutes, or until mixture boils, stirring once.
— Arrange chicken breast, skin side down, in (10 x 8-inch) glass baking dish, with meatiest portions to outside.
— Cover and Microwave 10 minutes on high, turning chicken over after 5 minutes.
— Pour sauce over chicken.
— Cover and Microwave 10 to 15 minutes, on high, or until chicken is fork tender.

(4 servings)

NEW DELHI CHICKEN

¼ cup butter
1 tablespoon curry power
¼ teaspoon ginger
2½ to 3-lb. frying chicken, cut up
Salt
Pepper
1 medium onion, chopped
1 green apple, peeled and chopped
½ cup raisins
2 cups hot cooked rice

— Place butter in 2-quart glass baking dish.
— Microwave on medium for about 1½ minutes or until melted.
— Stir in curry powder and ginger.
— Place chicken pieces, skin side down and thick edges toward outside, in curried butter.
— Sprinkle with salt and pepper; top with onion, apple and raisins.
— Cover with plastic wrap.
— Microwave on high for 20 minutes.
— Turn chicken oven and continue cooking on high for 5 to 6 minutes or until chicken is fork tender.
— Let stand 5 minutes before serving.
— Stir cooked rice into hot seasoned drippings.
— Serve with chicken.

(4-6 servings)

ROAST TURKEY

1. Select a turkey between 8 and 12 pounds. A large bird can be cooked in the oven, if you can easily get it in and out of the oven when it is raised on saucers or on a Microwave roasting rack (Trivet) with both breast-side up and breast-side down. A small bird is easier to maneuver and will not require any forcing.
2. Remove giblets and neck from turkey and rinse body cavity with water.
3. Pat turkey dry with paper towels. If stuffing is desired, stuff main cavity and neck cavity with desired stuffing. Secure neck skin and body opening with wooden skewers. Tie wings to body loosely with string. Tie legs together, loosely. Cover wings and legs with small pieces of foil to prevent over cooking.
4. Place inverted saucer or small casserole lids or a Microwave roasting rack (Trivet) in the bottom of a shallow 2- or 3-quart baking dish. Turkey should not extend over sides of dish. Start turkey cooking breast-side down.
5. Cook, uncovered on medium for half the allotted cooking time, remove turkey and turn

breast-side up. Remove foil pieces and baste as desired.

6. Continue cooking for remaining half of cooking time on high. During last half of cooking time watch turkey carefully. If it develops dark brown spots, this indicates overcooking; these spots should be covered with a small piece of aluminum foil to prevent further overcooking.
7. Remove turkey and insert a meat thermometer in the heavy part of the thigh or in the heavy part of the breast, making sure that it does not touch the bone. The thermometer should register about 170°, 10° to 15° lower than the final temperature. Cover turkey with foil and let stand about 20 minutes to bring temperature up to 185° and to make carving easier.

Cooking Time for Turkey

7½ to 9 minutes per pound

Note Do not use the conventional meat thermometer in oven while cooking in a Microwave. Insert when turkey is out of the oven. If you have a special Microwave thermometer, or food sensor that is part of your oven; you can operate the oven while these devices are in the turkey.

Due to the long cooking time, the turkey will be browned, but the skin will not be crisp. If crisp skin is desired, reduce cooking time by about 30 seconds per pound. Crisp skin is obtained by baking about 15 minutes in a 450° conventional oven.

To thaw a turkey:

— Place turkey in plastic wrap in baking dish.
— Microwave for 1 minute per pound on high, turning turkey over once during cooking period.
— Remove from oven and let stand 10 to 15 minutes to allow heat to penetrate to the center of the turkey.
— Remove plastic wrap and metal staple that is used to hold down legs in some turkeys.
— Remove bag of giblets from turkey.
— Microwave turkey for 1 minute per pound on high again, turning over 2 or 3 times during cooking period.
— Check appearance and cover any brown spots with small pieces of aluminum foil.
— Remove from oven and let stand 10 to 15 minutes to alow heat to penetrate turkey.
— Microwave turkey for ½ minute per pound on high, turning turkey twice during cooking period.
— Be sure to cover any browned spots with small pieces of aluminum foil.

ORANGE-GLAZED TURKEY

1 cup orange juice
1 cup firmly packed brown sugar
¼ turkey (about 2-lbs), defrosted

— Combine orange juice and sugar in 2-cup glass measure.
— Mix well.
— Place dry turkey, skin side up, in an (8 x 8-inch) glass baking dish.
— Brush with orange glaze.
— Microwave, uncovered, 15 minutes on medium.
— Turn turkey skin side down.
— Brush with glaze.
— Microwave, uncovered, 15 minutes on medium.
— Turn turkey skin side up.
— Brush with glaze.
— Microwave, uncovered, 5 minutes on medium. Let stand 5 minutes.

(2 servings)

TURKEY TETRAZZINI

4 ounces thin spaghetti
3 tablespoons butter
1 can (4-oz.) sliced mushrooms, drained
⅓ cup finely minced onions
3 tablespoons flour
2 cups chicken broth or milk
½ cup cream
¼ cup dry vermouth
1 teaspoon salt
Dash of white pepper
¾ cup grated Parmesan cheese, divided
2 cups diced cooked turkey

— Cook spaghetti accoring to package directions. Drain immediately and rinse in cold water to stop cooking.
— Place butter in a 3-quart casserole.
— Add mushrooms and onion.
— Microwave, covered, for 2 to 3 minutes, on high or until onions are soft.
— Add flour and mix to form a smooth paste.
— Microwave, covered, for 30 seconds on high.
— Stir in chicken broth, cream, vermouth, salt, pepper, and ¼ cup Parmesan cheese.
— Blend well.
— Microwave, uncovered, for 3 to 4 minutes, on high, or until mixture comes to a boil and thickens.
— Stir once during cooking period.
— Add cooked spaghetti, turkey, and remainder of cheese. Toss lightly.
— Microwave, covered, for 5 minutes, on high, or until mixture is piping hot.
— Let stand for 2 to 3 minutes, before serving.

(6 servings

BARBECUED CHICKEN

1 (2 to 3-lbs) frying chicken, cut up
1 cup catsup
¼ cup cider vinegar
1 tablespoon Worcestershire sauce
2 tablespoons finely chopped onion
3 tablespoons firmly packed brown sugar
1 tablespoons paprika
1 teaspoon sugar
1 teaspoon salt
Pepper to taste

— Arrange chicken in a glass (12x8-inch) baking dish, with meatiest portion toward outside of dish. Set aside.
— Combine remaining ingredients in a 1-quart glass measure.
— Mix well and microwave, uncovered, 5 minutes on high, or until sauce is hot and thick, stirring after 3 minutes.
— Pour barbecue sauce over chicken.
— Cover with plastic wrap and microwave 20 to 25 minutes on high, or until chicken is fork tender.

(4 servings)

SWEET 'N SOUR CHICKEN

4 chicken thigh-legs (9-oz. each)
1 teaspoon poultry seasoning
2 teaspoons salt
¼ teaspoon pepper
1 can (10¾ oz.) condensed cream of mushroom soup
1 can (4 oz.) mushroom stems and pieces, drained
½ cup sour cream
½ cup dry sherry or water
½ teaspoon finely chopped garlic

— Place chicken thigh-legs, skin side down and thick edges toward outside, in 2-quart (12 x 7) glass baking dish.
— Season with poultry seasoning, salt and pepper
— Cover.
— Microwave on high for 15 minutes; drain.
— Combine remaining ingredients in small mixing bowl.
— Turn chicken over; pour on cream soup mixture; recover, and continue cooking on medium for 6 to 8 minutes or until fork tender.
— Let stand, covered, 5 minutes before serving.

(4 servings)

LEMON CHICKEN WINGS

¼ cup butter or margarine
2 tablespoons all-purpose flour
1 tablespoon lemon juice
1 green onion, finely chopped
½ teaspoon paprika
¼ teaspoon salt
⅛ teaspoon ground thyme
Dash pepper
¾ lb. chicken wings

— Place butter in 2-quart (8 x 8) glass baking dish.
— Microwave on medium for about 1½ minutes or until melted.
— Stir in remaining ingredients, except chicken wings.
— Fold chicken wings tip under drumstick joint.
— Coat wings with lemon butter.
— Place wings, thick edges toward ouside, in baking dish.
— Cover with plastic wrap.
— Microwave on high for 8 minutes. Turn wings over and continue cooking on high for 5 to 6 minutes or until fork tender.
— Let stand 5 minutes before serving.

(2-3 servings)

SHERRIED CHICKEN LIVERS

2 tablespoons butter
2 packages (8-oz. each) frozen chicken livers, defrosted
3 tablespoons flour
¼ cup finely chopped onion
½ teaspoon salt
¼ teaspoon pepper
¾ cup cream sherry

— Place butter in a 2 quart casserole.
— Microwave 1 to 2 minutes on high or until butter is melted.
— Dredge livers in flour that has been seasoned with salt and pepper.
— Arrange in a casserole in a single layer.
— Cover loosely with waxed paper.
— Microwave 5 to 6 minutes, on high, turning livers every 2 minutes.
— Stir in onions and wine.
— Cover with waxed paper and Microwave 4 minutes, on high, stirring twice, or until livers are tender.
— Serve hot on a bed of rice.

(4 servings)

CHICKEN 'N DUMPLINGS

3 to 3 ¼-lb. stewing chicken, cut up
3 ½ cups water
½ cup diced celery
1 medium onion, sliced
1 bay leaf
4 peppercorns
1 tablespoon salt
4 carrots, sliced
⅓ cup unsifted all-purpose flour
½ cup water

DUMPLINGS:
1 ½ cups unsifted all-purpose flour
2 teaspoons baking powder
½ teaspoon salt
1 teaspoon dried parsley flakes
⅔ cup milk
1 egg
2 tablespoons cooking oil

— Combine all ingredients, except flour, ½ cup water and Dumpling ingredients, in 3-quart glass casserole.
— Cover with glass lid or plastic wrap.
— Microwave on high for 15 minutes. Stir in a mixture of flour and ½ cup water.
— Microwave on low for 50 to 60 minutes or until chicken is fork tender.
— Spoon Dumplings over hot chicken mixture.
— Recover and continue cooking on low for 10 to 12 minutes or until dumplings are no longer doughy.
— Let stand, covered, 5 minutes before serving
— *Dumplings:* Combine dry ingredients in medium mixing bowl. Blend milk, egg and oil in 2-cup measure. Pour into flour mixture. Stir until moistened.

(5-6 servings)

CHICKEN A LA KING

¼ cup butter or margarine
¼ cup flour
1 can (10 ½-oz.) chicken broth
1 cup milk
1 ½ cups cooked diced chicken or turkey
1 cup frozen peas, defrosted
1 jar (2-oz.) chopped pimento
½ teaspoon accent
⅛ teaspoon pepper
½ teaspoon seasoned salt
1 tablespoon grated sharp cheese

— Place butter in a 1 ½ quart casserole.
— Microwave 1 to 2 minutes, on high, or until butter is melted.
— Sir in flour to make a paste.
— Add chicken broth and milk beating with a wire whip.
— Microwave 5 to 6 minutes, on high, stirring every 2 minutes.
— Add chicken, peas, pimento, accent and pepper.
— Cover and Microwave 4 minutes, on high, or until hot.
— Just before serving, stir in seasoned salt and grated cheese.
— Serve on hot biscuits or buttered toast.

(4-6 servings)

COQ AU VIN

1 cup all-purpose flour
2 teaspoons salt
¼ teaspoon pepper
3 pound frying chicken, cut in serving pieces
3 slices bacon, cut in 1-inch pieces
1 large onion, cut in quarters
1 package (8-oz.) fresh mushrooms, sliced
1 clove garlic, pressed or finely chopped
1 cup red wine
2 tablespoons brandy
1 bay leaf
1 tablespoon snipped parsley

— Combine flour, salt and pepper in a shallow dish. Roll chicken in flour mixture.
— Set aside.
— Place bacon in 2-quart glass casserole. Microwave 2 minutes on high, or until almost crisp.
— Add chicken and remaining seasoned flour to bacon and drippings.
— Mix in onion, mushrooms, garlic, wine, brandy, bay leaf and parsley. Cover tighly.
— Microwave 15 minutes on high.
— Stir. (Do not cover)
— Microwave 10 minutes on high, or until chicken is fork tender.
— Let stand 5 to 10 minutes, covered.
— Remove bay leaf before serving.

(4-6 servings)

CHICKEN CACCIATORE

¼ cup cooking oil
1 broiler-fryer chicken, cut in serving pieces
1 medium onion, coarsely chopped
1 clove garlic, minced
1 medium green pepper, seeded and coarsely chopped
1 ¼ teaspons salt
⅛ teaspoon pepper
½ bay leaf
1 can (16-oz.) tomatoes
2 tablespoons dry white wine
Chopped parsley

— Pour oil into an (8 x 8-inch) square baking dish.
— Cut large pieces of chicken in half.
— Put in baking dish and turn so that all pieces are coated with oil.
— Place breasts in center and surround with other pieces of chicken.
— Sprinkle onion and garlic on top of chicken.
— Microwave for 5 minutes on high.
— Combine green pepper, salt, pepper, bay leaf, tomatoes, and wine.
— Stir with a fork and mash tomatoes into small pieces.
— Pour over top of chicken.
— Cook, covered, for 23 to 25 minutes, on high, or until chicken is fork-tender.
— Garnish with parsley and serve with cooked spaghetti.

SMOTHERED PHEASANT

2 tablespoons butter or margarine
1 pheasant (2 lbs.), cut up
All-purpose flour
Salt
Pepper

⅛ teaspoon celery salt
¼ teaspoon ground sage
½ cup thinly sliced carrots
¼ cup finely chopped onion
⅓ cup milk

— Place butter in a shallow 2-quart glass baking dish.
— Microwave, uncovered, on medium for about 1 minute or until melted.
— Roll pheasant in flour.
— Place, thick edges toward outside, in buttered baking dish.
— Season with salt, pepper, celery salt and sage
— Top with carrots and onion.
— Cover with plastic wrap.
— Microwave on medium for 10 to 12 minutes.
— Turn pheasant over; recover, and continue cooking on medium for 8 to 10 minutes.
— Add milk; recover, and continue cooking on medium for 2 to 3 minutes or until fork tender.
— Let stand, covered, 5 minutes before serving.

(3-4 servings)

ROAST DUCKLING

5 lb. duckling, thawed
Stuffing if desired
1 teaspoon Kitchen Bouquet dissolved in 1 teaspoon water

— Remove giblets from bird and wash cavity.
— If duckling is defrosted, keep in original wrapping; prick plastic bag with a fork near backbone.
— Place duckling on a roasting rack in shallow, 2-quart glass dish breast side up
— Microwave 10 minutes on high, or until duckling begins to exude fat.
— Let stand 5 minutes to allow fat to run out.
— Remove duckling from bag.
— Drain fat from glass dish.
— Wash duckling and pat dry.
— If desired, stuff cavity, packing loosely.
— Secure cavity with string or wooden picks.
— Lift wing tips up and over back.
— Place duckling breast side down on rack.
— Brush with Kitchen Bouquet mixture. Microwave, uncovered, 14 minutes on medium.
— Turn duckling breast side up.
— Brush with Kitchen Bouquet mixture.
— Microwave, uncovered, 22 minutes on medium or until duckling is fork tender.
— Let stand 10 minutes tented with aluminum foil, shiny side in.

(4 servings)

ORIENTAL CHICKEN

1 3 lbs. frying chicken, cut up
¼ teaspoon salt
Dash of pepper
¼ cup sake, or cooking sherry
¼ cup soy sauce
1 medium onion, cut into wedges
2 teaspoons cornstarch
1 tablespoon sugar
2 tablespoons water
¾ cup (5 oz. can) drained bamboo shoots
⅔ cup (5 oz. can) drained and sliced water chestnuts

— Cut larger pieces of chicken so all pieces are the same size.
— Combine salt, pepper, sake, soy sauce and onion in a shallow 2-quart glass baking dish.
— Place chicken in the dish, skin side up.
— Microwave, covered with wax paper, 28 minutes on high, turning chicken over once after 15 minutes.
— Place chicken on serving platter. Set aside.
— Add cornstarch, sugar and water, and juices.
— Microwave, covered, 2 minutes on high, stirring after 1 minute.
— Add bamboo shoots and water chestnuts. Re-cover.
— Microwave, covered, 2 minutes on high, stirring once. Serve over rice.

POLYNESIAN CHICKEN

1 3 lbs. frying chicken, cut up
1 can (6 oz.) frozen orange juice concentrate, thawed
1 tablespoon cornstarch
1 teaspoon salt
¼ teaspoon cinnamon
1 tablespoon lime juice
4 sliced bananas
½ cup macadamia nuts
Watercress sprigs for garnish

— Cut larger pieces of chicken so all pieces are the same size.
— Arrange in a shallow 2-quart glass baking dish, skin side up. Set aside.
— In a small bowl, mix juice concentrate, cornstarch, salt, cinnamon and lime juice. Pour over chicken.
— Microwave, covered with wax paper, 28 minutes on high, basting sauce over chicken after 15 minutes of cooking time.
— Microwave, uncovered, 1 minute, after adding bananas and nuts.
— Garnish with sprigs of watercress.

(4 servings)

DUCK A L'ORANGE

4 to 5 lb. fresh or frozen duckling, defrosted
1 orange, quartered
1 small onion, quartered
2 stems celery, cut in thirds
Orange sauce (below)
Orange segments

— Remove giblets and wash cavity of bird.
— If duckling is defrosted, keep in original wrappings; prick plastic bag with a fork near backbone.
— Place duckling on roasting rack in shallow 2-quart glass dish, breast side up. Microwave 7 to 9 minutes on high, uncovered, or until duckling begins to exude fat.
— Let stand 5 minutes to allow fat to run out.
— Prepare orange sauce (see below).
— Remove duckling from bag.
— Drain fat from glass dish.
— Secure neck skin of duckling to back with wooden picks. Lift wing tips up and over back.
— Fill cavity with the orange, onion quarters and celery pieces.
— Place duckling breast side down on rack.
— Microwave, uncovered, 12 to 17 minutes on medium.
— Turn breast side up.
— Brush with orange sauce.
— Microwave, uncovered, 20 to 25 minutes on medium.
— Let stand 5 minutes, tented with aluminum foil shiny side in.
— Serve with remaining orange sauce and garnish with orange segments if desired.

ORANGE SAUCE:

1 orange
1 cup orange juice
2 tablespoons corn starch
2 tablespoons soy sauce
¼ cup orange liqueur or sherry
3 tablespoons honey

— Pare orange thinly, being careful not to take white membrane.
— Cut peel in julienne strips. Set aside.
— Combine orange juice, corn starch and soy sauce in glass 2-cup measure. Mix well.
— Microwave 2 to 3 minutes on high, uncovered.
— Stir and add orange peel, liqueur and honey.
— Microwave, uncovered, 2 minutes on high or until sauce is thick and glossy.

(3-4 servings)

FISH AND SEAFOOD

Fish/Seafood	Quantity	Setting	Cooking Time
White Fish, fillets:			
Sole, Halibut,	1 lb.	high	6 to 7 minutes
Snapper, Flounder	2 lbs.	high	8 to 9 minutes
Whole Fish	1 ½ to 2 lbs.	high	10 to 12 minutes
Salmon Steaks	1 lb.	high	9 to 10 minutes
Shrimp or Scallops	8 oz. pkg.	high	6 to 7 minutes
Lobster Tails	1 lobster tail	high	4 to 5 minutes
(9 oz.) tails	2 lobster tails	high	7 to 8 minutes
	4 lobster tails	high	11 to 12 minutes

***high — 100% power : medium — 60% power : low — 30% power.

SEAFOOD

COOKING HINTS

Your family's enjoyment of fish and seafood will be increased by the enhanced flavor and texture from microwave cooking.

Fish and seafood require only a short cooking time since there is no tough tissue. Baked fish may be brushed with melted butter and sprinkled with paprika for enhanced flavor and appearance. Most fish and seafood should be covered during cooking and standing time. Avoid overcooking! After several minutes of standing time, fish should be easily flaked with a fork. This indicates that the fish is done.

Shellfish has completed cooking when the meat appears opaque and the shell is pink.

Fish is generally cooked on high. If a white sauce is added, reducing the setting to medium is suggested.

FRESH STEAMED LOBSTER

½ cup water
½ teaspoon salt
1 lemon, sliced
2 1½-lb. live lobsters, pegged

— In a deep, 3-quart casserole place water, salt and lemon.
— Microwave, uncovered for 3 minutes on high, or until water boils.
— Place live lobsters, head first, into boiling water; this will render them immobile.
— Microwave, covered, for 12 minutes on high.
— Let stand, covered, 4 minutes to finish cooking.
— Drain.
— With a sharp, heavy knife, split tail.
— If meat is still translucent in center, Microwave, covered, about 1 minute longer or until meat is opaque.
— Continue to cut up the center towards the head.
— Remove the stomach and the intestinal tract.
— The green liver and the red roe are considered to be delicacies.

(2 servings)

LOBSTER NEWBURG

2 (9-oz.) lobster tails, removed from shells
Melted butter
¼ cup butter
2 tablespoons flour
½ teaspoon salt
Pinch cayenne pepper
1½ cups light cream or milk
2 egg yolks
¼ cup dry white wine
1 teaspoon lemon juice

— Place lobster tails in a shallow, heat-resistant, non-metallic baking dish and brush liberally with melted butter.
— Microwave, covered, on high 4 minutes or until tender.
— Cut lobster into bite-sized pieces.
— Set aside.
— In a deep, 1½-quart, heat-resistant, non-metallic casserole melt the ¼ cup butter, uncovered, on high 30 seconds.
— Blend in flour, salt and cayenne.
— In a small bowl, beat cream and egg yolks until well blended.
— Gradually stir cream mixture into flour mixture until smooth.
— Microwave, covered, on medium for 6 to 7 minutes or until sauce thickens. Stir occasionally.
— Stir in wine, lobster pieces and lemon juice. If necessary, heat on medium for 2 to 3 minutes or until heated through.
— Serve over rice or toast points.

If desired, shrimp, scallops, crabmeat or any combination of these may be substituted for lobster.

(4 servings)

FROZEN LOBSTER TAILS

1 lb. frozen lobster tails
1 teaspoon lemon juice
¼ cup butter or margarine
¼ teaspoon grated lemon peel

— Place frozen lobster tails in an (8x8-inch) square baking dish.
— Sprinkle with lemon juice. Microwave for 4 minutes to thaw lobster.
— Cut away soft shell-like surface on underside of tail with a sharp knife or scissors.
— Insert wooden skewers into each lobster tail to keep flat while cooking.
— Drain liquid from dish and arrange lobster in dish shell side down.
— Microwave, uncovered, on high for 4 minutes or until tender.

(4 servings)

CRAB MEAT IN SHELLS

1 tablespoon chopped parsley
1 tablespoon chopped green pepper
1 chopped scallion, reserve shells
1 can (4-oz.) sliced mushrooms, well drained
1 teaspoon butter
1 can (10¾-oz.) condensed cream of celery soup
1 can (7½-oz.) crab meat
1 tablespoon lemon juice
1 tablespoon dry sherry
2 tablespoons dry bread crumbs
2 tablespoons grated Cheddar cheese
Paprika

— Combine parsley, green pepper, scallion, mushrooms, and butter in a glass 1-quart casserole.
— Microwave, covered, for 3 minutes on high.
— Add celery soup and blend well.
— Microwave, covered, for 1 minute on high.
—Add crab meat to mixture with lemon juice and sherry.
— Divide mixture into 4 scallop shells.
— Combine bread crumbs and cheese. Spread over top of crab mixture.
— Sprinkle generously with paprika.
— Microwave 2 shells at a time for 6 minutes, uncovered, on high.

(4 servings)

CRAB MORNAY

2 cups (12-oz.) cooked crab meat
2 cups white sauce
½ pound Swiss or cheddar cheese, grated
Parsley
Paprika

— Layer half of crab meat, half of sauce and half of cheese in (8 x 8-inch) baking dish.
— Repeat with second layers. Microwave 14 minutes, uncovered on medium. Garnish with parsley and paprika, if desired.

(5-6 servings)

SHRIMP CREOLE

3 tablespoons butter or margarine
½ cup chopped onions
½ cup chopped green pepper
½ cup diced celery
1 clove garlic, minced
1 can (1 lb.) tomatoes, mashed
1 can (8-oz.) tomato sauce
1 tablespoon Worcestershire sauce
1½ teaspoons salt
1 teaspoon sugar
½ teaspoon chili powder
Dash of hot-pepper sauce
1 tablespoon cornstarch
2 tablespoons cold water
1 lb. cooked shrimp

— Combine butter, onion, green pepper, celery, and garlic in a 2- or 3-quart glass casserole.
— Microwave for 3 minutes, uncovered, on high, stirring after 1 minute.
— Add tomatoes, tomato sauce, Worcestershire, salt, sugar, chili powder, and hot-pepper sauce.
— Microwave on high for 7 minutes, uncovered, stirring after every 3 minutes.
— Combine cornstarch with 2 teaspoons cold water.
— Stir into casserole.
— Microwave, uncovered, for 3 minutes, on high, stirring every 1 minute.
— Add shrimp.
— Microwave, uncovered, for 2 minutes, on high, or until shrimp is piping hot.
— Serve with wild rice or plain boiled rice.

(6 servings)

SHRIMP CURRY

¼ cup butter or margarine
¼ cup chopped onion
½ cup chopped celery
2 tablespoons chopped green pepper
3 tablespoons all-purpose flour
2 teaspoons curry powder
1 teaspoon instant chicken bouillon
½ cup water
½ cup milk
1 package (12-oz.) frozen uncooked shrimp, thawed

— Combine butter, onion and celery in a deep 2-quart glass casserole.
— Microwave, uncovered, on medium for 3 to 4 minutes or until vegetables are partly cooked. Stir in remaining ingredients. Cover with glass lid or plastic wrap.
— Microwave on high for 13 to 14 minutes or until shrimp turns pink. Serve over hot rice.

Note: If serving curry with rice, cook rice in microwave oven while mixing together other ingredients. Cook curry while rice rests, covered. Condiments to pass with curry: toasted coconut, chopped peanuts, pickle relish, chunky sliced green onions, raisins or crumbled crisp bacon.

(4-6 servings)

SCALLOPS CACCIATORE

1 medium onion, chopped
1 medium green pepper, chopped
¼ cup salad oil
1 can (1 lb.) tomatoes, drained
1 pound bay scallops
1 can (8-oz.) tomato sauce
¼ cup dry white wine
1 ¼ teaspoons salt
⅛ teaspoon pepper
2 bay leaves
2 tablespoons chopped parsley

— Combine onion, green pepper, garlic, and oil in a deep 1 ½- to 2-quart glass casserole.
— Microwave for 3 minutes, uncovered, on high, stirring after 2 minutes.
— Mash tomatoes with a fork to break into small pieces.
— Add to casserole with scallops, tomato sauce, wine, salt, pepper and bay leaves.
— Microwave, covered, 6 minutes on high or until scallops are tender.
— Sprinkle with parsley.
— Serve with hot cooked rice, if desired.

SHRIMP CONTINENTAL

1 package (6 oz.) herb seasoned rice mix
1 can (16 oz.) tomatoes, undrained
2 tablespoons butter or margarine
1 cup water
1 package (12 oz.) frozen uncooked shrimp, thawed
1 can (10¾ oz.) condensed cream of chicken soup
2 tablespoons milk
1 tablespoon dry white wine or lemond juice
½ teaspoon salt
Dash cayenne pepper
1 tablespoon dried parsley flakes

— Combine rice mix, tomatoes, butter and water in a deep 2-quart glass casserole.
— Cover with glass lid or plastic wrap.
— Microwave on high for 6 minutes; stir and recover.
— Microwave on medium for 12 to 15 minutes or until rice is tender.
— Let stand, covered, until rice is cooked, about 5 minutes.
— Combine shrimp, soup, milk, wine and seasonings in another 1 ½-quart glass casserole.
— Cover with glass lid or plastic wrap.
— Microwave on high for 5 minutes.
— Stir and recover, and continue cooking on high for 3 to 4 minutes.
— Let stand, covered, 5 minutes before serving.
— Serve over hot rice mixture.

(4-5 servings)

SHRIMP IN PAPAYA

2-3 ripe papayas (½ papaya per serving)
2 cups cooked shrimp
1 can condensed cream of shrimp soup
2 tablespoons sherry wine
2 tablespoons raisins
1 teaspoon (or to taste) curry powder
¼ cup shredded coconut
Paprika

— Peel papayas and cut in half lengthwise.
— Spoon out seeds and place shells on a large baking dish.
— Stir together all other ingredients except coconut and paprika.
— Spoon into shells and top with coconut and paprika.
— Cover with waxed paper and cook on high, 6 minutes, turning dish once.
— Let stand 5 minutes before serving.

(4-6 servings)

SHRIMP ORIENTAL

1 pkg. (7 oz.) frozen shrimp
1 pkg. (7 oz.) frozen green peas
¼ teaspoon salad oil
Small piece of ginger root
1 cup chopped leeks
1 cup sliced mushrooms
1 cut sliced celery
4 oz. cashew nuts
½ cup chicken stock cube dissolved in hot water
1 teaspoon salt
Dash of pepper
1 teaspoon cornstarch
Water
2 tablespoons sesame oil

— Thaw frozen shrimp and green peas by cooking 2 minutes, on high.
— Grease a shallow 2-quart glass baking dish with salad oil and add thawed shrimp and ginger.
— Microwave 1 minute.
— Add green peas, chopped leeks, sliced mushrooms, sliced celery and cashew nuts.
— Microwave 1 minute, uncovered, on high.
— Add soup, season with salt and pepper and cook 2 minutes, uncovered, on high
— Make a paste with the cornstarch and a little water and stir in sesame oil.
— Add to shrimp mixture.
— Microwave 30 seconds, on high, uncovered, until piping hot.

(4 servings)

COQUILLE ST. JACQUES

¼ cup butter or margarine
¼ cup chopped celery
1 can (4 oz.) sliced mushrooms, drained
2 medium green onions, sliced
2 tablespoons chopped green pepper
2 tablespoons all-purpose flour
½ teaspoon salt
⅛ teaspoon pepper
1 bay leaf
½ cup dry white wine
1 lb. sea scallops
1 tablespoon chopped pimento
¼ cup light cream
1 egg yolk
Buttered bread crumbs:
2 tablespoons butter or margarine
2 tablespoons dry bread crumbs
2 tablespoons grated Parmesan cheese

— Combine butter, celery, mushrooms, onions and green pepper in shallow 2-quart glass casserole.
— Microwave, uncovered, on medium for 3 to 4 minutes or until onion is tender.
— Stir in flour, salt, pepper, bay leaf and wine; mix well.
— Add scallops and pimento.
— Microwave, uncovered, on medium for 6 minutes.
— Stir and continue cooking on Medium for 2 to 3 minutes or until thickened.
— Mix together in small bowl, cream and egg yolk; stir into scallop mixture.
— Microwave, uncovered, on medium for 2 to 3 minutes or until piping hot.
— Remove bay leaf.
— Spoon into 4 natural shells or 1-cup glass serving dishes.
— Sprinkle about 1 tablespoon Buttered Bread Crumbs on each serving.
— Microwave, uncovered, on low for 1 to 2 minutes or until heated through.
— Let stand, covered, 5 minutes before serving.
— Buttered Bread Crumbs: Place 2 tablespoons butter in 1-cup glass measure.
— Microwave, uncovered, on medium for 1 to 1½ minutes or until melted. Stir in bread crumbs and Parmesan cheese.

(4 servings)

MAUNA LOA SOLE

2 lbs. boneless fillet of sole
¼ teaspoon salt
2 teaspoons chopped onion
1½ teaspoons water
¾ cup mayonnaise
1½ teaspoon lemon juice
¼ teaspoon seasoned salt
2 tablespoon finely chopped parsley
1 cup chopped macadamia nuts or
⅓ cup slivered almonds

— Dry fillets and sprinkle with salt.
— Roll fish and secure with toothpicks.
— Place fish in a shallow (10x6-inch) glass baking dish and cover loosely with waxed paper.
— Microwave 4 minutes on high.
— Mix together onion, water, mayonnaise, lemon juice, seasoned salt and parsley in a separate bowl.
— Coat fillets with sauce and return to microwave
— Cover with waxed paper and microwave 1 minute on high or just until sauce is hot.
— Sprinkle with nuts and serve immediately.

(4-6 servings)

STEAMED CLAMS

1 quart steamed clams
1 cup melted butter or margarine

— Scrub clams with a stiff brush to remove all sand and grit.
— Discard all clams that are even the least bit open.
— Put scrubbed clams in a deep 2-quart glass casserole.
— Add 2 tablespoons water.
— Microwave, covered, for 8 minutes on high, or until clam shells are all open and clams are cooked.
— Discard clams with closed shells.
— Serve clams in flat bowls.
— Divide clam liquid into 2 custard cups and fill a second set of 2 cups with melted butter.
— Remove clams from shells, dip in clam liquid, and then in butter.
— You can drink clam broth when clams have been eaten.

(2 servings)

SCALLOPS SUPREME

¼ cup butter or margarine
1 tablespoon finely chopped onion
¼ cup unsifted all-purpose flour
½ teaspoon salt
⅛ teaspoon pepper
½ cup dry white wine or chicken broth
1 can (4 oz.) mushroom stems and pieces, drained
1 package (12-oz.) frozen sea scallops, thawed
1 bay leaf
½ cup light cream
1 egg yolk
1 teaspoon dried parsley flakes

— Combine butter and onion in 2-quart glass casserole.
— Microwave, uncovered, on medium for 3 to 4 minutes or until onions are partly cooked.
— Blend in flour, salt and pepper.
— Stir in wine, mushrooms, scallops and bay leaf.
— Cover with glass lid or plastic wrap.
— Microwave on medium for 5 minutes.
— Stir and continue cooking on medium for 5 to 6 minutes or until scallops are fork tender.
— Combine cream and egg yolk in small mixing bowl.
— Gradually stir into hot scallop mixture.
— Recover.
— Microwave on medium for 3 to 4 minutes or until hot.
— Let stand, covered, 5 minutes before serving.
— Add parsley and serve.

(4 servings)

CREOLE HALIBUT

2 lbs. sliced halibut
Salad oil
1 cup chopped green pepper
1½ cups chopped onion
½ cup chopped celery
½ cup butter
1 clove chopped garlic
1 can (3-oz.) thinly sliced mushrooms
1 can (1 lb.) stewed tomato
1¼ teaspoons salt
1 teaspoon sugar
Dash of Tabasco
1 tablespoon green peas
A little lemon juice

— Arrange halibut in a shallow 2-quart baking dish with enough salad oil to coat bottom of dish.
— Put green peppers, onion, celery, butter and garlic in a separate bowl and microwave, uncovered, 3 minutes, 30 seconds on high, stirring every minute.
— Mix mushrooms, tomato stew, salt, sugar and Tabasco in another bowl.
— Spread mixture on the halibut and microwave, uncovered, 10 minutes, on high.
— Sprinkle with green peas and lemon juice.

(6 servings)

SUNRISE SOLE

1 ½ lb. sole fillets
Dash of salt and pepper
2 tablespoons lemon juice
2 tablespoons orange juice
1 ½ tablespoons catsup
2 ¼ tablespoons soy sauce
Chopped garlic
½ teaspoon orange peel

- Sprinkle sole with salt and pepper.
- Mix lemon juice, orange juice, catsup, soy sauce and garlic in a shallow 2-quart baking dish.
- Mix well.
- Cut sole into halves and place in sauce.
- Spoon sauce over sole.
- Microwave, covered, 5 minutes on high.
- Let stand 3 minutes.
- Decorate with thinly sliced orange peel before serving.

(4 servings)

FILLET OF SOLE VERONIQUE

1 ½ lbs. pre-cooked frozen breaded fish fillets
1 can (10¾-oz.) cream of celery soup, undiluted
½ cup mayonnaise
⅓ cup dry vermouth
2 tablespoons lemon juice
¼ teaspoon salt
¼ teaspoon pepper
Dash Tabasco sauce
½ cup fresh or canned seedless grapes
Parsley
Paprika

- Place fish in a large 3-qt. glass baking dish and microwave 5 minutes to thaw on high, uncovered.
- Turn fish over and microwave 5 minutes longer on high, uncovered, or until hot (depending on size).
- Meanwhile, combine soup, mayonnaise, vermouth, lemon juice, salt, pepper and Tabasco in a separate bowl.
- Turn fish fillets again and spoon over sauce mixture, being sure to coat each piece.
- Microwave, uncovered, 5 minutes longer on high, or until sauce is bubbly.
- Sprinkle over grapes and garnish with parsley and paprika.

(4-6 servings)

SHRIMP-STUFFED TROUT

2 tablespoons chopped green onion
¼ cup finely chopped celery
1 tablespoon finely chopped pimento
2 tablespoons butter or margarine
1 teaspoon lemon juice
1 tablespoon white wine
⅛ teaspoon celery salt
¼ teaspoon chervil
Dash white pepper
1 ½ cups dry bread cubes, coarsely crushed
¾ cup (4½ oz. can) chopped shrimp
1 egg, beaten
4 trout (6-8-oz.)

- Mix onion, celery, pimento, butter, lemon juice, wine and seasonings in a 1-quart glass bowl.
- Microwave, covered, 2 minutes on high, stirring after 1 minute.
- Add bread cubes and shrimp and mix together.
- Add beaten egg, blend thoroughly into mixture.
- Fill each fish with ⅓ cup of stuffing.
- Secure openings with toothpicks or small metal skewers.
- Wrap each fish individually in wax paper.
- Microwave 11 minutes on high, or until fish can be flaked easily.
- Turn each fish over after 5 minutes.
- Let stand, covered, 2 minutes to finish cooking.

(4 servings)

SEAFARER'S SALMON CROQUETTES

1 lb. can red salmon, drained and flaked
3 eggs, beaten
1 cup bread crumbs
½ cup chopped celery
¼ cup chopped green pepper
3 green onions chopped, including tops
1 tablespoon butter, melted
¾ cup milk

- Mix all ingredients in large mixing bowl.
- Divide mixture into four greased, 10-ounce custard dishes.
- Heap mixture lightly, do not pack down.
- Cover each cup with plastic wrap and Microwave 10 to 12 minutes on high.
- Croquettes may be served with a white sauce or a cocktail sauce.

(4 servings)

HALIBUT STEAKS

2 halibut steaks, about ¾ inch thick
½ lemon
1 egg, beaten
½ can (10¾-oz.) condensed cream of celery soup
2 tablespoons milk
2 tablespoons grated Parmesan cheese, divided
2 tablespoons fine dry bread crumbs
2 teaspoons melted butter or margarine

— Wipe fish with a damp paper towel.
— Cut each steak in 2 portions.
— Place in a glass (8x8-inch) square baking dish.
— Squeeze lemon over top of fish.
— Set aside.
— In a 2-cup measure beat together egg, soup, milk, and 1 tablespoon cheese.
— Microwave, covered, for 1 minute on high.
— Remove and stir well to melt cheese.
— Pour soup mixture over steaks.
— Combine bread crumbs and melted butter and sprinkle over top of fish.
— Top with remaining 1 tablespoon cheese.
— Microwave, covered, for 6 minutes on high, or until fish flakes when tested with a fork.

(4 servings)

STUFFED BASS

1 whole bass, cleaned, about 3-lbs
2 cups fresh bread cubes
1 tablespoon melted butter or margarine
Salt and pepper to taste
1 tablespoon chopped parsley
1 teaspoon lemon juice
3 slices bacon

— Wash fish in cold water.
— Pat dry with paper towels.
— Combine bread cubes, butter, salt and pepper, parsley, and lemon juice. Toss lightly.
— Stuff cavity of fish with bread mixture.
— Close with toothpicks or tie with string.
— Place fish in an oblong 2-quart glass baking dish.
— Place bacon slices on fish.
— Microwave, covered, for 5 to 6 minutes on high.
— Drain liquid and fat from bottom of dish.
— Microwave, covered with paper towels, for about 5 minutes on high, or until fish flakes easily when tested with a fork.
— Let fish stand covered with paper towels 5 minutes before serving.

(4-6 servings)

SALMON STEAKS WITH LEMON DILL SAUCE

4 salmon steaks, ¾ inch thick
1 medium onion, sliced
1 cup chicken bouillon
1 tablespoon lemon juice
1 teaspoon dill weed
½ teaspoon salt
4 parsley sprigs

— Arrange salmon steaks in a shallow 2-quart glass baking dish with thick edges.
— Top with onion bouillon, lemon juice, dill and salt.
— Cover with plastic wrap.
— Microwave on high for 10 to 12 minutes or until fish flakes easliy.
— Let stand, covered, 5 minutes and serve with hot sauce.
— Garnish with parsley.

SAUCE:

2 tablespoons butter
2 tablespoons flour
½ teaspoon salt
½ cup cream
2 tablespoons lemon juice

— Place butter in 2-cup glass measure.
— Microwave, uncovered, on medium for about 1 minute or until melted. Blend in flour and salt.
— Stir in cream, lemon juice, fish liquid; mix until smooth.
— Microwave on medium for 3 minutes, uncovered. Stir and continue cooking on medium for 2 to 3 minutes or until mixture bubbles.

(4 servings)

SWEET-SOUR SAUCE

½ cup pineapple juice
¼ cup distilled white vinegar
¼ cup firmly packed brown sugar
2 tablespoons salad oil
2 teaspoons soy sauce
½ teaspoon pepper

— Combine all ingredients in 1-quart glass measure.
— Microwave, uncovered, 2 minutes on high, or until sauce boils.
— Serve with eggs, fish, poultry or vegetables.

(1 cup)

PEKING HALIBUT

2 packages (12-oz. each) frozen Halibut steaks, defrosted
1 cup Peking sauce (see page 101)
1 can (8-oz.) crushed pineapple drained (reserve juice)
1 cup fine dry bread crumbs
3 tablespoons lemon juice
½ teaspoon curry powder
1 can (8-oz.) pineapple rings, drained (reserve juice)
4-6 tomato wedges
4-6 parsley sprigs

— Cut Halibut in serving pieces
— Arrange in (8x8-inch) glass baking dish.
— Set aside.
— Prepare Peking sauce as noted in recipe on page 101, using juice from crushed pineapple and pineapple chunks.
— Reserve ½ cup sauce.
— Combine remaining ½ cup Peking sauce, crushed pineapple, bread crumbs, lemon juice and curry powder.
— Spread mixture on Halibut.
— Pour reserved sauce evenly over top. Cover with plastic wrap. Microwave 12 to 15 minutes on high, or until fish flakes easily.
— Garnish each serving with 1 pineapple ring. Place a tomato wedge and parsley sprig in center of ring.

(4-6 servings)

RED SNAPPER ALMANDINE

1 lb. frozen red snapper, thawed
1 teaspoon lemon juice
Salt

Sauce:
⅓ cup slivered almonds
⅓ cup butter or margarine

— Place red snapper in 1½-quart (10x6-inch) glass baking dish.
— Rub lemon juice on top and salt lightly.
— Cover with plastic wrap.
— Microwave on high for 6 to 7 minutes or until fish flakes easily.
— Let stand, covered, while making sauce.
— Sauce: Combine almonds and butter in 1-cup glass measure.
— Microwave on high, uncovered, for about 2 minutes or until butter is melted.
—Stir and continue cooking, uncovered, on high for 2 to 3 minutes or until almonds are lightly browned.
— Serve over fillets.

(About 4 servings)

SALMON STUFFING

4 salmon steaks, cut ¾ inch thick
¼ teaspoon salt
¼ cup butter
½ cup chopped celery
¼ cup chopped onion
3 cups soft bread cubes
2 cups fresh sliced mushrooms
2 teaspoons dried parsley flakes
¼ teaspoon salt
⅛ teaspoon pepper
1 tablespoon lemon juice
½ cup milk
4 lemon slices

— Arrange salmon steaks in a shallow 2-quart glass baking dish with thick edges toward outside of dish.
— Sprinkle with salt; set aside.
— Combine butter, celery and onion in large glass mixing bowl.
— Microwave on medium for 3 to 4 minutes, uncovered, or until vegetables are partly cooked.
— Stir in bread cubes, mushrooms, parsley, salt, pepper and lemon juice; mix well.
— Sprinkle on top of salmon steaks.
— Pour milk over all.
— Cover with plastic wrap.
— Microwave on high for 12 to 14 minutes or until salmon flakes easily.
— Let stand, covered, 5 minutes before serving.
— Garnish with lemon slices.

(4 servings)

GIOVANNI'S POACHED FISH

2 tablespoons chopped parsley
1 clove garlic, pressed or finely chopped
1 to 1½ tablespoons olive oil
¼ cup hot water
1 lb. white fish fillets, fresh or frozen, defrosted.
⅛ teaspoon oregano leaves
Salt and pepper to taste

— Place parsley, garlic, olive oil and water in a shallow 2-quart glass baking dish.
— Microwave 30 seconds on high, uncovered.
— Arrange fillets in dish with thickest portions to outside of dish, and spoon sauce over fish.
— Sprinkle with oregano, salt and pepper.
— Cover tightly with plastic wrap.
— Microwave 5 to 6 minutes on high, or until fish flakes easliy.
— Let stand 2 minutes, covered, before serving.

(4 servings)

SEAFOOD NEWBURG

¼ cup butter or margarine
1 ½ tablespoons all-purpose flour
½ teaspoon salt
1 ½ cups light cream
2 egg yolks
¼ cup dry sherry or water
1 package (12 oz.) cooked lobster, crab or shrimp

— Place butter in deep 1 ½-quart glass casserole.
— Microwave, uncovered, on medium for 2 to 3 minutes or until melted.
— Blend in flour and salt. Set aside.
— In a small mixing bowl combine cream and egg yolks; mix well.
— Stir into flour mixture to form smooth paste.
— Add sherry and seafood.
— Cover with glass lid or plastic wrap.
— Microwave on medium for 6 minutes.
— Stir, re-cover and continue cooking on medium for 5 to 6 minutes or until mixture thickens.
Let stand, covered, 5 minutes before serving.
— Serve over toast points, patty shells or cooked rice.

(5-6 servings)

FISH FILETS IN ALMONDS AND WINE

⅓ cup slivered almonds
⅓ cup butter
2 tablespoons lemon juice
2 tablespoons white wine
½ teaspoon dill weed or seed
½ teaspoon salt
1 lb. fresh or frozen halibut, perch or sole fillets, thawed
4 lemon wedges
4 parsley sprigs

— In a 2-quart shallow glass baking dish, combine almonds and butter.
— Microwave, uncovered, 5 minutes on high, or until butter and almonds are golden brown.
— Stir in lemon juice, wine, dill and salt.
— Arrange fish in butter, with thickest sections facing outside.
— Spoon sauce over fillets.
— Microwave, covered, on high, with plastic wrap, 5 minutes on high, or until fish is no longer transparent.
— Allow to stand 2 minutes, covered, before serving.
— Garnish with lemon wedges and parsley.

(4 servings)

SOLE ALMONDINE

½ cup slivered almonds
½ cup butter or margarine
1 lb. fresh or frozen fillet of sole
½ teaspoon salt
⅛ teaspoon pepper
1 teaspoon chopped parsley
1 tablespoon lemon juice
4 lemon wedges
4 sprigs of parsley

— Place almonds and butter in glass (8x8-inch) square baking dish.
— Microwave, uncovered, for about 5 minutes, on high, or until almonds and butter are golden brown.
— Remove almonds with a slotted spoon and set aside.
— Arrange sole in dish with butter, turning to coat both sides of fish.
— Sprinkle with salt, pepper, parsley, and lemon juice.
— Microwave, covered with waxed paper or plastic wrap, for 4 minutes on high.
— Remove waxed paper.
— Sprinkle fish with toasted almonds.
— Microwave, covered, for 1 minute on high, or until fish flakes easily when tested with a fork.
— Let stand 1 to 2 minutes before serving.
To serve, garnish with lemon wedges and sprigs of parsley.

(4 servings)

TUNA LUAU

3 cups white sauce
2 cans (7-oz.) tuna, flaked
1 tablespoon pimiento, diced
1 cup crushed pineapple, drained
½ teaspoon salt
½ cup shredded coconut
Parsley or watercress

— Combine all ingredients except coconut, and parsley or watercress.
— Spoon mixture into greased large 10-ounce glass custard dishes.
— Sprinkle with coconut.
— Cover dishes loosely with waxed paper and cook 10 minutes on high, or until heated through.
— Let stand a few minutes before serving.
— Serve with parsley or watercress garnish.

(4-6 servings)

BREAD MIXES

Breads and Quick Breads	Package Size	Number of Muffins	Setting #1 and Time	Setting #2 and Time
Apple Cinnamon Coffee Cake Mix	19 oz.		medium 6 minutes	high 3 to 4 minutes
Date Bread Mix	17 oz.		medium 10 minutes	high 2 minutes
Banana Bread Mix	15 1/2 oz.		medium 8 minutes	high 2 to 3 minutes
Corn Muffins in cupcake liners	8 1/2 oz.	2	medium 1 to 1 1/2 minutes	
		4	medium 2 to 3 minutes	
		6	medium 4 to 5 minutes	
Blueberry Muffins Mix	13 1/2 oz.	2	medium 2 to 2 1/2 minutes	
		4	medium 4 to 4 1/2 minutes	
		6	medium 6 to 6 1/2 minutes	
Bran Muffins		2	medium 2 to 2 1/2 minutes	
		4	medium 4 to 4 1/2 minutes	
		6	medium 6 to 6 1/2 minutes	

***high — 100% power : medium — 60% power : low — 30% power.

BREADS

COOKING HINTS FOR BREADS

A variety of breads can be cooked and raised in your Microwave Oven.

When reheating breads, the center will be hotter than the outside, since the center contains more moisture than the crust. Overcooking can make bread items tough and rubbery. Breads should be heated on a paper napkin or towel to absorb moisture.

Muffins may be prepared in coffee cups lined with paper muffin liners, or lined plastic coffee cup holders may be used. Custard cups may also serve as holders. Fill with batter no more than half-way, as the volume of baked goods is greater when cooked by microwaves.

Breads and baked goods are not usually covered. Leaving them uncovered prevents the surface from becoming too moist.

The surface of breads does not brown; doneness cannot be based on surface appearance. Color will depend on ingredients and toppings. If more browning or crisping is desired, breads may be placed in a hot conventional oven or under a conventional broiler for a few minutes. Opening the oven door while baking will not cause the bread to fall permanently as it would when baked conventionally.

Cooking continues during cooling, so breads should be slightly damp when removed. As bread cools, it may pull away from the side of the dish.

Loaf breads should cool 10 to 15 minutes in the baking dish. Muffins should be removed immediately from the cooking containers.

Day-old or slightly dry rolls or breads may be freshened very quickly in your Microwave Oven. Fully baked breads, rolls, and pastries should be reheated on paper toweling to absorb excess moisture. Reheat bread products on medium. Eight ounces of rolls reheat in approximately 1 minute, 15 seconds on medium. Frozen baked goods may be defrosted and heated on low.

The texture and volume of most bread products is best when medium setting is used for baking, which is approximately 60 per cent of power.

DUTCH CARROT BREAD

2 cups flour
2 teaspoons baking soda
1 teaspoon ground cinnamon
1 ½ cups sugar
3 eggs
1 ½ cups vegetable oil
2 teaspoons vanilla extract
2 cups finely grated carrots

— Lightly grease two 8 ½x4 ½x2 ½-inch loaf pans and set aside.
— Sift flour, baking soda, cinnamon and sugar together into a large bowl.
— Stir with a spoon.
— Make a well in center with the back of the spoon.
— Place eggs in well and beat just the eggs with a rotary beater or electric hand mixer until thoroughly blended.
— Try to keep dry ingredients on the side of the bowl.
— Add vegetable oil and beat thoroughly with eggs, again trying to keep dry ingredients on the side of the bowl.
— Add vanilla to egg-oil mixture.
— Beat in flour mixture until all ingredients are combined and smooth.
— Fold carrots into mixture.
— Pour mixture into prepared loaf pans.
— Bake each loaf, uncovered, on medium for 10 minutes. Bread is done when a toothpick inserted in the bread comes out clean.
— Allow bread to cool 10 minutes before removing from loaf pans.

(2 loaves)

WHITE BREAD

1 envelope active dry yeast
½ cup warm water
½ cup butter or margarine
¼ cup sugar
1 teaspoon salt
½ cup evaporated milk
3½ cups sifted all-purpose flour

— Sprinkle yeast over warm water in a large bowl. Stir until yeast dissolves.
— In a medium-size bowl melt butter on high 1 minute.
— Add sugar, salt and evaporated milk and stir until sugar dissolves.
— Stir into yeast mixture..
— Add flour all at once and beat until batter is smooth and very stiff.
— Knead until elastic.
— Cover and let rise in a warm place until double in bulk.
— Punch dough down and place in a heat-resistant, non-metallic, loaf pan.
— Cover and let rise again until double in bulk.
— Microwave, uncovered, on low for 11 to 12 minutes.

(If desired, bread may be placed in a very hot conventional oven (475°F.) for a few minutes to brown.)

(1 loaf)

MUFFIN JEWELS

½ cup all-purpose flour
¼ cup sugar
½ teaspoon salt
4 teaspoons baking powder
1 cup whole wheat flour
1 egg, beaten
1 cup milk
3 tablespoons butter or margarine, melted

— Sift flour, sugar, salt and baking powder together.
— Stir in whole wheat flour.
— Combine beaten egg, milk and melted butter.
— Make a well in dry ingredients and add liquid ingredients all at once.
— Stir just until flour mixture is moistened.
— Spoon batter into paper muffin lined plastic coffee cup holders or custard cups.
— Place 6 muffins at a time in oven.
— Microwave, uncovered, on medium for 3 minutes or until muffins test done with a toothpick.
— Repeat above steps for the remaining muffins.

(8 muffins)

FAST CHEESE FRENCHIES

1 loaf (1-lb.) French bread
French or Italian salad dressing
Grated Parmesan cheese

— Cut bread diagonally in 1-inch slices, leaving bottom crust intact.
— Place on sheet of waxed paper large enough to wrap loaf.
— Spread dressing between slices and over top of loaf.
— Sprinkle generously with Parmesan cheese.
— Bring sides of paper up over top of loaf.
—Twist ends to close loosely.
— Microwave 45 seconds on high, or until bread is warm.

(24 ½-inch slices)

BANANA BREAD

3½ cups unsifted flour
3 teaspoons baking powder
1 teaspoon baking soda
1 teaspoon salt
2 cups mashed ripe bananas
2 tablespoons lemon juice
¾ cup softened butter or margarine
1½ cups sugar
3 eggs
¾ cup milk
1 cup coarsely broken walnuts

— Lightly grease two 8½x4½x2½-inch loaf pans and set aside.
— Sift together flour, baking powder, baking soda and and salt; set aside.
— In a small bowl, combine mashed bananas and lemon juice and set aside.
— In the large bowl of an electric mixer, cream butter and sugar until light and fluffy.
— Add eggs, 1 at a time, beating well after each addition.
— Add milk and dry ingredients alternately, beginning and ending with dry ingredients.
— Fold in walnuts and banana mixture.
— Pour batter into prepared loaf pans and bake each loaf, uncovered on medium for 11 to 12 minutes.
— Bread is done when a toothpick inserted in the bread comes out clean.
— Allow bread to cool 10 minutes before removing from loaf pans.

(Makes 2 loaves)

CHILI CHEESE CORNBREAD

2 eggs
1 ½ teaspoons salt
1 tablespoon baking powder
¼ teaspoon pepper
1 cup sour cream
¼ cup melted butter or margarine
1 cup corn meal
1 cup drained whole kernel corn
3 drops Tabasco sauce (optional)
1 ½ cups grated sharp Cheddar cheese
2 to 4-oz. canned green chilies, drained and chopped

— In a large bowl, thoroughly blend together all but the last two ingredients.
— Grease a shallow, 8-inch, round, heat-resistant, non-metallic baking dish.
— Pour half the batter into the greased baking dish.
— Spread chopped chilies and ½ cup of cheese over the batter.
— Top with remaining batter, then cheese.
— Microwave, uncovered, on medium for 14 to 16 minutes.
— Let stand 5 minutes before serving.

(If desired, bread may be placed in a very hot conventional oven (475°F.) for a few minutes to brown.)

(8-10 servings)

FAST MUFFINS

¾ cup milk
¼ cup sugar
1 egg
2 tablespoons salad oil
2 cups sifted buttermilk biscuit mix

— In a medium-sized bowl, combine milk, sugar, egg and oil. Blend well.
— Add sifted biscuit mix to milk mixture and stir vigorously until all the flour is moistened.
— Divide batter into 12 plastic coffee cup holders or custard cups that have been lined with paper muffin liners.
— Place 6 of the muffins in oven. Microwave, uncovered, on medium for 3 to 4 minutes or until toothpick inserted in the center of muffin comes out clean.
— Place remaining 6 muffins in oven and cook, uncovered, on medium for 3 to 4 minutes.

(12 muffins)

CORNBREAD FROM A MIX

1 (8½-oz.) package cornbread mix

— Prepare cornbread according to package instructions.
— Grease an 8-inch, round, heat-resistant, non-metallic baking dish.
— Heat, uncovered, on medium for 6 minutes or until a toothpick inserted in center comes out clean.
— Let stand 3 to 4 minutes before serving.

(6-8 servings)

CORN BREAD

1 cup sifted flour
1 cup corn meal
¼ cup sugar
1 teaspoon baking powder
1 teaspoon baking soda
1 teaspoon salt
1 egg
1 cup sour milk
2 tablespoons melted shortening

— Sift flour, corn meal, sugar, baking powder, baking soda and salt together into a large mixing bowl.
— In a medium-sized bowl beat the egg.
— Add the sour milk to the egg and blend together well.
— Add milk mixture to flour mixture.
— Stir to combine.
— Add melted shortening to flour-milk mixture and beat well.
— Pour into an 8-inch, round, heat-resistant, non-metallic baking dish.
— Microwave, uncovered, on medium for 7 to 8 minutes or until done.

To make sour milk: Place 2 tablespoons lemon juice into glass measuring cup. Add milk till it measures 1 cup. Let stand 5 minutes.

(6 servings)

PUMPKIN BREAD WITH PUMPKIN TOPPING

1 ½ cups unsifted flour
1 ½ cups sugar
1 teaspoon soda
¾ teaspoon salt
½ teaspoon nutmeg
½ teaspoon cinnamon
1 cup mashed cooked pumpkin
½ cup cooking oil
⅓ cup water
2 eggs
½ cup chopped walnuts
½ cup chopped dates

Pumpkin Topping:
1 cup whipping cream
¼ cup powdered sugar
¼ teaspoon nutmeg
¼ teaspoon cinnamon
¾ cup mashed cooked pumpkin

— Combine all bread ingredients, except walnuts and dates, in large mixer bowl.
— Beat at medium speed about 1 minute.
— Fold in walnuts and dates.
— Pour batter into 2-quart glass loaf dish.
— Microwave on low for 20 minutes.
— Microwave on high for 5 to 6 minutes or until toothpick inserted near center comes out clean.
— Let stand 2 minutes; unmold.
— Serve with Pumpkin Topping.
— Pumpkin Topping: Whip cream with powdered sugar and spices. Fold in pumpkin.

(1 loaf)

ONION-CHEESE STICKS

1 cup quick biscuit mix
⅓ cup milk
⅓ cup grated American cheese
1 package (1 ¼-oz. dry onion soup mix)

— Measure biscuit mix into 1-quart bowl.
— Stir in milk to make soft dough.
— Mix in cheese.
— Turn out on lightly floured pastry cloth.
— Knead lightly several times.
— Pinch off 1-inch balls of dough. Roll into sticks.
— Roll sticks in soup mix to coat.
— Arrange 6 to 8 at a time on microwave roasting rack in (12x8-inch) utility dish, or paper towels.
— Microwave 2 to 3 minutes on high, or until firm to touch.

(16 pieces)

STREUSEL COFFEE CAKE

⅓ cup butter or margarine
¾ cup sugar
2 eggs
1 teaspoon almond or vanilla extract
1 ½ cups all-purpose flour
2 ½ teaspoons baking powder
½ teaspoon salt
½ cup milk
Steusel topping below

— Place butter in large mixing bowl. If necessary, Microwave 20 seconds on medium to soften.
— Cream sugar with butter until fluffy.
— Beat in eggs and almond extract.
— Stir in flour, baking power, salt and milk
— Pour all coffee cake mixture in pan. Microwave 5 minutes on high.
— Then sprinkle on streusel topping and Microwave 3 to 4 minutes on high or untl wooden pick inserted in center comes out clean.

Topping:
1 cup firmly packed brown sugar
¼ cup flour
¼ cup granulated sugar
½ teaspoon cinnamon
½ cup chopped nuts
2 tablespoons butter or margarine, melted

— Blend all ingredients in small bowl.

(9-12 servings)

BISCUIT MIX COFFEE CAKE

2 cups biscuit mix
2 tablespoons sugar
⅔ cup water
1 egg

Topping:
⅓ cup biscuit mix
⅓ cup packed brown sugar
½ teaspoon cinnamon
¼ cup butter or margarine

— Combine 2 cup biscuit mix, sugar, water and egg in medium mixing bowl; mix well.
— Spread in 9-inch round glass baking dish. Sprinkle with Topping.
— Microwave on low for 7 minutes.
— Microwave on high for 4 to 4 ½ minutes or until toothpick inserted near center comes out clean.
— Topping: Combine ⅓ cup biscuit mix, brown sugar and cinnamon; cut in butter.

(6 servings)

IRISH SODA BREAD

4 cups unsifted all-purpose flour
¼ cup sugar
1 tablespoon baking powder
1 teaspoon salt
½ cup butter or margarine
2 cups dark raisins
1 ⅓ cups buttermilk
1 egg
1 teaspoon baking soda
1 egg yolk
1 tablespoon water

— Grease a deep, 2½-quart, heat-resistant, non-metallic caserole and set aside.
— Sift flour, sugar, baking powder and salt together into a large bowl.
— With a pastry blender or 2 knives, cut in butter until mixture resembles cornmeal.
— Stir in raisins.
— Combine buttermilk, egg and baking soda in a small bowl until thoroughly blended.
— Stir buttermilk mixture into dry ingredients until well blended.
— Turn out onto a lightly floured board and knead lightly about 3 minutes or until dough is smooth.
— Shape dough into a ball and place in prepared casserole.
— With a sharp knife cut an "X" about ½-inch deep into the top of the dough.
— Beat egg yolk and water together.
— Brush mixture over top of dough.
— Cook, uncovered, on medium for 14 minutes or until a cake tester inserted in the center comes out clean.
— Cool 10 minutes in casserole; turn out of pan and allow to cool completely.

(If desired, bread may be placed in a very hot conventional oven (475°F.) for a few minutes to brown.)

DRESSED UP GINGERBREAD

1 package gingerbread mix
Sweetened whipped cream or ice cream
¼ cup crushed peppermint candy

— Prepare gingerbread as directed on package.
— Pour into (8x8-inch) baking dish.
— Microwave 4 to 6 minutes on high or until top is slight firm to touch.
— Cool slightly.
— Serve warm topped with whipped cream or ice cream.
— Sprinkle with crushed candy.

(9 servings)

CORNMEAL MOLASSES BREAD

¾ cup boiling water
3 tablespoons vegetable shortening
¼ cup dark molasses
½ cup cornmeal
2 teaspoons salt
1 envelope active dry yeast
¼ cup lukewarm water
1 egg, beaten
3 cups sifted all-purpose flour

— Combine boiling water and shortening in a large bowl and set aside until shortening has melted.
— Add molasses, cornmeal and salt.
— Let stand until mixture is lukewarm.
— Sprinkle yeast over the ¼ cup lukewarm water and stir to dissolve.
— Stir dissolved yeast, egg and half of the flour into the cornmeal mixture.
— Beat until thoroughly mixed.
— Stir in remaining flour and mix dough forms a soft ball. Transfer dough to a greased, 1½-quart, heat-resistant, non-metallic loaf pan.
— Cover with greased wax paper and place cloth on top.
— Set in warm place to rise until dough is double in bulk.
— Microwave, uncovered, on low for 18 to 20 minutes or until bread tests done with a toothpick.
— Cool before slicing.

(1 large loaf)

DATE NUT BREAD

1 package (17-oz.) Date Nut Bread mix

— Prepare bread as directed on package.
— Grease loaf dish and line bottom with waxed paper.
— Pour batter into loaf dish.
— Microwave 6 to 7 minutes on high, or until top is slightly moist and wooden pick inserted in center comes out clean, rotating dish once.
— Let stand 10 minutes.
— Remove from loaf dish.

NOTE: Top will be slightly irregular.

(1 loaf)

MACADAMIA NUT BISCUITS

1/3 cup brown sugar
3 tablespoons butter
4 tablespoons water
1/3 cup chopped macadamia nuts
1 tablespoon rice powder
10 refrigerator biscuits (uncooked)

— Combine brown sugar, butter and water in a baking dish.
— Microwave 1 minute, 30 seconds on high.
— Add macadamia nuts and rice powder.
— Stir well.
— Cut each biscuit in half and coat well with the mixture.
— Place on glass dish and microwave 4 minutes on high, uncovered.

(4 servings)

PLUM AND NUT BREAD

1 tablespoon salad oil
1 cup plums in syrup, finely chopped
1 cup finely chopped pecan nuts
4 teaspoons baking powder
1/4 teaspoon salt
3/4 cup boiling water
3 tablespoons shortening
2 beaten eggs
3/4 cup sugar
1 1/2 cups flour
1/2 teaspoon vanilla
1/2 teaspoon lemon juice

— Grease a 3 x 9 inch wide loaf pan with salad oil.
— Mix plums, pecan nuts, baking powder and salt well in a deep bowl.
— Add boiling water, shortening, and stir roughly.
— Cover with wet cloth and let stand for 1 hour.
— Add eggs, sugar, sifted flour, vanilla and lemon juice. Whisk well.
— Pour the mixture into the oiled pan. Microwave 8 minutes on high.
— Let stand 10 minutes; then remove from the oven and cool.
— Chill in the refrigerator about 8 hours.
— Slice and serve.

(1 loaf)

EVIE'S STICKY BUNS

1 cup quick biscuit mix
1/3 cup milk
2 tablespoons butter or margarine, melted
1/4 cup sugar
1 teaspoon cinnamon
2 tablespoons butter or margarine, softened
2 tablespoons firmly packed brown sugar
1/4 cup walnut or pecan pieces

— Measure biscuit mix into 1-quart bowl.
— Stir in milk to make a soft dough.
— Turn out on lightly floured pastry cloth.
— Knead lightly several times.
— Roll out in 8-inch square.
— Brush with melted butter.
— Mix together sugar and cinnamon and sprinkle on dough. Roll up.
— Cut in 1-inch pieces.
— Combine softened butter and brown sugar in 8-inch cake dish. Spread to cover bottom.
— Scatter nuts over sugar mixture.
— Arrange rolls in dish.
— Microwave 5 to 6 minutes on high, or until wooden pick inserted in center comes out clean.
— Let stand 5 minutes. Invert onto serving plate.

(8 pieces)

DEPENDABLE DUMPLINGS

2 1/2 cups stock or lightly salted water
1 cup flour
1 1/2 teaspoons baking powder
1/2 teaspoon salt
3 tablespoons shortening
2/3 cup milk

— Pour stock in 1 1/2-quart casserole.
— Microwave 6 to 8 minutes on high, or until boiling.
— Measure flour, baking powder and salt into mixing bowl.
— Cut in shortening until mixture looks like corn meal.
— Stir in milk until mixture is moistened but not smooth.
— Drop dough by rounded teaspoonfuls onto boiling stock. (Do not cover).
— Microwave 6 minutes on high, uncovered.
— Cover.
— Microwave 5 minutes on high, or until dumplings are firm.
— Remove dumplings to serving dish with slotted spoon.

(8 servings)

GARLIC BREAD

1 loaf French bread
2 cloves garlic
½ cup softened butter
½ teaspoon chopped parsley
½ teaspoon salt

— Slice French bread diagonally into 1 inch thick slices, but do not cut from loaf completely. Leave about ¼ inch uncut at the bottom.
— Peel garlic, and crush with a garlic press or bottle.
—Mix well with butter, chopped parsley and salt.
— Butter French bread by inserting butter mixture between slices.
—Place bread on a baking dish covered with wet paper towel.
— Cover bread with dampened paper towel.
— Microwave 1 minute on medium.

(1 loaf)

CARAMEL BISCUIT RING-A-ROUND

⅓ cup packed brown sugar
3 tablespoons butter or margarine
1 tablespoon water
⅓ cup chopped nuts
1 can (8 oz.) refrigerated biscuits

— Combine brown sugar, butter and water in 1-quart glass casserole.
— Microwave on medium for about 2 minutes or until butter is melted.
— Stir in nuts.
— Separate biscuits; cut each one into quarters.
— Add biscuits to sugar mixture; stir to coat each piece.
— Push biscuits and coating away from center of casserole and set a custard cup or glass open end up, in center.
— Microwave on medium for 5 to 5½ minutes or until biscuits are not longer doughy.
— Let stand 2 minutes; twist out custard cup and invert biscuit ring on serving plate.
— Serve warm with forks to pull sections apart into individual servings.

(6 servings)

IT'S NOT MAGIC

THE EVOLUTION OF MODERN-DAY COOKING

After using your microwave oven for just a short time, you'll find it difficult to imagine doing without it. Such was the case with other important advances in the history of cooking. The twelfth century development of open-hearth cooking made outdoor fire pits appear to be "camping," harking back to cave-man times. Invention of the wood and coal-burning stove in the early 1800's made the open hearth appear primitive. Gas and electric ranges of the present day, with their many refinements, have been responsible for making all other cooking equipment obsolete. That is, until the microwave.

IN THE BEGINNING . . .

Imagine coming home after a hard day's work realizing that firewood must be collected, cut and assembled to build an open fire for the evening meal. The day's game (say, a wild hen) is placed on a spit and turned for several hours until the cook guesses it is ready. Potatoes and breads are baked in the pit lining, against the hot rocks. Water waiting to be boiled rests beside the fire in a water-tight basket or animal hide bag. Later, hot rocks from the fire will be added until water comes (or nearly comes) to a boil.

FIRE PIT

The addition of wood has caused the fire to vary between hot and cool causing the game meat to have parts overcooked and parts which are nearly raw. The uneven texture and doneness goes unnoticed, however, because of the long wait for dinner, the gentle basting of the meal with fine wood ash from the fire, and perhaps a little sand mixed in with the drumsticks. We have a tendency to romanticize the scene, but if it were a daily event,the romance would soon disappear.

In the following centuries, conditions improved somewhat as the fire pit was brought inside with a flue to the outside of the home. This modernization was a great boon to the cook because the elements of nature (wind, rain, darkness, cold) were no longer so significant to the meal's outcome. Coals were maintained continuously over great periods of time, from meal to meal, and development of heat resistant pottery allowed containerized cooking directly over the fire.

WOOD STOVE

Once brought indoors, handicaps to the open-pit method of cooking became obvious to the whole family. Necessity, being the mother of invention, soon placed the pit at a strategic wall within the home so that smoke could be vented outside and cooking itself could be set aside from other household activities. Further refined, the open hearth was just a short step away; the stage was set for a manufactured product that could obviate the construction required to contain indoor fires.

Cast iron wood-burning stoves came into use early in the nineteenth century. Some of us know people who can remember "stoking" a fire in the wood stove to heat the morning coffee and prepare bacon and eggs for breakfast. In days when bread was made "like grandma used to make," a good cook had to be an expert in fire building as well as in the culinary skills. Quality of wood, draft and cooking time varied in such a way that an easy breakfast could be spoiled by a mistakenly hot fire.

The wood stove was a significant innovation, however. For the first time a cooking surface was present, different sections of the stove could be heated simultaneously to different temperatures for different foods, and all cooking was self-contained. But how would you like to spend Saturday morning cleaning a wood and grease blackened stove, or preparing baked goods in a wood-fueled oven on an unbearable summer day?

GAS RANGE

The modern range has done a great deal to facilitate daily cooking needs — and to make good cooks much more prevalent than before. Even heat and controlled heat are an accepted fact of modern-day cooking equipment, and it is possible to predict when food will be fully cooked. Later model ovens turn on and off automatically; some even have self-cleaning features. Food cooked on a stove top can be put on a "burner with a brain" achieving the ultimate in cooking predictibility.

The gathering of firewood and removal of ashes is a thing of the past, although utility bills are replacing the pile of firewood in the kitchen. Kitchens still become uncomfortable from lengthy oven-cooked meals. Food still stands out for hours to thaw or defrost. Scouring of pots and pans, lessened from earlier times, remains one of the tasks least liked by cooks everywhere.

Lifestyles have changed considerably from the time cooking was done over an open fire, and it will continue to change! In more households than ever before, the cook is also a family "breadwinner" No one really wants to slave over the stove after a day's work.

MICROWAVE

With your microwave oven, a meal can be prepared in a fraction of the time it used to take — to the total enjoyment of family and guests. Clean-up is minimized through the use of different utensils and containers. Speed, comfort, cleanliness, flexibility, and food quality are all possible now. It's not magic . . . it only seems that way.

SAUCES

SAUCES

The French often say, "The dish is only as good as the sauce." A bit extreme in American kitchens, but something to remember in microwave cooking.

Because of exceptionally fast cooking, some foods do not naturally brown, tenderize, or develop a rich broth as in conventional slow cooking. The microwave cook can compensate for this and at the same time enhance her dish through the use of sauces.

Rich colored sauces, such as Basic Browning Sauce, and "brown" meats and poultry as well as glaze surfaces for eye appeal. Marinades and basting sauces will tenderize meats. And foods that may tend to get dry can be kept moist and flavorful with carefully selected cooking sauces.

Many cooking sauces are interchangeable in this book. If you prefer Barbecue Sauce to Teriyaki, or Apricot chutney glaze to Orange-honey glaze, switch the recipies, or make up a sauce of your own.

GARNISH

Almost any dish can use a touch of garnish. It's the secret of every chef and very important in making microwave cooking attractive. Since there is not the same amount of color change as experienced in conventional cooking, some foods may tend to appear "unfinished" when done. Simple garnish is the answer.

The standard is a dish of paprika, a sprig of parsley, or a cherry tomato. But there are a number of other colorful garnishes easily found in most kitchens. Try sliced olives, orange or lemon wedges or slices, nuts, canned fruits, grated cheese, or seasoned bread crumbs.

It's that little extra touch that counts!

— Give two good cooks the same recipe to follow and chances are the finished results will be different. And that's just fine — especially in microwave cooking!

It's the individual flair that each cook imparts to a dish that makes it personal, whether a simple vegetable or an elegant main dish. And this is the secret in making often drab looking recipes into specialties of the house.

— There are three ways to impart personal touches to every recipe: seasonings, sauces, and garnish.

SEASONINGS

The kitchen-tested recipes in this book were seasoned to appeal to average family tastes. They may be altered in any way to match your liking, though a few simple rules should be kept in mind.

Salt, or seasoned salt combinations, are best added at the end of cooking as they tend to draw moisture from foods, especially meats, during cooking.

Recipes calling for herbs and spices may have to be adjusted due to far shorter cooking times with microwave compared to conventional cooking. For example, a bay leaf in a stew kettle has hours to flavor the food. Herbs added to microwave cooking have only minutes to do their flavoring. The best rule is to season microwave cooking as you would "stove-top" or conventional "quick-cooking" recipes.

Many seasonings, such as seasoned salt, soy sauce, brown gravy sauce and paprika also add color to microwave cooking. Seasoning mixtures that contain sugar will tend to carmelize during cooking and can act as a browning factor as well as a flavoring.

SPAGHETTI SAUCE

1 tablespoon butter or margarine, melted
½ lb. ground beef
2 teaspoons salt
½ cup chopped onion
2 teaspoons oregano
2 cloves garlic, chopped
¼ teaspoon basil
1 can (28 oz.) tomatoes
¼ teaspoon ground thyme
2 cans (6 oz. each) tomato paste
Freshly ground pepper
2 tablespoons butter or margarine
1 tablespoon chopped parsley
Grated Parmesan cheese

— In a deep, 2-quart glass casserole dish place butter, crumbled beef, salt, onion, oregano and garlic.
— Microwave, uncovered, about 6 minutes, on high, stirring every 2 minutes to break up meat.
— Cut whole tomatoes into smaller pieces.
— Add remaining ingredients except parsley and Parmesan cheese.
— Microwave, covered, about 15 minutes on high or until mixture is well blended and thickens slightly.
— Cover and let stand about 5 minutes.
— Serve steaming hot over hot cooked spaghetti.
— Top with chopped parsley and Parmesan cheese.

(2 quarts)

ITALIAN MEAT SAUCE

1 pound lean ground beef
1 clove garlic, peeled and crushed
½ teaspoon dried oregano leaves
½ teaspoon dried basil leaves
½ teaspoon sugar
1 teaspoon salt
¼ teaspoon pepper
1 (15-oz.) can tomato sauce

— In a medium-size glass bowl crumble beef.
— Heat, uncovered, on medium for 6 minutes, stirring frequently until meat is browned.
— Drain off excess fat.
— Add remaining ingredients and stir to blend well.
— Cook, uncovered, on medium 7 to 8 minutes, stirring occasionally.
— Serve over spaghetti.

(4 servings)

MORNAY SAUCE

2 tablespoons butter or margarine
2 tablespoons flour
¼ cup light cream
1 cup chicken stock or broth
¼ cup Romano cheese
¼ cup shredded Swiss cheese
2 tablespoons dried parsley flakes

— In a 2-cup measuring cup melt butter on high for 30 seconds.
— Blend in flour.
— Gradually stir in light cream and chicken stock.
— Microwave, uncovered, on medium for 4 to 5 minutes or until thickened and smooth.
— Stir frequently.
— Add cheese and parsely flakes and Microwave, uncovered, on medium for 1 minute, or until cheese is melted and sauce is smooth.
— Alow sauce to stand until cheese has completely melted.

(1 ½ cups)

BROWN GRAVY

2 tablespoons grease separated from drippings
1 ½ tablespoons all-purpose flour
1 cup drippings
¼ teaspoon MSG (monosodium glutamate)
Dash of mustard, allspice, nutmeg and tarragon
Dash of salt and pepper

— Mix grease and flour in a shallow 2-quart glass baking dish and stir until smooth.
— Microwave, uncovered, 3 minutes or until browned on high. Stir every 30 seconds.
— Add drippings, MSG and remaining ingredients to the dish.
— Microwave, uncovered, again 2 minutes on high, stirring every 30 seconds.
— Milk can be added according to taste.

(1 ½ cup)

ORANGE GLAZE

½ cup orange marmalade
3 tablespoons honey
1 tablespoon lemon juice
1 tablespoon cinnamon

— Combine marmalade and honey in a small bowl.
— Add lemon and cinnamon. Mix until smooth.
— Heat, uncovered, on high for 1 minute.
— Use as a glaze on poultry.

(½ cup)

HOT FUDGE SAUCE

2 squares unsweetened chocolate
¼ cup butter or margarine
¼ cup evaporated milk
½ cup powdered sugar
1 teaspoon vanilla

— Combine chocolate and butter in 1-quart glass measure or bowl.
— Microwave 2 minutes on high, uncovered, or until chocolate and butter are melted. Stir.
— Stir in milk. Add sugar and beat until smooth and creamy.
— Add vanilla.

(1 cup)

SPICY PINEAPPLE SAUCE

2 tablespoons brown sugar
1 tablespoon cornstarch
1 (8-oz.) can pineapple chunks in unsweetened juice, undrained
¼ teaspoon cinnamon
2 tablespoons butter

— Combine sugar and cornstarch in a deep, 1-quart glass casserole.
— Gradually add juice from pineapple, stirring constantly.
— Add pineapple, cinnamon and butter.
— Cook, uncovered, on high 3 minutes.
— Stir and heat on high an additional 4 minutes or until sauce has thickened. Stir occasionally.
— Serve with meat or as a dessert sauce.

(¾ cup)

BASIC BROWNING SAUCE

½ cup unsulphured molasses
⅓ cup dark corn syrup (Karo)
1½ teaspoons soy sauce
1½ teaspoons carmel color
½ teaspoon monosodium glutamate (MSG)

— Combine ingredients in a 2 cup glass measure and cook 2 minutes on high, or until mixture boils.
— Stir and cook 2 more minutes on high.
— Pour into a jar and refrigerate covered. (Sauce will keep for weeks.)
— Rub or baste on meats, poultry and game. (Use during the final 15 minutes of cooking on large poultry. Sauce imparts a delicate flavor as well as aids in browning.)

1 cup)

CHEESE SAUCE

3 tablespoons butter or margarine
3 tablespoons flour
¼ teaspoon mustard powder
Dash of salt and pepper
1¼ cups milk
½ cup grated cheese

— Melt butter, cook in a cup for 20 seconds on high.
— Mix in flour, mustard, salt, pepper and nutmeg.
— Stir in milk gradually.
— Microwave 2 minutes, on high, stirring after 1 minute.
— Add cheese and stir until it melts.

CARAMEL SAUCE

½ cup light cream
⅔ cup white corn syrup
1¼ cups packed brown sugar
2 tablespoons butter or margarine

— Combine all ingredients in 4-cup glass measure; mix well.
— Microwave on medium for 8 minutes. Stir and continue cooking on medium for 4 to 6 minutes or until hot.
— Beat until smooth.

(1½ cups)

WHITE SAUCE

2 tablespoons butter or margarine
2 tablespoons flour
½ teaspoon salt
1 cup milk

— Place butter in custard cup.
— Microwave on high until butter is melted.
— Blend in flour and salt to make a smooth paste. Set aside.
— Place milk in 1-quart measure or bowl.
— Microwave 2 minutes, 30 seconds on high, or until milk is about to boil.
— Beat in butter-flour paste, using a wire whip. Microwave 2 minutes on high or until thickened, stir about 1 minute.
— Mix well before using.

CHEDDAR CHEESE SAUCE
— Add ½ cup grated sharp cheddar cheese and pinch of cayenne to white sauce.
— Stir until melted.

CURRY SAUCE
— Add 1 teaspoon or more curry powder to white sauce.

(1 cup)

WHITE CLAM SAUCE

½ cup olive oil
2 cloves garlic, peeled and quartered
2 (8-oz.) cans chopped clams, undrained
¼ cup chopped parsely
1 teaspoon dried oregano leaves

— Place oil and garlic, to taste, in a small, glass bowl and heat, uncovered, on high 3 minutes.
— Remove garlic pieces.
— Add remaining ingredients and heat, uncovered, on high 4 minutes or until heated through.
— Sir occasionally.
— Serve over spaghetti.

(4 servings)

LEMON SAUCE

1 cup water
½ cup sugar
1 tablespoon corn starch
2 tablespoons butter or margarine
1 ½ teaspoons lemon juice
½ teaspoon lemon rind
⅛ teaspoon salt

— Measure water into 2-cup measure. Stir in sugar and cornstarch unil dissolved.
— Microwave 4 minutes on high, or until slightly thickened.
— Add butter, lemon juice, rind and salt.
— Sir until buter is melted.
— Serve warm or cold over pudding or cake.

(1 ½ cups)

CHOCOLATE FONDUE

1 can (14 oz.) sweetened condensed milk
1 jar (10 oz.) marshmallow creme
½ cup milk
1 teaspoon vanilla
1 package (12 oz.) semi-sweet chocolate pieces

— Combine all ingredients in medium glass mixing bowl.
— Microwave on medium for 4 to 6 minutes. Beat until well blended and creamy.

Keep fondue sauce warm in a chafing dish or in a heavy pottery crock over very low heat.

(4 cups)

BARBECUE SAUCE FOR FRANKFURTERS

¼ cup bottled chili sauce
¼ cup grated Cheddar cheese
1 can (16 oz.) barbecued beans
¼ cup chopped sauerkraut
¼ teaspoon Tabasco

— Combine chili sauce and cheese in a casserole.
— Add barbequed beans and sauerkraut with a dash of Tabasco on top.
— Microwave 3 minutes on high, stirring every 1 minute.

(6-8 servings)

TERIYAKI SAUCE

½ cup soy sauce
¼ cup sherry
2 tablespoons brown sugar
¼ teaspoon dry mustard
1 clove garlic, crushed
1 tablespoon fresh ginger or ¼ tablespoon powdered ginger

— Mix ingredients and Microwave on high for 2 minutes, just until mixture boils and sugar is dissolved.
— Cool and use as a baste for meats, poultry and seafood during final 5 to 10 minutes of cooking.

HOLLANDAISE SAUCE

⅓ cup butter
⅓ cup cream
3 egg yolks, beaten
1 tablespoon lemon juice or white vinegar
¼ teaspoon salt
½ teaspoon mustard

— Melt butter in a 2 cup measure or glass bowl, about 30 seconds on high.
— Stir in remaining ingredients, mixing well.
— Microwave 1 minute on high, or until mixture starts to thicken, stirring twice.
— Whip or beat until smooth.

(1 cup)

ORANGE HONEY SAUCE & GLAZE

⅓ cup undiluted frozen orange juice concentrate, thawed
⅓ cup honey
⅓ cup sherry

— Brush mixture on meats and poultry during final 10 minutes of cooking, or heat and serve as a table sauce.

SHRIMP SAUCE

1 can (10 oz.) frozen shrimp soup
Water
⅔ cup milk
1½ teaspoons chopped onion
Dash of celery seeds and pepper
Dash of chili sauce and salt

— Place opened can of soup in a bowl.
— Pour water into the bowl. (Do not pour water into can.)
— Let stand until one third of contents thaw.
— Blend shrimp soup and milk in a blender.
— Pour blended soup and milk into a bowl.
— Mix in onion, celery seeds, pepper, chili sauce and salt.
— Microwave 3 minutes, on high, stirring once every minute.

PEKING SAUCE

3 tablespoons corn starch
1¼ cups pineapple juice
1 tablespoon soy sauce
3 tablespoons vinegar
⅓ cup water
½ cup brown sugar
2 cups pineapple chunks
2 green peppers, chopped

— Combine all ingredients except pineapple and peppers.
— Cook until mixture thickens, 3 minutes on high, stirring after every 30 seconds.
— Add pineapple and peppers and cook 1 minute longer, on high, or just until mixture boils.
— Serve with pork, lamb or poultry.

BARBECUE SAUCE

1 cup catsup
¼ cup cider vinegar
1 tablespoon Worcestershire sauce
2 tablespoons finely chopped onion
2 tablespoons firmly packed brown sugar
1 tablespoon paprika
1 teaspoon sugar
1 teaspoon salt
Pepper to taste

— Combine all ingredients in a 1-quart measure or bowl. Mix well.
— Microwave 5 minutes on high, or until sauce is hot and thick enough to coat a spoon, stirring after three minutes.

(1½ cups)

CHOCOLATE TOPPING

3 squares unsweetened chocolae
¼ cup water
1 cup sugar
½ cup light corn syrup
⅛ teaspoon salt
⅔ cup heavy cream

— Combine chocolate and water in 1½-quart casserole.
— Microwave 1 minute, 30 seconds on high, or until chocolate is melted.
— Add sugar, corn syrup and salt. Blend well.
— Microwave 1 minute on high, or until a little dropped in cold water forms a soft ball.
— If necessary, Microwave 1 minute more on high.
— Stir, test again.
— Gradually stir in cream. (Serve warm)

(2 cups)

FLUFFY HOLLANDAISE

¼ cup butter or margarine
¼ cup whipping cream
2 egg yolks, well beaten
1 tablespoon lemon juice
½ teaspoon dry mustard
¼ teaspoon salt

— Place butter in 1-quart bowl.
— Microwave on high 1 minute or until melted.
— Add remaining ingredients.
— Mix well.
— Microwave 1 minute to 1 minute, 30 seconds on medium, or until thickened, stirring halfway through.
— Beat with wire whip or rotary beater until light and fluffy.
— Serve with eggs, fish or vegetables. (Over cooking will curdle sauce.)

(⅔ cup)

HOT MUSTARD SAUCE

1 egg, beaten
½ cup prepared mustard
⅓ cup sugar
⅓ cup vinegar
½ teaspoon salt
Pepper

— Combine all ingredients in 2-cup glass measure.
— Microwave on medium for 3 minutes. Stir and continue cooking on medium for 1 to 2 minutes or until thickened.
— Stir before serving.

(1¼ cups)

BUTTERSCOTCH FROSTING

1 ½ cups firmly packed brown sugar
½ cup granulated sugar
½ cup cream
1 teaspoon vanilla
2 tablespoons butter

— Blend sugars and cream in 2-quart glass casserole.
— Microwave 5 to 6 minutes on high, uncovered, or until sugar is dissolved and mixture is no longer grainy, stirring after 3 and 4 minutes.
— Immediately add vanilla and butter.
— Stir until butter melts.
— Cool thoroughly.
— Beat to spreading consistency.
— Thin with a little cream if necessary.

(Frosts 8 or 9-inch layer cake)

STRAWBERRY SAUCE

1 ½ pounds strawberries, cleaned and hulled
1 ½ cups sugar
1 teaspoon lemon juice

— Place strawberries in a medium-size bowl.
— Pour sugar on top and stir to mix thoroughly.
— Microwave, uncovered, on high 5 minutes. Stir.
— Microwave, uncovered, an additional 5 minutes on high.
— Add lemon juice and stir to mix thoroughly.
— Cool before serving.

(2 ½ cups)

VELVET CUSTARD SAUCE

½ cup sugar
2 tablespoons corn starch
1 teaspoon salt
2 cups milk
4 egg yolks, well beaten
1 teaspoon vanilla, (other flavorings can be used)

— Combine sugar, corn starch and salt in 1-quart bowl.
— Mix well.
— Gradually add milk to dry ingredients, stirring until mixture is smooth.
— Add egg yolks, beating until well combined.
— Microwave 3 to 4 minutes on high, uncovered, or until mixture coats a metal spoon, stirring after 2 minutes.
— Stir in vanilla or other flavoring and chill thoroughly.
— Serve over cake or ice cream.

(2 cups)

ORANGE SAUCE

2 tablespoons butter or margarine
1 ½ tablespoons cornstarch
¼ cup sugar
¼ cup packed brown sugar
1 cup water
1 tablespoon grated orange peel
⅓ cup orange juice
1 to 2 tablespoons Grand Marnier or other orange flavored liqueur, if desired

— Combine all ingredients, except liqueur, in 4-cup glass measure; mix well.
— Microwave on high for 3 minutes. Stir and continue cooking on high for 1 to 1 ½ minues or until boiling.
— Stir in Grand Marnier.

(1 ½ cups)

LEMON SAUCE

1 tablespoon cornstarch
½ cup sugar
1 cup water, at room temperature
2 tablespoons butter or margarine
1 ½ teaspoons lemon juice
½ teaspoon grated lemon peel
Few grains salt

— In a deep, 1-quart casserole combine sugar and cornsarch.
— Gradually stir in water.
— Cook, uncovered, on high 3 to 4 minutes or until sauce has thickened and is smooth. Stir occasionally.
— Add butter, lemon juice, lemon peel and salt.
— Serve warm or cold.

(1 cup)

BECHAMEL SAUCE

2 tablespoons butter or margarine
1 tablespoon flour
½ cup light cream
½ cup chicken broth
2 teaspoons grated onion
½ teaspoon salt
Pepper
Pinch thyme

— Place butter in custard cup.
— Microwave 30 seconds on high until butter is melted.
— Blend in flour to make a smooth paste; set aside.
— Combine cream, chicken broth and onion in 1-quart measure or bowl.
— Microwave 2 minutes, 30 seconds on high.

(1 cup)

FANCY CHOCOLATE SAUCE

1 package (12-oz.) semisweet chocolate bits
2 squares (2-oz.) unsweetened chocolate
¼ cup honey
1 cup heavy cream
3 tablespoons brandy

— Combine chocolate bits and unsweetened chocolate in a small mixing bowl.
— Microwave, covered, for 2½ minutes, on high, or just until chocolate melts. (Watch carefully during last 1 minute so that chocolate does not burn.)
— Stir in honey and cream with a wire whisk to make a smooth paste.
— Microwave, covered, on high for 30 seconds to 1 minute, until hot.
— Stir in brandy.
— Serve hot over vanilla ice cream or cake squares.

(2 cups)

CURRANT-RAISIN SAUCE

½ cup orange juice
½ cup water
½ cup currant jelly
⅓ cup raisins
½ teaspoon grated orange rind
1 tablespoon corn starch
1 tablespoon water
2 tablespoons packed brown sugar
¼ teaspoon cinnamon
Dash of salt

— Combine orange juice, water, jelly, raisins and orange rind in 1-quart glass measure or casserole.
— Microwave, uncovered, 3 to 4 minutes on high, or until boiling. Set aside.
— Blend corn starch with water in a small bowl to make a smooth paste.
— Add brown sugar, cinnamon and salt. Mix well.
— Stir into hot orange juice mixture.
— Microwave 4 minutes, uncovered, on high, or until thick and clear, stirring after 2 minutes.
— Serve with ham or duck.

(2 cups)

HEATING PRECOOKED AND CANNED CASSEROLES

Main Dish	Serving Size	Setting	Cooking Time
Precooked Beef, Chicken, Pork, Lamb, and Veal casseroles. (from refrigerator)	1 serving	high	3 to 4 minutes
	1 quart serving	high	6 to 8 minutes
	1½ quart serving	high	10 to 12 minutes
	2 quart serving	high	12 to 15 minutes
	3 quart serving	high	14 to 17 minutes
Precooked Beef, Chicken, Pork, Lamb, and Veal casseroles. (frozen)	1 serving	high	5 to 6 minutes
	1 quart serving	high	12 to 16 minutes
	1½ quart serving	high	20 to 24 minuets
	2 quart serving	high	24 to 30 minutes
Canned Meat and Vegetables in sauce or Pork Beans (from room temperature)	15 to 16-oz.	high	4 to 6 minutes
	31 to 42-oz.	high	6 to 8 minutes

high — 100% power : medium — 60% power : low — 60% power.

CASSEROLES

CASSEROLE BASICS

Casseroles may require occasional stirring to distribute heat. They cook more evenly when made with ingredients of similar size and shape. Because of their shorter cooking time, casseroles cooked in the microwave oven generally need less liquid. Casseroles with cream and cheese sauces, or meats which need slower cooking to tenderize, do best on lower heat control settings.

A number of these casserole recipes call for leftover meats, because leftovers remain flavorful and fresh tasting when reheated in the microwave oven. Any casserole leftovers can be frozen in individual servings.

When cooking a favorite casserole, make two and freeze the second for future use. Line a casserole or basting dish with plastic wrap. Transfer the cooked food to the lined container and freeze. As such, as the food is frozen in the shape of the dish, remove it and wrap with freezer paper. Later it can be unwrapped and returned to the container for defrosting and heating.

HEARTY BEEF HASH

2 cups cooked rice
2 cups diced cooked beef
1 small onion, chopped
½ cup snipped parsley
1 can (10½-oz.) condensed cream of tomato soup, undiluted
2 teaspoons Worcestershire sauce
⅛ teaspoon pepper
4 to 5 thin slices cheddar cheese

— Combine rice, beef, onion, parsley, soup, Worcestershire sauce and pepper in 1½-quart casserole.
— Cover.
— Microwave 8 to 10 minutes on high, or until hot and bubbly.
— Let stand 3 minutes, covered.
— When serving, top each serving with thin slice of cheese.
— Serve with dinner rolls and Whipped Herb Butter.

(4-5 servings)

HAMBURGER HASH BURGUNDY

Excellent — to double use time duration 1½

1 lb. ground beef
½ cup chopped onions
2 tablespoons all-purpose flour
1 can (10½ oz.) condensed beef consomme, undiluted
½ cup dry red wine
2 cups diced raw potatoes
½ cup diced celery
Salt and pepper to taste

— Crumble ground beef into a 2-quart casserole
— Stir in onion.
— Microwave, uncovered, for 3 minutes on high.
— Stir with a fork to break up meat.
— Microwave for about 2 minutes on high or until meat loses its red color.
— Sprinkle flour on meat; Stir in well.
— Add consomme and wine.
— Microwave, covered, for about 3 minutes on high, or until liquid becomes warm.
— Add potatoes and celery, and salt and pepper to taste.
— Microwave, covered, for about 25 minutes, again on high or until potatoes are tender.
— Let stand 5 minutes before serving.

(4 servings)

INTERNATIONAL BEEF CASSEROLE

3 tablespoons flour
1 ½ lbs. beef round steak, cut in ¾-inch cubes
½ cup finely chopped onion
1 cup thinly sliced carrots
2 ½ cups water
1 teaspoon instant beef bouillon
½ teaspoon salt
1 teaspoon pepper

— Measure flour into paper bag.
— Add beef cubes and toss to coat evenly.
— Combine all ingredients in 3-quart casserole.
— Cover.
— Microwave 5 minutes on high.
— Reduce setting. Microwave 36 minutes on medium, or until meat and vegetables are tender.

(4-6 servings)

VARIATIONS:

CHINESE BEEF

Add:

½ lb. fresh or frozen green beans, defrosted, cut in ½-inch lengths
1 green or sweet red pepper, cut in juilenne strips
2 ½ tablespoons soy sauce

— Serve with boiled rice.

AUSTRALIAN BEEF

Add:

¼ cup firmly packed brown sugar
1 ½ tablespoons Worcestershire sauce
1 ½ tablespoons catsup
1 ½ tablespoons vinegar
½ teaspoon nutmeg

— Serve with a green vegetable and mashed or baked potatoes.

BELGIAN BEEF

Substitute 2 ½ cups beer for water
Add 1 clove garlic, finely chopped

— Serve with boiled potatoes.

ENGLISH BEEF

Add:

1 small turnip, peeled and finely chopped
2 stems celery, finely chopped
1 cup fresh shelled peas
2 tomatoes, peeled and coarsely chopped
Garnish with snipped parsley

— Serve with boiled or baked potatoes.

HUNGARIAN BEEF

Add:

4 medium carrots, thinly sliced
4 medium boiling potatoes, sliced
1 tablespoon papdika
1 clove garlic, pressed or finely chopped
Stir in 3 tablespoons dairy sour cream just before serving

— Serve with macaroni, noodles or rice.
— Top each serving with additional sour cream, if desired.

INDIAN BEEF

1 to 1 ½ tablespoons curry power (add with flour
2 tomatoes, peeled and chopped
1 apple, peeled, cored and chopped
Stir in 1 tablespoon lemon juice and 2 tablespoons chutney just before serving

— Serve with rice, sliced bananas in lemon juice and fruit chutney.

ONE DISH MACARONI BEEF

½ lb. ground beef
1 small onion, finely chopped
1 cup uncooked macaroni
1 can (8 oz.) tomato sauce
1 ½ cups water
⅓ cup catsup
1 can (7 oz.) whole kernel corn, undrained
1 tablespoon packed brown sugar
½ teaspoon salt
¼ teaspoon pepper
¼ teaspoon chili powder

— Crumble ground beef in 2-quart glass casserole.
— Stir in onion.
— Cover with glass lid or plastic wrap.
— Microwave on high for 3 minutes.
— Drain and stir in remaining ingredients; recover.
— Microwave on low setting for 30 to 35 minutes or until macaroni is tender.
— Let stand, covered, 5 minutes before serving

(4 to 6 servings)

LIMAS AND BEEF CASSEROLE

1 lb. lean ground beef
1 clove garlic, crushed
1 medium onion, chopped
1 small green pepper, seeded and chopped
¼ teaspoon chili powder
½ teaspoon dry mustard
2 teaspoons Worcestershire sauce
½ teaspoon salt
2 cans (1 lb. each) lima beans
1 can (8-oz.) tomato sauce

— Combine beef, garlic, onion, and green pepper in a 2- or 3-quart casserole.
— Microwave, uncovered, for about 5 minutes, on high, or until beef loses its pink color.
—Stir once or twice during cooking period to break up meat.
— Add remaining ingredients.
— Toss lightly.
— Microwave, covered, for about 8 minutes, on high, stirring once during cooking period.
— Let stand, covered, 3 to 4 minutes before serving.

(4-6 servings)

NUTTY BEEF CASSEROLE

1 ½ lbs. ground beef
1 large onion, chopped
1 teaspoon salt
¼ teaspoon pepper
½ teaspoon leaf basil
½ cup chopped green pepper
½ cup pimento stuffed olives
1 can (4 oz.) mushroom stems and pieces, drained
½ can (11 oz.) condensed Cheddar cheese soup
½ cup salted Spanish peanuts, if desired

— Crumble ground beef in 2-quart glass casserole.
— Stir in onion.
— Cover with glass lid or plastic wrap.
— Microwave on high for 6 minutes.
— Drain and stir in remaining ingredients except salted nuts; recover.
— Microwave on low for 6 to 8 minutes or until hot.
— Let stand, covered, 5 minutes.
— Sprinkle nuts on top and serve.

(4-6 servings)

FIESTA TAMALE PIE

1 tablespoon vegetable oil
1 clove garlic, peeled and crushed
1 small onion, minced
1 lb. lean ground beef
¼ lb. bulk pork sausage
1 (16-oz.) can stewed tomatoes, undrained
1 (16-oz.) can whole kernel corn, drained
1 ½ teaspoons salt
1 ½ teaspoons chili powder
18 pitted ripe olives
2 eggs, well beaten
1 cup corn meal
1 cup milk
1 cup grated Cheddar cheese

— Combine vegetable oil, onion and garlic in a large mixing bowl; heat, uncovered, on high 2 minutes or until onion is tender.
— Add ground beef and sausage to onion and garlic.
— Heat, uncovered, on medium for 7 minutes or until meat is browned.
— Stir occasionally.
— Dain excess fat.
— Add tomatoes, corn, salt and chili powder to meat mixture.
— Heat, uncovered, on medium for 6 minutes or until mixture comes to a boil.
— While meat mixture is cooking, combine eggs, corn meal and milk in a medium-sized bowl.
— Blend thoroughly; set aside.
— Pour meat mixture into an 8-inch square baking dish.
— Press olives into meat mixture.
— Spoon corn meal mixture over meat mixture.
— Sprinkle grated cheese on top.
— Heat, uncovered, on medium for 12 minutes or until cheese melts.

(6 servings)

BEEF CHIP CASSEROLE

real Good

1 lb. lean ground beef
1 large onion, chopped
2 cups corn chips
1 can (15-oz.) chili with beans
1 can (8-oz.) tomato sauce
¼ cup grated cheddar cheese

— Crumble meat into 1-quart mixing bowl.
— Add onion.
— Microwave 4 minutes on high, or until meat is set.
— In 2-quart casserole, layer half the corn chips, half the meat, half the chili and half the tomato sauce.
— Repeat layers and cover.
— Microwave 6 minutes on high
— Sprinkle grated cheese on top.
— Microwave 30 seconds on high, or until cheese melts.

(3-4 servings)

ZUCCHINI-GROUND BEEF ITALIAN STYLE

excellent
kid hate it

1 lb. lean ground beef
1 medium sized onion, chopped
1 can (1 lb., 13 oz.) solid packed tomatoes
1 can (8 oz.) tomato sauce
1 can (6 oz.) tomato paste
1 small green pepper, seeded and chopped
¼ lb. shredded cheddar cheese
6 medium size zucchini, sliced ½ inch thick
½ cup pitted ripe olives
½ teaspoon salt
¼ teaspoon pepper
¼ teaspoon garlic salt
⅛ teaspoon oregano
Grated Parmesan cheese

— Crumble ground beef in a 2 quart casserole.
— Microwave 3 minutes on high.
— Add onion and cook 2 minutes more on high.
— Add rest of ingredients except Parmesan cheese.
— Microwave, covered 4 minutes on high.
— Place all the ingredients in a 8x12 glass baking dish.
— Sprinkle top generously with parmesan cheese.
— Microwave on high 15 minutes or until sauce is thickened.

(6-8 servings)

SUNDAY-NIGHT SPECIAL

1 can (7-oz.) green chilies
1 cup coarsely crushed corn chips
Meat (optional)
2 mild Italian sausages, cooked and broken up, or
½ lb. ground chuck, cooked, or
1 cup ground cooked pork or ham
½ cup cottage cheese or ricotta
4 oz. Monterey Jack cheese, cut in strips
2 eggs
1 cup milk
½ teaspoon salt
½ cup grated Cheddar or Parmesan cheese

— Wash and dry chilies.
— Remove any remaining seeds.
— Cut into strips 1 inch wide.
— Put half the corn chips in bottom of an 8-inch round cake pan.
— Arrange about one-third of the chilies on top of corn chips.
— Place meat, if desired, on top of chilies.
— Dot cottage cheese on top of meat.
— Add another third of the chilies.
— Arrange Monterey Jack cheese over top of chilies.
— Arrange remaining chilies on top of cheese.
— Beat together eggs, milk, and salt.
— Pour over top of mixture in casserole.
— Sprinkle top with Cheddar or Parmesan cheese.
— Sprinkle remaining corn chips on top of cheese.
—Microwave, uncovered, for 9 to 10 minutes, on high, or until custard is set.
— Remove from oven and let stand, covered, for 3 to 4 minutes.

(4-6 servings)

BUSY DAY CASSEROLE

O.K. boys

1 can (10½-ounces) cream of onion soup, undiluted
1 can (10¾-ounces) chicken gumbo soup, undiluted
2½ to 3 cups large chunks cooked turkey or chicken
½ cup seasoned croutons

— Combine soups in 2-quart casserole.
— Stir until well blended.
— Stir in turkey.
— Sprinkle with croutons.
— Microwave 8 to 10 minutes on high, or until hot.

(6 servings)

CHILI CHICKEN

4 tablespoons butter or margarine
1 3 lbs. frying chicken, cut up
1 onion, thinly sliced
½ cup chopped celery
3 tablespoons chopped parsley
1 can (10¾ oz.) concentrated tomato soup
1½ tablespoons flour
1½ teaspoons chili powder
Dash of paprika, rosemary and pepper
½ teaspoon salt
¼ cup red wine
2 tablespoons sour cream

— Heat butter 30 seconds and saute chicken in the casserole.
— Add onion, celery, parsley and tomato soup
— Add flour and mix well.
— Sprinkle with chili powder, paprika, rosemary, salt and pepper.
— Add red wine and stir well.
— Microwave, covered, 20 minutes on high, stirring every 5 minutes.
— Spread sour cream on top.

(6 servings)

ITALIAN BEEF STEW

2 lbs. beef stew meat
1 teaspoon Italian seasoning
½ teaspoon oregano
2 teaspoons salt
¼ teaspoon garlic salt
¼ teaspoon pepper
3 large carrots, cut into chunks
2 medium onions, sliced ½ inch thick
2 tablespoons cornstarch
2 tablespoons water
2 cans (4 oz. each) whole mushrooms, drained
1 can (28 oz.) Italian pear-shaped tomatoes
1 carton (8 oz.) sour cream

— Place meat in 3-quart glass casserole.
— Cover.
— Microwave on high for 10 minutes.
— Drain and stir in seasonings.
— Layer carrots and onions on top.
— Microwave on low for 20 minutes.
— Blend cornstarch with water.
— Stir into meat mixture with mushrooms and tomatoes; mix well.
— Recover and continue cooking on low for 35 to 40 minutes or until meat is fork tender.
— Fold in sour cream.
— Let stand, covered, 5 minutes before serving.

(4-6 servings)

VEAL AND ARTICHOKE STEW

2 tablespoons all-purpose flour
½ teaspoon salt
¼ teaspoon pepper
1½ lbs. boneless veal, cubed
2 tablespoons butter or margarine
½ teaspoon basil
1 teaspoon paprika
1 clove garlic, chopped
1 tablespoon parsley flakes
¼ lb. fresh mushrooms, sliced
1 jar (2 oz.) chopped pimento, drained
1 package (9 oz.) frozen artichokes
2 tablespoons cornstarch
1 can (10¾ oz.) chicken broth

— Combine flour, salt and pepper in flat dish.
— Coat veal cubes in seasoned flour.
— Place butter in 2-quart glass casserole with coated meat. Cover.
— Microwave on medium for 10 minutes.
— Stir in remaining ingredients, except cornstarch and broth.
— Blend cornstarch and broth in small mixing bowl.
— Mix into meat and vegetables;
— Microwave on low for 26 to 28 minutes or until meat is fork tender.
— Let stand, covered, 5 minutes.
— Stir well before serving.

(4-6 servings)

CHICKEN-BROCCOLI CASSEROLE

½ cup mayonnaise
1 tablespoon lemon juice
½ teaspoon curry powder
2 cans cream of chicken soup
2 packages (10 oz. each) chipped broccoli
4 cups cooked chopped chicken
¾ cup bread crumbs
¾ cup grated cheese

— Combine mayonnaise, lemon juice, curry powder and chicken soup.
— Set aside.
— Cook broccoli 8 to 10 minutes, in a 3 quart casserole, covered, or until done stirring once.
— Spread chicken over top of broccoli and then top with soup mixture spreading evenly over the chicken.
— Sprinkle bread crumbs and cheese over the top.
— Cook, covered, 8 to 10 minutes on high or until hot.

(4-6 servings)

MACARONI GOULASH

1 cup uncooked macaroni
1 pound ground beef
1 can (1 lb.) tomato puree, or 1 can (1 lb.) tomatoes packed in puree
½ teaspoon sugar
½ teaspoon basil
1 teaspoon salt
Pepper to taste
1 tablespoon chopped parsley

— Cook macaroni on conventional range according to package directions. Set aside.
— Crumble beef into a 2- or 3-quart casserole.
— Microwave, uncovered, for about 5 minutes, on high, stirring once to break up meat.
— Add puree, sugar, basil, salt, pepper to taste, and parsley.
— Stir in macaroni.
— Microwave, covered, for about 8 minutes, on high, stirring once during cooking time.
— Let stand, covered, about 3 to 4 minutes before serving.

(6-8 servings)

GROUND BEEF DINNER

1 tablespoon salad oil
1 lb. ground beef
1 package (7-oz.) "add meat" dinner mix for hamburger

— To preheat browning dish, microwave 4 minutes on high.
— Add oil.
— Crumble beef into browner.
— Microwave 3 to 5 minutes on high, or until meat loses its pink color.
— Remove meat from browner to 3-quart casserole.
— Add mix and hot tap water as directed on package.
— Cover.
— Microwave 20 to 22 minutes on high.
— Stir well, let stand 5 minutes, covered.

(4 servings)

SATURDAY SPECIAL

1 lb. lean ground beef
½ cup chopped onion
1 cup dairy sour cream
1 can (10¾-oz.) condensed cream of mushroom soup, undiluted
1 can (16-oz.) whole kernel corn, drained
1 jar (2-oz.) chopped pimento
1 teaspoon salt
⅛ teaspoon pepper
1 large tomato, thinly sliced

— Crumble ground beef into 2-quart casserole.
— Add onion.
— Microwave 5 minutes on high until beef is set and onion is transparent.
— Add sour cream, soup, corn, pimiento, salt and pepper.
— Cover with waxed paper.
— Mcrowave 3 minutes on high, or until
— Top with tomato slices.
— Microwave 3 minutes on high, or until tomatoes are slightly softened.
— Garnish with canned French fried onion rings, if desired.
— Let stand 3 minutes, uncovered.

(6 servings)

SUPER BEEF CASSEROLE

¼ cup flour
1 pound beef top round steak, cut in ¾-inch cubes
1 can (10½-oz.) condensed beef bouillon, diluted with water to make 2 cups
1 can (6-oz.) tomato paste
1 small onion, thinly sliced
1 teaspoon salt
⅛ teaspoon pepper
Add meat to flour, coat evenly

— Combine meat, bouillon, tomato paste, onion, salt and pepper in 2-quart casserole.
— Stir until tomato paste is mixed with broth.
— Cover.
— Microwave 5 minutes on high.
— Reduce setting. Microwave 25 minutes on medium, or until meat is fork tender, stirring after 15 minutes.

(3-4 servings)

VEAL WITH NOODLES

2 cups cubed cooked veal
1 can (10¾ oz.) condensed cream of mushroom soup
¼ cup milk
1 cup cooked noodles
1 teaspoon salt
2 teaspoons parsley flakes
½ teaspoon garlic salt
½ teaspoon paprika
¼ teaspoon marjoram
¼ teaspoon pepper

— Combine all ingredients in 1½-quart glass casserole; mix well.
— Cover.
— Microwave on low for 10 to 12 minutes or until heated through.
— Let stand, covered, 5 minutes before serving

(4 servings)

KIDNEY CASSEROLE

1 ½ lbs. beef kidney, trimmed and cut into small pieces
2 tablespoons butter or margarine
2 carrots, thinkly sliced
2 teaspoons salt
1 can (10¾ oz.) peas, undrained
1 jar (16 oz.) whole onions, undrained
1 can (4 oz.) mushroom stems and pieces, drained

— Wash kidneys well before placing in 2-quart glass casserole.
— Add butter, carrots, seasonings and juice from peas and onions.
— Cover.
— Microwave on low for 20 minutes.
— Stir in peas, onions and mushrooms.
— Recover and continue cooking on low for 10 to 12 minutes.
— Let stand, covered, 5 minutes before serving.

(6-8 servings)

FIJI BEEF CHUNKS

2 lbs. beef round steak, cut in ¾-inch cubes
1 clove garlic, finely chopped
¼ cup wine vinegar
1 can (10½-oz.) beef broth
½ cup sliced celery
1 green pepper, chopped
1 large onion, sliced
2 large tomatoes, diced
1 can (13½-oz.) pineapple chunks, with juice
4 tablespoons firmly packed brown sugar
3 tablespoons cornstarch
2 tablespoon soy sauce
1 teaspoon paprika
¼ cup water

— Sprinkle beef cubes with chopped garlic and 2 tablespoons of the vinegar.
— Pour beef broth over meat.
— Cover.
— Microwave 8 minutes on high, stirring after 5 minutes.
— Add celery, green pepper and onion.
— Cover.
— Microwave 20 minutes on medium.
— Stir in tomatoes and pineapple chunks.
— Blend brown sugar, corn starch, soy sauce, paprika, water and remaining vinegar.
— Stir into sauce.
— Microwave 4 to 6 minutes on medium, or until sauce has thickened and meat is fork tender.

(4-6 servings)

TURKEY AND WILD RICE CASSEROLE

4 cups cubed cooked turkey
1 cup finely chopped celery
1 ½ cup finely chopped onion
1 ½ cups cooked wild rice
1 can (10¾ oz.) condensed cream of chicken soup
6 oz. water chestnuts, sliced
1 can (4 oz.) mushroom stems and pieces, undrained
3 tablespoons soy sauce
¼ teaspoon pepper
2 tablespoons butter or margarine
½ cup dry bread crumbs

— Combine all ingredients, except butter and bread crumbs, in 2-quart glass casserole; mix well; set aside.
— Place butter in small glass mixing bowl.
— Microwave on medium for about 1 minute or until melted.
— Stir in bread crumbs.
— Sprinkle buttered crumbs over turkey mixture
— Cover with glass lid or plastic wrap.
— Microwave on low for 24 to 26 minutes or until hot.
— Let stand, covered, 5 minutes before serving

(4-6 servings)

SEATTLE SALMON LOAF

4 cups cooked or canned salmon
2 tablespoons lemon juice
1 cup milk
3 cups soft bread crumbs
2 eggs, beaten
¼ cup minced onion
1 teaspoon salt
¼ teaspoon pepper
1 tablespoon dried parsley flakes

— In a large bowl sprinkle lemon juice over salmon.
— In medium-sized bowl combine milk, bread crumbs, eggs, onion, salt, pepper and parsley flakes.
— Pour over salmon and blend well.
— Pour into a greased loaf pan.
— Microwave, uncovered, on high 12 minutes.
— Cool 5 minutes; place on serving platter

(4-5 servings)

MARCIA'S MARZETTI

5 cups hot water
1 tablespoon salt
3 cups uncooked egg noodles
¼ cup butter
1 cup fine dry bread crumbs
1 lb. lean ground beef
½ cup finely chopped onion
¼ cup finely chopped green pepper
½ teaspoon garlic salt
1 teaspoon salt
⅛ teaspoon pepper
1 cup grated Swiss cheese
1 (8-oz.) can tomato sauce
1 ((4-oz.) can mushroom stems and pieces, drained

— In a deep, 3-quart casserole place 5 cups water, 1 tablespoon salt and 3 cups uncooked noodles.
— Cook, covered, on high 12 minutes or until noodles are tender.
— Stir occasionally.
— Drain noodles and set aside.
— In a large mixing bowl, melt ¼ cup butter on high 30 seconds.
— Add bread crumbs and heat, uncovered, on high 1½ minutes or until bread crumbs are golden brown.
— Add meat to bread crumb mixture and mix to combine well.
— Heat on medium, uncovered, 6 minutes or until meat is borwned, stirring occasionally so meat crumbles.
— Add onions, green pepper, garlic salt, salt and pepper.
— Blend into meat mixture thoroughly.
— Cook, uncovered, on medium for 4 minutes.
— In a 2-quart casserole layer cooked noodles with meat mixture.
— Top with cheese, tomato sauce and mushrooms (in that order).
— Heat, uncovered, on medium for 10 minutes or until cheese melts.

(4-6 servings)

ENCHILADA CASSEROLE

1 lb. lean ground beef round
1 tablespoon instant minced onion
1 clove garlic, peeled and crushed
1 teaspoon pepper
2½ teaspoons chili powder
⅔ cup water
1 (8-oz.) can tomato sauce
2 cups shredded sharp Cheddar cheese
¼ teaspoon salt
6 tortillas or taco shells

— Crumble beef into a shallow, 2½-quart casserole. Sprinkle meat with minced onion and crushed garlic.
— Heat, uncovered, on medium for 6 minutes.
— Stir occasionally to break up meat.
— Drain excess fat.
— Add pepper, chili powder, water and tomato sauce. Stir to combine.
— Heat, uncovered, 5 minutes on medium.
— Alternately layer tortillas, meat sauce and cheese in a round, 1½-quart casserole (Last layer should be cheese).
— Heat, covered, on Medium for 9 to 11 minutes or until cheese is melted.

(4-6 servings)

CHILI PIE

1½ lbs. lean ground beef
1 medium-sized onion, thinly sliced
1 (12-oz.) can, whole kernel corn, drained
1 (16-oz.) can whole peeled tomatoes
1 (8-oz.) can tomato sauce with cheese
1 to 2 teaspoons dried chili powder
1 teaspoon salt
¼ teaspoon pepper
⅓ cup sliced stuffed olives
½ cup shredded Cheddar cheese
1½ cups coarsely crumbled tortilla chips or corn chips

— Crumble meat into a deep, 2 quart casserole.
— Add onion and heat, uncovered, for 8 to 9 minutes on high or until meat is browned and onions are tender.
— Stir occasionally.
— Drain off excess fat.
— Add corn, tomatoes, tomato soauce, chili powder to taste and salt and pepper. Stir to combine.
— Heat, uncovered, for 5 minutes on high, stirring once.
— Arrange olive slices on top of meat mixture and sprinkle with cheese.
— Heat, uncovered for 5 minutes on high.
— Sprinkle with tortilla chips and heat, uncovered, for 1 minute on high.

(4-6 servings)

SAUCY TURKEY AND RICE

Rice:
½ cup uncooked rice
¼ cup chopped onion
¼ cup chopped celery
¼ cup chopped green pepper
1 ½ cups chicken broth
¼ teaspoon seasoned salt
Turkey Sauce:
2 tablespoons butter or margarine
¼ cup flour
2 cups milk
½ teaspoon salt
Dash paprika
1 teaspoon instant chicken bouilllon
2 cups cubed cooked turkey

— Combine rice, onion, celery and green pepper in 2-quart casserole.
— Add chicken broth and salt and cover.
— Microwave 13 minutes on high.
— Let stand, covered, while preparing sauce.
— Place butter in 1 ½-quart casserole.
— Microwave on high, until melted.
— Stir in flour to make a smooth paste.
— Gradually add milk, stirring util blended.
— Microwave 8 minutes on medium, or until thickend, stirring after 5 minutes.
— Beat in salt, paprika and bouillon with a wire whip until bouillon is dissolved and sauce is smooth.
— Stir in turkey and cover.
— Microwave 6 minutes on medium, or until hot.

(4 servings)

CHOW MEIN TUNA CASSEROLE

2 tablespoons butter or margarine
1 cup chopped celery
¼ cup chopped onion
2 tablespoons chopped green pepper
1 tablespoon butter
1 (7-oz.) can tuna
1 (10 ½-oz.) can condensed cream of mushroom soup
1 cup chow mein noodles
⅛ teaspoon pepper
⅓ cup chow mein noodles

— In a deep, 1 ½-quart, heat-resistant, non-metallic casserole, melt 2 tablespoons butter or margarine on high 30 seconds.
— Add celery, onion and green pepper to melted butter.
— Cook, uncovered, on high 3 minutes or until vegetables are tender.
— Combine remaining ingredients except ⅓ cup chow mein noodles with vegetables.
— Blend well.
— Top with ⅓ cup of chow mein noodles.
— Heat on medium for 12 minutes or until sauce bubbles.

(4 servings)

TUNA-SPINACH CASSEROLE

1 package (10 ounces) raw spinach
1 can (7 ounces) solid pack tuna
1 can (4 ounces) sliced mushrooms
2 tablespoons lemon juice
3 tablespoons butter or margarine, divided
1 tablespoon minced onion
2 tablespoons all-purpose flour
½ teaspoon salt
⅛ teaspoon pepper
1 egg, lightly beaten

— Rinse spinach in fresh, cold water.
— Drain well and break in pieces, removing tough center stems.
— Put in a 2-quart casserole.
— Microwave, covered, for 3 to 4 minutes, until spinach is limp.
— Drain well and set aside.
— Drain tuna and set aside.
— Drain mushrooms, reserving liquid.
— Put mushroom liquid in a 1-cup measure.
— Add lemon juice and enough water to make 1 cup of liquid.
— Put 2 tablespoons of the butter in a 1-quart casserole.
— Microwave for 30 seconds on high or just long enough to melt butter.
— Add onion, flour, salt, and pepper. Microwave uncovered, for 30 seconds on high.
— Stir in mushroom liquid.
— Microwave, uncovered on high, for about 3 minutes, or until thick, stirring occasionally during cooking time.
— Add a small amount of sauce to egg, beat well, and return to hot sauce.
— Stir mushrooms into sauce.
— Put drained spinach in a 2- to 3-quart casserole.
— Break tuna in big chunks and place over top of spinach.
— Pour sauce over top.
— Dot with remaining 1 tablespoon of butter.
— Microwave, uncovered, for about 6 minutes on high.
— Let stand covered with waxed paper 3 to 4 minutes before serving.

(Serves 4)

DUCK STEW

4 lbs. duckling, cut up
2 tablespoons salad oil
1 tablespoon olive oil
¼ cup all-purpose flour
2 teaspoons paprika
½ cup white wine
1 ½ cup chicken bouillon
1 clove garlic, crushed
1 sliced onion
1 sliced green pepper
6 small tomatoes
⅓ cup chopped stuffed olives
2 tablespoons chopped parsley

— Pour salad oil in a casserole and Microwave 30 seconds on high.
— Fry a half of the duckling in the preheated casserole until brown, this process should take approximately 6 minutes on high, and Microwave again for 1 minute on high. Microwave the rest of the duckling in the same way.
— (The amount may be too large to cook all at once in the oven).
— Reserve cooking liquid produced in the casserole.
— Place duckling on a paper towel to drain oil.
— Pour reserved cooking liquid and olive oil into a casserole and Microwave 45 seconds on high.
— Add flour and paprika, stir well until smooth. Add white wine a little at a time, stirring constantly.
— Pour chicken bouillon in while stirring.

(4 servings)

CHRISTY'S CRAB SALAD

¾ cup mayonnaise or salad dressing
2 tablespoons lemon juice
1 can (6 ½ oz.) crab meat, drained
1 can ((6 ½ oz.) water-packed white tuna, drained
1 can (6 oz.) water chestnuts, drained and sliced
4 green onions, finely chopped
½ teaspoon salt
2 teaspoons dill weed

— Combine all ingredients in 1 ½-quart glass casserole; mix well.
— Cover with glass lid or plastic wrap.
— Microwave on medium for 7 to 9 minutes or until hot; stir to blend.
— Let stand, covered, 3 minutes before serving.

(4 servings)

TURKEY NOODLE BAKE

1 can (10¾ oz.) condensed cream of chicken soup
¼ cup water
2 cups cubed cooked turkey
1 cup chopped celery
½ cup coarsely chopped nuts
¼ cup chopped onion
1 tablespoon chopped pimento
1 can (3 oz.) chow mein noodles

— Combine all ingredients, including 1 cup chow mein noodles, in 2-quart glass casserole.
— Mix well.
— Cover with glass lid or plastic wrap.
— Microwave on low for 8 to 10 minutes or until hot.
— Let stand, covered, 5 minutes.
— Sprinkle top with remaining noodles and serve.

(4 servings)

TUNA NOODLE CASSEROLE

1 cup water
1 ½ cups uncooked noodles
1 can (10¾ oz.) condensed cream of mushroom soup
1 can (4 oz.) mushroom stems and pieces, drained
1 can (17 oz.) green beans, drained
½ cup coarsely crushed potato chips

— Pour water into 2-quart casserole.
— Cover with glass lid or plastic wrap.
— Microwave on high for 3 to 5 minutes or until water comes to a boil.
— Stir in noodles.
— Recover and cook on lowest setting for 11 to 12 minutes or until noodles are tender.
— Drain and stir in remaining ingredients except potato chips; recover.
— Microwave on low for 8 to 10 minutes or until hot.
— Let stand, covered, 5 minutes.
— Sprinkle potato chips on top and serve.

(6-8 servings)

SALMON SPAGHETTI

4 oz. spaghetti
1 can (10½ oz.) cream of mushroom soup
½ cup milk
1 can (7 oz.) salmon
1 can (3 oz.) mushrooms (boiled)
½ cup chopped onion
1 cup grated Cheddar cheese
Chopped parsley

— Break spaghetti into 2½ inch lengths and boil on high for 5 minutes and drain.
— Put spaghetti in a casserole and mix with mushroom soup and milk.
— Add salmon, mushrooms, onion and ½ cup Cheddar cheese and mix.
— Microwave covered, 8 minutes on high, stirring every 3 minutes.
— Uncover, sprinkle with ½ cup Cheddar cheese and Microwave again, uncovered, 8 minutes, 10 seconds on high.
— Sprinkle with parsley.

ARKANSAS CRAB GUMBO

½ cup onion, chopped
½ cup celery, chopped
2 tablespoons green pepper, finely chopped
1 clove garlic, pressed or minced
2 tablespoons butter or margarine
1 package (10-oz.) frozen okra, partially defrosted and sliced
1 can (14½-oz.) stewed tomatoes
¼ teaspoon sugar
1 bay leaf
¼ teaspoon thyme
1 teaspoon salt
1 can (6½-oz.) crab meat, drained and broken up with fork
1½ cups cooked rice

— Combine onion, celery, green pepper, garlic and butter in 2-quart casserole.
— Microwave 3 to 4 minutes on high, or until onion is transparent.
— Add okra, tomatoes and seasoning; Cover tightly. Microwave 12 minutes on high, or until okra is tender and mixture is bubbly.
— Remove bay leaf.
— Add crab meat.
— Cover and let stand 5 minutes.
— Serve over rice.

(4 servings)

SALMON CASSEROLE

4 cups cooked noodles
1 (16-oz.) can salmon, drained and flaked
1 (4-oz.) can mushrooms slices, drained
1 (10¼-oz.) can condensed cream of celery soup
½ cup thinly sliced celery
1 (5¼-oz.) can sliced water chestnuts, drained
1 (17-oz.) can green peas, drained
1 cup coarsely broken potato chips

— In a deep, 2½-quart casserole, combine noodles, salmon, mushroom slices, celery soup, celery, water chestnuts and green peas until well blended.
— Cook, covered, on medium for 8 to 10 minutes or until heated through. Stir occasionally.
— Just before serving, sprinkle with potato chips.

(4-6 Servings)

A number of substitutions may be made in this casserole:

— Tuna may be substituted for salmon.
— Cream of mushroom or cream of asparagus soup may be substituted for cream of celery soup.
— Green beans or corn may be used in place of peas.
— Pimientos or green pepper may be added for color and flavor.
— Chinese noodles, fried onion rings, broken crackers or nuts may be used in place of potato chips.

TURKEY ORIENTAL

2 tablespoons cooking oil
1 cup finely chopped onion
1 cup finely chopped celery
2 cups cubed cooked turkey
1 can (6 oz.) water chestnuts, drained and sliced

— Combine oil, onion and celery in 2-quart glass casserole.
— Microwave on high for 4 to 5 minutes or until onions are partly cooked.
— Stir in remaining ingredients, except rice; mix well.
— Cover.
— Microwave on low for 10 to 12 minutes or until heated through and thickened.
— Let stand, covered 5 minutes.
— Serve with hot cooked rice.

(4-6 servings)

TEXAS CRAB CASSEROLE

1 cup grated sharp Cheddar cheese
2 cups medium white sauce
2 beaten egg yolks
2 cups crab meat
¼ cup toasted crumbs
2 tablespoons grated Parmesan cheese
2 tablespoons butter or margarine
½ teaspoon paprika
or ½ teaspoon prepared mustard (optional)

— In ½ quart casserole, stir cheese into warmed white sauce.
— Microwave 30 seconds to 1 minute on high, or until cheese is completely melted, stirring every 10 seconds. (Reserve 1 cup).
— Blend egg yolks into cheese sauce until smooth.
— Add crab meat.
— Sprinkle with crumbs and cheese and dot with butter.
— Top with reserved cheese sauce.
— Microwave 8 to 9 mnutes on high.

(4 Texas sized servings)

OYSTERS AND MACARONI AU GRATIN

3 tablespoons butter or margarine
3 tablespoons flour
1 ½ cups milk
1 cup macaroni, cooked and drained
2 cans (8-oz.) oysters, drained
Salt and pepper
1 cup grated Cheddar cheese

— Place butter in 1-quart measure.
— Microwave on high until butter melts.
— Blend in flour to make a smooth paste.
— Gradually stir in milk.
— Microwave 2 minutes, 30 seconds to 3 minutes, 30 seconds on high, or until thickened, stirring once with wire whip.
— Layer half the macaroni and half the oysters in 1 ½-quart casserole.
— Season with salt and pepper.
— Sprinkle with one-third of the cheese.
— Repeat layers.
— Pour sauce over mixture and top with remaining cheese. Microwave 8 minutes on high or until heated through.
— Garnish with parsley if desired.

(6 servings)

FISH AND WINE CASSEROLE

2 tablespoons butter
1 onion, thinly sliced
½ cup dry white wine
2 lbs. halibut fillets, cut into 2-inch pieces
Milk
3 tablespoons butter
3 tablespoons flour
1 ½ teaspoons salt
⅛ teaspoon pepper
1 (8 ½-oz.) can small peas, drained
1 ½ cups Chinese fried noodles

— In a shallow, 1 ½-quart casserole melt the 2 tablespoons of butter on high 30 seconds.
— Add onion and heat, uncovered, on high 3 minutes or until onion is tender but not browned.
— Add wine and fish and cook, covered, on high 6 minutes or until fish flakes easily with fork.
— Drain pan juices into a measuring cup and add enough milk to pan juices to equal 2 cups. Set fish and liquid aside.
— In a small bowl, melt the 3 tablespoons of butter on high for 30 seconds.
— Stir in flour, salt and pepper.
— Gradually stir in reserved fish liquid mixture.
— Cook, uncovered, on medium for 8 minutes, stirring twice until thickened and smooth.
— Add peas to sauce.
— Add sauce to fish in the casserole and stir gently.
— Cook, uncovered, on medium for 3 minutes.
— Sprinkle noodles over fish and heat, uncovered, on medium for 2 minutes.

(4-6 servings)

MACARONI BAKE

2 tablespoons butter or margarine
4 cups cooked shell macaroni
½ cup sour cream
4 oz. sliced ham, cut into pieces
½ teaspoon dried parsley flakes
Salt
Pepper

— Combine all ingredients in 2-quart glass casserole.
— Cover with glass lid or plastic wrap.
— Microwave on medium for 4 minutes.
— Stir; recover, and continue cooking on medium for 4 to 6 minutes or until hot.

(4-6 servings)

SEAFOOD CREOLE

3 tablespoons butter or margarine
1 cup finely chopped onion
½ cup finely chopped green pepper
½ cup finely chopped celery
1 clove garlic, finely chopped
1 ½ tablespoons all-purpose flour
1 can ((28 oz.) whole tomatoes, undrained
1 can (6 ½ oz.) chunk tuna, drained
1 can (6 ½ oz.) crabmeat, drained
1 can (4 ½ oz.) shrimp, drained
1 teaspoon salt
2 bay leaves
½ teaspoon leaf thyme
¼ teaspoon allspice
1 tablespoon Worcestershire sauce
¼ teaspoon Tabasco
2 tablespoons dried parsley flakes

— Combine butter, onion, green pepper, celery and garlic in 2-quart glass casserole.
— cover with glass lid or plastic wrap.
— Microwave on medium for about 5 minutes or until vegetables are partly cooked.
— Blend in flour.
— Stir in remaining ingredients; recover.
— Microwave on low for 10 to 12 minutes or until hot.
— Let stand, covered, 5 minutes before serving.

(6-8 servings)

LOBSTER CASSEROLE

2 tablespoons butter
1 cup soft bread crumbs
1 tablespoon butter
½ clove garlic, peeled and crushed
2 tablespoons finely chopped onion
⅔ cup canned condensed Cheddar cheese soup
1 (4-oz.) can sliced mushrooms, drained
¼ cup milk
2 tablespoons dry sherry
1 tablespoon chopped parsley
½ cup cooked peas, drained
1 ½ cups canned, fresh or frozen cooked lobster, cubed

— In a small bowl melt the 2 tablespoon butter on high for 30 seconds.
— Place soft bread crumbs in melted butter and coat with butter. Set aside.
— In deep, 2 ½-quart casserole place the 1 tablespoon butter.
— Heat 15 seconds on high.
— Add onion and garlic to melted butter and cook, uncovered, on high 2 minutes or until onion is tender.
— Stir soup and mushrooms into onions and garlic.
— Gradually blend in milk, sherry and parsley.
— Add peas to soup mixture.
— Add lobster and bread crumb mixture to soup mixture. Stir to combine all ingredients.
— Cook, uncovered, on medium for 7 minutes or until sauce bubbles.

(4 servings)

HAM CASSEROLE

2 cups diced cooked ham
2 tablespoons chopped onion
⅛ teaspoon tarragon
3 tablespoons butter or margarine
1 can (10 ½-oz.) condensed cream of chicken soup, undiluted
1 ½ cups cooked narrow egg noodles
½ cup cooked French-style green beans
3 tablespoons buttered bread crumbs

— Combine ham, onion, tarragon, and butter in a 1 ½-quart casserole.
— Cook, covered, for 2 minutes on high, or just long enough to melt butter and cook the onion a little.
— Add chicken soup, egg noodles, green beans, and ½ cup water. Toss lightly.
— Cook, covered, for 5 to 6 minutes on high, or until piping hot.
— Stir once during cooking period.
— Top with crumbs.
— Cover and let stand 2 to 3 minutes.

SEAFOOD TETRAZZINI

2 tablespoons butter or margarine
3 tablespoons finely chopped onion
1 (10 1/2-oz.) can condensed cream of mushroom soup
1/2 cup water
1 cup elbow macaroni, cooked and drained
1/4 cup grated Parmesan cheese
1 cup drained tuna, shrimp or crabmeat
1/2 cup sliced ripe olives
3 teaspoons lemon juice
1/8 teaspoon dried thyme leaves
1/8 teaspoon dried marjoram leaves
1/2 cup grated Parmesan cheese

— In a shallow, 1 1/2-quart baking dish, place 2 tablespoons butter.
— Cook, uncovered, on high 30 seconds.
— Add minced onion to melted butter and cook, uncovered, on high 2 minutes or until onion is tender.
— Add soup, water and cooked macaroni to onions.
— Blend well.
— Add remaining ingredients, except the second 1/4 cup Parmesan cheese to macaroni mixture.
— Combine well.
— Sprinkle remaining Parmesan cheese on top.
— Cook, uncovered, on medium for 12 minutes.
— If desired, top can be browned by placing under conventional broiler 3 minutes.

(4 servings)

RAINBOW HAM CASSEROLE

1 tablespoon butter
1 large onion, chopped
1/2 green pepper, chopped
1 1/2 cups cubed, cooked ham
1 can (10 3/4-oz.) condensed cream of mushroom soup, undiluted
1 can (4-oz.) sliced mushrooms, drained
1 can (2-oz.) chopped pimento, drained
8 pitted black olives, quartered
1/3 cup broken cashews
2 cans (15-oz.) each) macaroni and cheese

— Combine butter, onion and pepper in (12x8-inch) baking dish.
— Microwave 3 minutes on high, or until onion is transparent.
— Mix in ham, soup, mushrooms, pimento, olives, cashews and macaroni and cheese.
— Cover with plastic wrap.
— Microwave 10 to 12 minutes on high, or until hot and bubbly.

(4-6 servings)

HAM DELIGHT

3 slices bacon, cut up
1/2 cup finely chopped onion
2 cups cubed cooked ham
2 cups cooked noodles
1 can (10 3/4 oz.) condensed tomato soup
1 can (16 oz.) stewed tomatoes
1 can (16 oz.) whole kernel corn, drained
1 can (17 oz.) lima beans, drained
1 cup shredded Cheddar cheese

— Place bacon and onions in 3-quart glass casserole.
— Cover with glass lid or plastic wrap.
— Microwave on high for 5 minutes.
— Stir in remaining ingredients except cheese; mix well.
— Microwave on low for 14 to 16 minutes or until hot in center.
— Sprinkle cheese on top.
— Let stand, covered, 5 minutes or until cheese melts.

(8-10 servings)

Variation: Substitute 1 can (16 oz.) cut green beans for lima beans.

SCALLOPED BOLOGNA BAKE

1 package (5 1/2-oz.) scalloped potato mix
1 ring (1-lb.) coarse ground bologna, skinned and cut in 3/4-inch skices

— Use 1/4 cup less water than amount recommended in mix.
— Pour water over potatoes in 2-quart casserole.
— Let stand 20 minutes.
— Add bologna slices, sauce mix and milk, omit butter or margarine.
— Cover.
— Microwave 12 to 17 minutes on medium or until potatoes are tender.

(4-6 servings)

MISSY'S LAZY BEEF STEW

2 cups diced roast beef
1 cup chopped onion
1 cup sliced carrots
1 cup diced potatoes
1 package brown gravy mix
1/2 teaspoon salt
1/2 teaspoon celery salt
2 teaspoons instant beef bouillon dissolved in 1 1/2 cups hot water
1 bay leaf

— Combine all ingredients in 2-quart casserole.
— Cover.
— Microwave 20 minutes on high, or until vegetables are tender crisp, stirring twice.
— Remove bay leaf.

(4-5 servings)

SWISS AND ONION PIE

4 slices bacon
1 large onion, thinly sliced
1 tablespoon butter
1 9-inch baked pastry shell
½ pound Swiss cheese, grated
1 tablespoon flour
3 eggs, lightly beaten
1 cup milk
½ teaspoon salt
⅛ teaspoon pepper

— Place bacon slices on 2 paper towels. Cover with another paper towel.
— Microwave for about 3 minutes on high, or until almost crisp; reserve bacon.
— Combine onion and butter in a 1-quart casserole.
— Microwave, covered, for 3 to 4 minutes on high or until onion is limp.
— Place cooked onion in prebaked pastry shell.
— Toss together cheese and flour and sprinkle over onion.
— Beat together eggs, milk, salt, and pepper.
— Pour over cheese.
— Microwave for 10 minutes on high, rotating every 2 minutes.
— Place bacon strips on top of pie.
—Microwave for 2 to 3 minutes, or until custard is almost set.
— Let stand 10 to 15 minutes to finish cooking.

(6-8 servings)

BAKED BEAN CASSEROLE

2 strips bacon
1 (16-oz.) can old fashioned baked beans in molasses and brown sugar sauce
2 tablespoons minced onion
2 tablespoons ketchup
1 teaspoon prepared mustard
2 tablespoons brown sugar

— Place bacon on a paper-towel-lined paper plate.
— Cover with paper towel.
— Cook for 3 minutes on high or until crisp.
— In a deep, 1½-quart casserole combine beans, onion, ketchup, mustard and brown sugar.
— Mix thoroughly.
— Crumble bacon and sprinkle over baked bean mixture.
— Microwave uncovered for 12 minutes on high or until sauce is bubbly.

Optional: Add 6 franks or 4 slices (½-inch thick) ham and heat an additional 2 minutes in last step.

(3-4 servings)

RATATOUILLE

¼ cup olive or salad oil
2 medium onion, thickly sliced
1 clove garlic, finely chopped
1 large green pepper, cut in strips
1 medium eggplant, peeled and cut into ½-inch cubes (about 1½-lbs.)
2 zucchini, cut in ¼-inch slices
3 to 4 large tomatoes, peeled and cut in wedges, or 1 can (16-oz.) tomatoes
2 teaspoons basil
2 teaspoons parsely flakes
1 teaspoon marjoram
1 teaspoon salt
⅛ teaspoon pepper

— Combine olive oil, onion, garlic and green pepper in 3-quart casserole.
— Microwave 4 to 5 minutes on high, or until onions are transparent.
— Mix in eggplant and zucchini.
— Cover.
— Microwave 4 to 5 minutes on high, or until eggplant softens.
— Gently stir in tomatoes, basil, parsley, marjoram, salt and pepper.
— Microwave 12 minutes on medium or until vegetables are tender.

(6-8 servings)

COWBOY'S BEEF STEW

3 tablespoons flour
1 teaspoon salt
½ teaspoon pepper
1½ lbs. beef stew meat
3 tablespoons butter
3 cups water
1 tablespoon soy sauce
1 tablespoon Worcestershire sauce
¼ teaspoon garlic salt
1 bay leaf
½ teaspoon thyme
2 cups cubed peeled potatoes
1½ cups sliced carrots

— Combine flour, salt and pepper in flat dish.
— Coat meat in seasoned flour.
— Place butter in 3-quart glass casserole with coated meat.
— Cover with glass lid or plastic wrap.
— Microwave on high for 8 minutes.
— Stir in remaining ingredients; recover.
— Microwave on low for 45 to 50 minutes or until meat is fork tender.

(Thicken meat juices by blending ¼ cup unsifted all-purpose flour with ½ cup water. Stir into hot stew; remove. Microwave on low for 5 to 6 minutes or until thickened. Let stand, covered, 5 minutes. Stir well before serving)

(4-6 servings)

BOLOGNA CHEESE BAKE

1 to 1½ cup diced raw potatoes
½ lb. bologna, diced
3 tablespoons minced green pepper
1 tablespoon minced onion
1 can (10¾-oz.) condensed cream of celery soup, undiluted
1 cup grated sharp cheddar cheese

— Combine potatoes, bologna, green pepper, onion and soup in 1½-quart casserole.
— Cover.
— Microwave 15 minutes on high, or until potatoes are tender.
— Top with grated cheese.
— Let stand, uncovered, until cheese is just melted .

(4-5 servinggs)

FRANKS AND MACARONI

1 lb. beef frankfurters
1 (8-oz.) package macaroni, cooked and drained
1 (8-oz.) jar processed cheese spread
¼ cup finely chopped onions
1 tablespoon prepared brown mustard

— Place frankfurters on a paper plate.
— Heat, uncovered, on high for 3 minutes.
— Slice each cooked frankfurter into five diagonal slices.
— Combine cooked macaroni, sliced frankfurters, cheese spread, onion, and mustard in a deep, 2½-quart, heat-resistant, non-metallic casserole.
— Heat, uncovered, on medium for 7 minutes, or until sauce is bubbly.

(4-5 servings)

BEANS 'N KRAUT

1 lb. weiners (10)
1 can (31 oz.) pork and beans
¼ cup chili sauce
1 can (16 oz.) sauerkraut, drained
1 teaspoon caraway seeds

— Cut half of weiners into ¼-inch slices.
— Combine with pork and beans and chili sauce in 2-quart glass casserole.
— Spread sauerkraut on top.
— Sprinkle with caraway seeds.
— Cover with glass lid or plastic wrap.
— Microwave on low for 10 minutes.
— Arrange remaining weiners on top in a spoke fashion.
— Recover and continue cooking on low for 4 to 5 minutes or until heated through.

(3-4 servings)

SAUERKRAUT 'N FRANK SALAD

4 cups prepared potato salad
1 1 can (8 oz.) sauerkraut, drained
1 package (8 oz.) cocktail franks
½ teaspoon salt
½ teaspoon caraway seed
Paprika

— Combine all ingredients, except paprika, in 2-quart glass casserole.
— Cover with glass lid or plastic wrap
— Microwave on low for 8 to 9 minutes or until hot.
— Let stand, covered, 3 minutes.
— Sprinkle paprika on top before serving.

(6 servings)

CHEDDAR CHEESE CASSEROLE

1 (4-oz.) can green chili peppers
2 tablespoons butter
1 medium-sized onion, finely chopped
1 (8-oz.) can tomato sauce
½ teaspoon salt
2 eggs, beaten
1 cup cream
1 (6-oz.) package corn chips
½ lb. Cheddar cheese, shredded
1 cup sour cream
½ cup shredded Cheddar cheese
3 ripe tomatoes, sliced

— Drain chili peppers.
— Remove seeds and chop peppers coarsely.
— In a medium-sized bowl melt butter on high 30 seconds.
— Add onion and heat, uncovered, on high 3 minutes or until tender.
— Add chili peppers, tomato sauce and salt to onion.
— Cook, uncovered, on high 6 minutes.
— In a small bowl beat eggs and cream together until well blended.
— Gradually add egg mixture to heated sauce mixture, very little at a time, stirring constantly.
— Layer ½ of corn chips, ½ of tomato mixture and half of the ½-lb. shredded Cheddar cheese in a shallow, 1½-quart casserole.
— Repeat
— Carefully spread the sour cream over the top of the entire casserole.
— Cook, uncovered, on medium for 7 minutes or until mixture begins to set.
— Sprinkle the ½ cup of Cheddar cheese over the sour cream.
Arrange tomatoes in a ring around the outside edge of the casserole.
— Cook, uncovered, on medium for 7 to 8 minutes or until cheese melts and tomatoes are cooked. (6 servings)

BASIC PORK CASSEROLE

1 tablespoon butter
1 onion, sliced
1 ½ lbs. lean boneless pork, cut in ¾-inch cubes
¼ cup flour
2 ½ cups water
1 teaspoon instant chicken bouillon
1 teaspoon salt
¼ teaspoon pepper

— Combine butter and onion in 3-quart casserole.
— Microwave 3 minutes on high, or until onion is transparent.
— Add pork.
— Sprinkle flour over pork.
— Toss to coat well.
— Add water, bouillon, salt and pepper. Cover.
— Microwave 5 mintues on high.
— Reduce setting; Microwave 36 minutes on medium, or until meat is fork tender.

(4-6 servings)

Variations:

AMERICAN PORK

Add:
1 can (16-oz.) baked beans or red kidney beans, drained and rinsed
4 slices bacon cut in pieces
— Serve with boiled potatoes

BELGIAN PORK

Substitute 1 ¼ cups wine for half the water
— Add:
½ lb. pitted prunes
— Just before serving, stir in 1 tablespoon currant jelly.
— Sprinkle with snipped parsley.

CHINESE PORK

Substitute salad oil for butter
— Add:
2 tablespoons firmly packed brown sugar
2 tablespoons catsup
2 tablespoons vinegar
2 tablespoons soy sauce
1 carrot cut in julienne strips
1 green pepper, cut in julienne strips
— During last 15 minutes, add:
1 cup unsweetened pineapple cubes
— Serve with boiled rice.

FRENCH PORK

— Add:
1 can (4-oz.) sliced mushrooms, drained
1 clove garlic, finely chopped
— Just before serving, add:
2 tablespoons brandy
2 tablespoons cream
— Microwave 2 minutes on high, or until hot but not boiling.
— Garnish with snipped parsley.
— Serve with new potatoes or egg noodles.
— Follow with tossed green salad.

ENGLISH PORK

— Substitute cider for half the water
— During last 15 minutes add:
1 teaspoon sage
2 apples, peeled, cored and sliced
— Serve with a green vegetable and mashed potatoes.

GERMAN PORK

— During last 15 minutes, add:
½ lb. frankfurters, cut in pieces
1 cup drained sauerkraut
½ teaspoon caraway seeds
1 teaspoon German mustard
— Serve with boiled or sauteed potatoes.

HUNGARIAN PORK

— Add:
4 carrots, sliced
4 medium boiling potatoes, peeled and sliced
2 tomatoes, peeled and quartered
1 tablespoon paprika
— Just before serving, stir in:
3 tablespoons sour cream

SCANDINAVIAN PORK

— During last 15 minutes add:
2 apples, peeled, cored and chopped
½ lb. cooked ham, diced
— Just before serving add:
⅓ cup cream
— Microwave 2 minutes on high, or until hot but not boiling.
— Serve with braised red cabbage and sauteed potatoes.

PORK AND BEAN CASSEROLE

1 lb. lean ground beef
1 small onion, chopped
1 can (16-oz.) pork and beans
1 can (8-oz.) tomato sauce
2 tablespoons prepared mustard
2 teaspoons Worcestershire sauce
¼ teaspoon salt
¼ teaspoon pepper

— Crumble ground beef into 2-quart casserole.
— Add onion.
— Microwave 4 to 5 minutes on high, or until meat loses its pink color.
— Stir in pork and beans, tomato sauce, mustard, Worcestershire sauce, salt and pepper.
— Cover.
— Microwave 6 minutes on high, or until hot.

(4 servings)

LAMB RIBLETS IN TOMATO HONEY SAUCE

2 lbs. lamb riblets
1 medium onion, sliced
1 can (10½-oz.) condensed golden mushroom soup
1 can (8-oz.) tomato sauce
2 tablespoons honey
½ teaspoon salt
⅛ teaspoon pepper
¼ teaspoon thyme

— Place riblets in 2-quart casserole.
— Cover with onion slices.
— Microwave 12 minutes on medium.
— Drain fat.
— Stir in soup, tomato sauce, honey, salt, pepper and thyme.
— Cover.
— Microwave 50 to 60 minutes on medium, or until riblets are tender, stirring twice.
— Serve over rice, noodles or biscuits.

(4 servings)

TOMATO BEEF STEW

1½ lbs. stew meat
2 teaspoons salt
½ teaspoon pepper
½ teaspoon tarragon
1 package frozen peas
2 cans (10¾ oz. each) condensed tomato soup
1 can (4 oz.) whole mushrooms, drained
1 whole fresh tomato, sliced

— Place meat in 3-quart glass casserole.
— Cover.
— Microwave on high for 8 minutes.
— Drain and stir in remaining ingredients, except tomato; recover.
— Microwave on low for 55 to 60 minutes or until meat is fork tender.
— Let stand, covered, 5 minutes before serving.
— Garnish with sliced fresh tomato.

(4 servings)

FULL O' BALONEY

1½ cups raw potatoes, cubed (about 1½ potatoes)
1½ cups cubed bologna (½ lb.)
2 tablespoons minced green pepper
1 (10½-oz.) can condensed cream of mushroom soup, undiluted
2 large slices of American cheese, quartered

— Combine all the ingredients except the American cheese, in a deep, 1½-quart casserole.
— Cook, covered, on medium for 17 minutes or until tender. Stir occasionally.
— Top casserole with cheese slices and heat, uncovered, on medium an additional 1 minute or just until cheese melts.

(4 servings)

SAUSAGE NOODLE CASSEROLE

1 lb. pork sausage roll, cut into ½-inch chunks
1 large onion, sliced
1 small green pepper, diced
½ cup diced celery
1 package (1½-oz.) dry chicken noodle soup mix
1 can (10¾-oz.) condensed cream of mushroom soup, undiluted
1 cup cooked rice
½ cup water

— Combine sausage and onions in 1½-quart casserole.
— Cover.
— Microwave 4 to 5 minutes on high, or until sausage is set.
— Drain fat.
— Add green pepper, celery, soup mix, soup, rice and water.
— Cover.
— Microwave 6 to 8 minutes on high, or until bubbly.

(4 servings)

MOUSSAKA
(Lamb and Eggplant Casserole)

4 (7 to 8-inch) eggplants, washed
1 tablespoon salt
2 tablespoons olive oil
2 lbs. lean ground lamb
Vegetable oil
⅔ cup finely chopped onion
1 (8-oz.) can sliced mushrooms, drained
1 teaspoon salt
1 teaspoon dried rosemary leaves
½ teaspoon dried thyme leaves
1 clove garlic, peeled and crushed
⅔ cup beef broth
1 ½ teaspoons cornstarch
3 tablespoons tomato paste (save remainder for sauce)
3 eggs, slightly beaten
Tomato Sauce

— Remove green caps from eggplants and slice eggplants in half lengthwise.
— Make deep slashes in eggplant pulp, but do not cut through skins.
— Sprinkle eggplant halves with the 1 tablespoon salt and allow to stand at room temperature ½ hour.
— Squeeze moisture out of eggplant halves and brush cut surfaces with the 2 tablespoons of olive oil.
— Cook 4 eggplant halves at a time on high 7 minutes or until pulp is tender.
— Repeat with remaining eggplant halves.
— Scoop pulp out of eggplant, being careful not to rip skins. Set skins aside.
— Chop eggplant pulp coarsely.
— Place pulp in a bowl and heat, uncovered, on high 4 minutes or until tender.
— Stir occasionally.
— In a large bowl, crumble the lamb.
— Cook, uncovered, on medium for 7 minutes stirring frequently to break up pieces until meat is no longer pink.
— Liberally oil a deep, 2-quart casserole.
— Line casserole with the reserve eggplant skins.
— Arrange skins with the purple sides toward the outside and wide ends of eggplant skins at the top of the casserole.
— Drain the lamb juices and discard.
— Add chopped eggplant, onion, mushrooms, the 1 teaspoon salt, thyme, rosemary and garlic to the cooked lamb.
— Stir to combine well.
— Cook, uncovered, on medium for 7 minutes or until onion is tender.
— In a small bowl combine beef stock and corn starch until smooth.
— Cook, uncovered, from 1-1 ½ minutes until thickened and clear; stir occasionally.
— Add thickened beef stock and remaining ingredients, except tomato sauce to lamb mixture.
— Pour lamb-eggplant mixture into eggplant-skin lined casserole.
— Fold eggplant skins over filling.
— Heat, covered with a plate, for 11 minutes or until knife inserted in the center of the mixture comes out clean.
— Place onto platter for serving.
— Serve with tomato sauce.

(6 servings)

SAUSAGE AND CABBAGE CASSEROLE

2 lbs. bulk breakfast sausage
1 onion, coarsely chopped
2 lbs. cabbage, cored and cut into 1-inch pieces
1 (16-oz.) can whole peeled tomatoes, undrained
1 tablespoon sugar
½ teaspoon dried oregano leaves
1 ½ teaspoons salt
¼ teaspoon pepper
2 tablespoons flour
¼ cup cold water

— Crumble sausage into a deep, 3-quart casserole and add onion.
— Heat, uncovered, on medium for 9 minutes or until sausage is cooked and onion is tender.
— Stir frequently.
— Drain off excess fat.
— Add cabbage, tomatoes, sugar, oregano, salt and pepper.
— Stir to combine.
— Cook, covered, on medium for 10 to 12 minutes or until cabbage is tender.
— In a small cup mix flour and water until smooth.
— Gradually stir flour mixture into sausage mixture.
— Cook, uncovered, on medium for 4 minutes, stirring frequently until thickened.

(6-8 servings)

INTERNATIONAL LAMB CASSEROLE

1 1/2 lbs. boneless lamb, cut in 3/4-inch cubes
2 onion, cubed
1/4 cup flour
2 1/2 cups water
1 teaspoon instant beef or chicken bouillon
1 teaspoon salt
1/4 teaspoon pepper

— Combine lamb and onions in 2-quart casserole.
— Stir in flour to coat meat.
— Add water, bouillon, salt and pepper.
— Cover.
— Microwave 5 minutes on high.
— Stir.
— Reduce setting. Microwave 30 to 36 minutes on medium, or until meat is fork tender.

(4 servings)

Variations:

FRENCH LAMB

Add:

8 small whole onions
1 clove garlic, chopped
1/3 cup tomato paste
1/2 cup fresh shelled peas
1/2 teaspoon thyme or rosemary
Bay leaf

— Garnish with snipped parsley.
— Remove bay leaf.
— Serve with mashed or new potatoes.

(Frozen peas may be substituted for fresh. Add during last 5 minutes of cooking).

GREEK LAMB

Add:

1/2 eggplant, peeled and diced
4 zucchini, sliced
2 tomatoes, peeled and chopped, or 2 tablespoons tomato paste
Finely grated rind and juice of 1 lemon

— Serve with boiled rice.

INDIAN LAMB

Add:

1 tablespoon curry powder (add with flour)
2 stems celery, chopped
1 clove garlic, finely chopped
2 tablespoons raisins
1/4 teaspoon ginger

— Stir in 1/3 cup plain yogurt just before serving
— Serve with boiled rice and chutney.

ITALIAN LAMB

Add:

1 can (16-oz.) Italian plum tomatoes
1 clove garlic, pressed or chopped
1/2 teaspoon basil
1/2 taspoon oregano

— Garnish with grated Parmesan cheese
— Serve with macaroni, noodles or rice.

IRISH LAMB

Add:

2 (additional) onion, cut in eighths
3 slices bacon, chopped
4 medium boiling potatoes, thinly sliced

— Garnish with snipped parsley.

(Microwave 5 to 10 minutes longer on medium or until potatoes are tender.)

AUSTRALIAN LAMB

Add:

1 carrot, thinly sliced
1 small turnip, diced
1 cup diced pumpkin or winter squash
1 teaspoon rosemary

— Garnish with snipped parsley.
—Serve with a green vegetable and mashed potatoes.

GERMAN PORK AND SAUERKRAUT STEW

2 lbs. boneless pork, cubed
1 can (16 oz.) sauerkraut, drained
1 teaspoon salt
1/4 teaspoon pepper
1 large onion, finely chopped
1 teaspoon garlic salt
2 teaspoons paprika
2 teaspoons dill weed
1 can (10 3/4 oz.) condensed chicken broth
1/2 cup sour cream

— Place pork in 2-quart glass casserole. Cover with glass lid or plastic wrap.
— Microwave for 15 minutes on high.
— Drain and stir in remaining ingredients, except sour cream.
— Microwave for 25-30 minutes on high or until meat is fork tender. Blend in sour cream.
— Let stand, covered, 5 minutes before serving.

(4-6 servings)

CHICKEN STEW

1 3 lbs. frying chicken, cut up
2 stalks celery, cut into 1-inch pieces
6 baby onions, peeled
1 bay leaf
4 peppercorns
1 tablespoon salt
3 cubes or teaspoons chicken bouillon
3 cups water
4 carrots, cut into thin slices
¼ cup flour

Dumplings:
1½ cups unsifted flour
2 teaspoons baking powder
½ teaspoon salt
1 teaspoon parsley flakes
⅔ cup milk
1 slightly beaten egg
2 tablespoons oil
2 tablespoons grated Parmesan cheese

— Combine chicken, celery, onion, bay leaf, peppercorn, salt, bouillon and water in 4-quart casserole or Dutch oven.
— Microwave, covered, 24 minutes on high, stirring once. Add carrots.
— Combine ¼ cup flour with ½ cup water.
— Stir into chicken mixture.
— Microwave, covered, 8 minutes on high.
— Meanwhile, prepare dumplings: combine flour, baking powder, salt and parsley flakes.
— Combine milk, egg and oil; add to dry ingredients and mix just until moistened. (Mixture will be soft.)
— Remove bay leaf and peppercorns from stew and if desired, meat from bone.
— Spoon dumplings by rounded teaspoons into hot chicken mixture.
— Microwave, covered, 6 minutes on high or until bottom of dumplings are no longer soft on underside.

(4-6 servings)

GOULASH

2 tablespoons salad oil
2 chopped onions
1 clove garlic, pressed or finely chopped
1 teaspoon paprika
2 lbs. beef stew meat, cut in ¾-inch cubes
4 medium boiling potatoes, peeled and cut in small cubes
4 medium tomatoes, peeled and chopped, or 1 can (14-oz.) stewed tomatoes
1 green pepper, chopped
½ teaspoon caraway seeds
4 cups beef broth, or ¼ cup instant beef bouillon dissolved in 4 cups hot water
Salt and pepper
Sour cream

— Combine oil, onion and garlic in 4-quart casserole.
— Microwave 2 to 3 minutes on High, or until onion is transparent.
— Stir in paprika.
— Add beef, potatoes, tomatoes, green pepper, caraway seeds and beef broth.
— Cover.
— Microwave 5 minutes on high.
— Reduce setting. Microwave 55 to 75 minutes on medium, or until meat is fork tender, stirring once.
— Season with salt and pepper.
— Let stand 5 minutes, covered.

(Serve in bowls with sour cream spooned on top.)

IRISH STEW

2 tablespoons flour
2 teaspoons salt
¼ teaspoon pepper
2 lbs. lamb stew meat, trim off fat
2 tablespoons butter
1 cup finely sliced carrots
1 cup finely sliced celery
1 cup finely sliced turnips
1 medium onion, chopped
2 cups cubed raw potatoes
1 bay leaf
2 teaspoons rosemary
2 tablespoons parsley
2 tablespoons cornstarch
2 cups water

— Combine flour, salt and pepper in flat dish.
— Coat meat in seasoned flour.
— Place butter in 2-quart glass casserole with coated meat.
— Cover.
— Microwave on medium for 10 minutes.
— Stir in remaining ingredients, except cornstarch and water.
— Blend cornstarch with water in small mixing bowl.
— Mix into meat and vegetables; recover.
— Microwave on low for 35 to 40 minutes or until meat is fork tender.
— Let stand, covered, 5 minutes.
— Stir well before serving.

(4-6 servings)

FRESH AND FROZEN VEGETABLE COOKING CHART

(Use high power for listings below)

Vegetables	Amount	Minutes
ARTICHOKES	1	5 to 6
(Fresh 3½	2	7 to 8
inches in diameter)	3	9 to 10
	4	11 to 12
Frozen Hearts	10-oz. package	5 to 6
BEANS: GREEN AND WAX		
Fresh	1 lb.	12 to 14
	2 lbs.	16 to 18
Frozen	9-oz. pouch	8 to 9
French Style or cut	10-oz. package	8 to 9
BROCCOLI		
Fresh	1½ lbs.	10 to 12
Frozen	10 oz. package	8 to 9
	10 oz. pouch	8 to 9
BRUSSELS SPROUTS		
Fresh	½ lb.	5 to 7
	1 lb.	7 to 8
Frozen	8-oz. package	8 to 9
	10-oz. pouch	6 to 7
CABBAGE		
Fresh - shredded	½ medium	5 to 6
	1 medium	8 to 9
CARROTS		
Fresh - Sliced, Diced, Slivered	2 medium	5 to 6
	4 medium	8 to 10
	6 medium	10 to 12
Frozen - Diced or Whole	10-oz. package	8 to 10
	10-oz. pouch	8 to 9
CAULIFLOWER		
Fresh - Broken into flowerests	1 medium	7 to 8
Whole	1 medium	8 to 9
Whole	1 large	12 to 14
Frozen	10-oz. package	8 to 9
	10-oz. pouch	8 to 9
CORN		
Fresh - Cut from cob	1½ cups	6 to 7
	3 cups	7 to 8
Frozen	10-oz. package	6 to 7
	10-oz. pouch	5 to 6
CORN ON THE COB		
Fresh	2	4 to 5
	4	7 to 8
	6	9 to 10
Frozen	2	6 to 8
	4	10 to 12

VEGETABLES

VEGETABLES

You can enjoy the fresh taste and vivid color of green vegetables by using the Microwave Oven. Moreover, due to the short cooking time, only a small quantity of water-soluble vitamins are lost, including considerable amounts of Vitamin C.

To cook leafy vegetables: Make vertical incisions with knife on thick part of stem. Place washed vegetables still wet, alternating stem and leaf on plastic wrap and wrap tightly before placing in the oven.

To cook root vegetables: In making potato salad, wash potatoes and wrap, unpeeled. Heat for the appointed cooking time. Remove and let stand a few minutes. Potatoes will further cook by retained heat. In making stew, preheat peeled and wrapped potatoes in the oven. Then place potatoes in casserole and boil in the oven. If potatoes of the same size are selected they will cook evenly.

To maintain the natural color of broccoli: Sprinkle washed broccoli with a little vinegar and heat, covered, in the oven. Broccoli will not lose its color.

DRUNK BEANS

1 can (15-oz.) kdney beans, drained
¼ cup finely chopped onion
2½ tablespoons dry red wine
½ teaspoon salt
1 tablespoon butter or margarine, cut in small bits

— Combine beans, onion, wine and salt in 1-quart casserole. Mix well.
— Dot with butter.
— Cover.
— Microwave 5 to 6 minutes on high, or until hot.

(3 servings)

PEPPERED BEANS

1 lb. green beans
⅔ cup water
2 tablespoons olive oil
½ sweet red pepper, seeded and cut in slivers
¼ cup slivered almonds
Salt and pepper to taste

— Cook beans in water 20 minutes
— Cover and let stand.
— Combine oil, red or green pepper, and almonds in a 1-quart casserole.
— Cook, uncovered, for 3 to 4 minutes, or until peppers are limp.
—Toss with green beans.
— Season to taste with salt and pepper.

3-4 servings)

FROZEN LIMA BEANS

— Place a 10-oz. package frozen baby lima beans in a 1-quart casserole.
— Add ¼ cup water.
— Cook, covered, for 9 to 10 minutes on high, or until tender.
— Stir once during cooking period.

(3-4 servings)

CAULIFLOWER MEDLEY

1 medium to large head cauliflower
½ cup water
1 zucchini
¼ cup onion, finely chopped
2 tablespoons butter
2 whole tomatoes, cut in wedges
½ teaspoon salt
⅛ teaspoon crushed thyme
1 cup sharp Cheddar cheese spread

— Cook cauliflower with water in 2 quart covered casserole 6 minutes on high or until barely tender.
— Remove cauliflower and place zucchini, onion, butter in casserole.
— Heat, uncovered, on high for 2 minutes on high or until vegetables are tender.
— Add cauliflower, cheese, and tomatoes to zucchini mixture, mix in salt and thyme.
— Heat covered on high 4 minutes or until tomatoes are tender.

TOMATO CASSEROLE

4 small tomatoes
2 tablespoons butter or margarine
2 tablespoons chopped onion
2 ½ teaspoons sugar
1 teaspoon salt
Dash of pepper
¾ cup bread crumbs
1 tablespoon grated Swiss cheese
Chopped parsley

— Pour boiling water over tomatoes, peel and cut into quarters.
— Preheat a casserole 2 minutes in Microwave on high power.
— Melt butter in the casserole, add tomatoes, onion, sugar, salt and pepper and mix.
— Microwave 1 minute, 30 seconds on high.
— Stir gently and cook 1 minute, 30 seconds more on high.
— Cut off bread crust and dice bread.
— Add diced bread to the casserole and cook on high 3 minutes. Sprinkle with cheese and parsley.

(6 servings)

RED CABBAGE

1 medium head red cabbage
4 cooking apples
2 tablespoons sugar
4 tablespoons red wine vinegar
1 tablespoon butter
1 ¼ teaspoons salt
¼ teaspoon pepper
¼ cup dry red wine

— Shred cabbage fine, core and cut apples in small pieces.
— Combine with sugar, vinegar, butter, salt and pepper in a 2 ½ quart casserole.
— Cook covered 9 to 10 minutes strring once, on high.
— Add wine and cook 2 minutes more again on high.
— This is delicious served with roast pork.

(6-10 servings)

SWEET-SOUR CELERY

2 cups thinly sliced celery
3 tablespoons red wine vinegar
1 tablespoon sesame seeds
2 tablespoons butter or margarine
3 whole cloves
½ cup water
Dash of salt and pepper
2 tablespoons sugar
Chopped parsley

— In a casserole, put celery, bay leaf, cloves, and ½ cup water.
— Cook, covered, 8 minutes, on high or until celery is only slightly crisp.
— Add sugar, vinegar, and butter and toss lightly
— Cook, covered, 1 minute, on high or until butter is melted and celery is piping hot.
— Season to taste. Sprinkle with chopped parsley.

Variation:

— Carrots can be prepared the same way using 1 ½ tablespoons of sugar.
— Very pretty served together with the celery.

(4 servings)

ARTICHOKE HEARTS WITH MUSHROOMS

1 package (10-oz.) frozen artichoke hearts
1 can (4-oz.) sliced mushrooms
1 ½ teaspoons cornstarch
2 tablespoons dry sherry
2 tablespoons butter or margarine
½ teaspoon lemon juice
Salt and pepper
Onion salt
Garlic salt
1 tablespoon chopped parsley

— Cook articoke hearts in a glass casserole dish for 5 to 6 minutes on high; set aside.
— Drain mushrooms, reserving liquid.
— Combine cornstarch, sherry, butter, lemon juice, and mushroom liquid in a 1-quart bowl
— Microwave, uncovered, for 30 seconds to 1 minute, on high, or until mixture is thckened and clear.. Blend well.
— Season to taste with salt, pepper, onion salt, and garlic salt. Stir in parsley. Cut artichoke hearts in half and add them, along with the mushrooms. stir gently.
— Cook, covered, for 2 to 3 minutes, on high, until mixtures is piping hot.

(3-4 servings)

LIMA BEANS PARMESAN

1 package (10-oz.) frozen baby lima beans
¼ cup chicken bouillon
1 bay leaf
1 clove garlic
Salt and pepper to taste
Grated Parmesan cheese

— Place lima beans in a 1½-quart casserole.
— Add chicken bouillon, bay leaf, and garlic.
— Cook, covered, for 9 to 10 minutes until beans are tender.
— Remove bay leaf and garlic.
— Season to taste with salt and pepper.
— Serve with Parmesan cheese sprinkled on top of beans.

(3-4 servings)

STUFFED ZUCCHINI RAMON

4 small zucchini (about 1 lb.)
½ lb. lean ground beef or pork
1½ tablespoons finely chopped onion
1½ teaspoon parsley flakes
Salt and pepper to taste
1 egg, beaten
½ cup bread crumbs
½ cup grated Parmesan cheese
2 cups tomato sauce
4 tablespoons chopped onion
1 clove garlic, peeled and crushed
1 teaspoon parsley flakes
¼ teaspoon sweet basil leaves
½ teaspoon salt

— Place zucchini in the Microwave Oven and heat on high 7 minutes, or until soft.
— Cut each zucchini in half and scoop out pulp and seeds and save.
— In a medium-sized bowl combine pulp and seeds, ground beef, the 2 tablespoons of onion, parsley flakes and salt and pepper, to taste.
— In a small bowl combine beaten egg, crumbled white bread and grated Parmesan cheese.
— Add egg-bread mixture to ground beef mixture and mix thoroughly.
— Stuff each zucchini half with some of the ground beef mixture.
— Place zucchini, stuffing side up, in a shallow, 3-quart, heat-resistant, non-metallic baking dish, leaving about ½-inch between each zucchini half.
— Sprinkle top of zucchini with Parmesan cheese.
— In a medium-sized bowl combine remaining ingredients.
— Heat, uncovered, 5 minutes on high or until sauce bubbles.
— Spoon sauce over zucchini.
— Heat, uncovered, on medium for 16 to 18 minutes.

(4 servings)

STUFFED EGGPLANT

2 medium eggplants
1 onions, chopped
1 lb. ground lamb
1 beef bouillon cube
1 can (8-oz.) tomato sauce
¼ teaspoon curry powder
½ teaspoon oregano
2 tablespoons chopped parsley
½ teaspoon salt
¼ teaspoon pepper
½ cup drp bread crumbs

— Wash eggplant and cut in half lengthwise.
— Scoop out insides, leaving a shell 1 inch thick.
— Chop eggplant pulp in medium chunks; set aside.
— Put onion in a 1½-quart casserole.
— Crumble in lamb.
— Cook, covered, for about 5 minutes, on high or just until lamb loses its pink color.
— Drain off fat.
— Dissolve bouillon cube in ½ cup hot water.
—Stir into cooked lamb with 3 tablespoons tomato sauce and the chopped eggplant pulp.
— Cook, covered, for about 5 minutes, on high stirring occasionally.
— Remove from oven; stir in oregano, parsley, salt, and pepper.
— Fill eggplant halves with mixture.
— Sprinkle bread crumbs over top.
— Streak remaining tomato sauce over top of crumbs.
— Place eggplant halves in a glass baking dish
— Cook, covered, for about 8 minutes, on high or just until eggplant is tender.

(4 servings)

ONION TOPPED BEANS

2 packages (10 oz. each) frozen French-cut green beans
1 can (5 oz.) water chestnuts, sliced
2 cans (10¾ oz. each) condensed cream of celery soup
1 can (3½ oz.) French-fried onion rings

— Place frozen beans in 2-quart (12x7) glass baking dish. Cover with plastic wrap.
— Microwave on high for 7 to 8 minutes or until beans are tender-crisp.
— Add water chestnuts. Spread soup over beans. Top with onion rings.
— Continue cooking on high for about 5 minutes or until hot. Let stand 2 to 3 minutes before serving.

(6-8 servings)

GREEN BEANS ITALIAN

2 packages (10-oz. each) frozen green beans
1 small onion, thinly sliced
¾ cup bottled Italian dressing
3 strips cooked bacon

— Place green beans in a 1½-quart casserole or saucepan.
— Cook, covered, for 7 to 8 minutes, on high, or until almost tender, stirring once.
— Add onion and Italian dressing.
— Cook, covered, for about 3 minutes, or until beans are just tender.
— Serve hot, topped with crumbled cooked bacon.

(6 servings)

ASPARAGUS VINAIGRETTE

2 dz. asparagus spears
7 tablespoons oil
4 tablespoons vinegar
⅛ teaspoon hot sauce
¾ teaspoon sugar
¼ teaspoon salt
⅓ cup onion, sliced

— Cook asparagus 6-7 minutes on high in covered glass casserole dish.
— Cool, place in shallow pan.
— Combine remaining ingredients except pimiento, blend well.
— Pour vinaigrette sauce over asparagus and refrigerate several hours or over night.

BEANS PARMESAN

10 oz. green beans
1 tablespoon butter
¼ cup cream
¼ cup chicken bouillon
Dash of sugar, salt and pepper
Parmesan cheese
1 bay leaf
½ clove garlic

— In a casserole, place green beans, butter, cream, chicken bouillon, bay leaf, garlic and pinch of sugar.
— Cook, covered, 9 to 10 minutes on high.
— Remove bay leaf and garlic.
— Season with salt and pepper to taste.
— Sprinkle Parmesan cheese on top of beans and serve.

(4 servings)

STUFFED TOMATOES

4 large ripe tomatoes
2 tablespoons butter or margarine
2 tablespoons finely chopped onion
2 tablespoons diced celery
1 cup dry bread crumbs
½ teaspoon salt
¼ teaspoon sage
⅛ teaspoon pepper
2 tablespoons butter or margarine, cut in small pieces
Paprika

— Scoop out center pulp and seeds of tomato.
— Place tomatoes in (8x8-inch) square baking dish; set aside.
— Combine butter and onion in a 1-quart covered casserole.
— Microwave 4 minutes on high, or until onion is transparent.
— Stir in bread crumbs, salt, poultry seasoning and pepper.
— Mix well.
— Spoon stuffing mixture into tomatoes.
— Dot with remaining butter.
— Sprinkle with paprika.
— Cover.
— Microwave 3 to 4 minutes on high, or until skins begin to break and tomatoes are heated through.

(4 servings)

PEAS AND ONIONS WITH MUSHROOMS

2 tablespoons butter or margarine
¼ cup chopped onion
1 can (4 oz.) mushrooms, chopped
1 package (10 oz.) frozen peas
¼ teaspoon salt
Dash pepper and allspice

— Combine butter and onion in 1-quart glass casserole. Cover.
— Microwave on high for 3 minutes or until onion is partly cooked.
— Add mushrooms, frozen peas, salt, pepper and allspice. Recover, and continue cooking on high for 4 minutes.
— Stir and continue cooking on high for 3 to 4 minutes or until peas are tender-crisp.
— Let stand, covered, 3 minutes before serving.

(4 servings)

CREAMY PEAS AND POTATOES

1 lb. small red potatoes
1½ cups fresh shelled peas
2 tablespoons water
2 tablespoons butter or margarine
1 tablespoon chopped onion
2 tablespoons all-purpose flour
1¼ teaspoon salt
½ teaspoon dill weed
⅛ teaspoon pepper
1½ cups milk

— Prick potatoes before cooking. Place in oven
— Microwave on high for 10 to 11 minutes or until potatoes are fork-tender; set aside.
— Combine peas and water in 2-quart casserole
— Cover with glass lid or plastic wrap.
— Microwave on high for 6 minutes or until peas are tender-crisp; set aside.
— Combine butter and onion in 4-cup glass measure.
— Microwave on medium for about 1 minute or until melted.
— Blend in flour, salt, dill and pepper.
— Stir in milk.
— Microwave on high for 4 to 5 minutes or until mixture thickens. Peel potatoes and add to peas in casserole.
— Pour hot cream sauce over vegetables; stir gently to thoroughly coat vegetables. high for 2 to 3 minutes or until piping hot.
— Let stand 3 minutes before serving.

(4-5 servings)

JOHN'S CORN DELICIOUS

1 (10-oz.) package frozen cut corn, defrosted
1 (17-oz.) can cream-style corn
3 eggs, well beaten
½ cup whole milk
1 teaspoon salt
¼ teaspoon pepper
½ cup cracker crumbs or fine dry bread crumbs
Butter

— In a 1½ quart bowl place cut corn.
— Add can of cream-style corn and mix together well.
— To corn mixture add milk, beaten eggs, salt and pepper. Stir until thoroughly blended.
— Lightly butter a 2-quart casserole.
— Pour ⅓ of corn mixture into casserole.
— Cover with ⅓ of the crumbs.
— Dot with butter.
— Repeat until all ingredients are used. Be sure to end with crumbs dotted with butter.
— Heat, covered, on medium for 8 to 9 minutes.
— Remove cover and heat on medium for an additional 2 minutes.

(6 servings)

STUFFED ONION BAKE

4 large white onions, peeled
1 can (5-oz.) boned chicken
2 tablespoons mayonnaise
Salt and pepper
¼ cup butter or margarine
2 cups catsup

— Hollow out the center of each onion leaving a half-inch thick shell; set aside.
— Finely chop center portions.
— Combine onion, chicken and mayonnaise in medium bowl.
— Season with salt and pepper.
— Mix well.
— Fill onion shells with stuffing and place in (8 x 8-inch) baking dish.
— Dot each onion with 1 tablespoon butter.
— Pour catsup around onions.
— Cover with plastic wrap. Microwave 9 minutes on high, or until onions are tender-crisp.

For Variety: substitute 1 can (10¾-ounces) double-strength chicken broth, undiluted, for catsup. (Can be prepared in advance and cooked later.)

(4 servings)

CORN PUDDING

2 tablespoons butter
2 tablespoons flour
1 can (1-lb.) whole kernel corn, drained
2 cups milk
2 eggs, beaten
½ teaspoon pepper

— Melt butter in a 1 ½-quart glass casserole for 30 seconds.
— Stir in flour to make a paste.
— Add remaining ingredients and blend.
— Cook, covered, for 9 minutes on high, stirring once.
— Let stand, loosely covered, 2 minutes before serving.

(4 servings)

CORN ON THE COB

— Just before cooking, remove husks, silk and any blemishes.
— Wrap each ear of corn in a piece of waxed paper and twist ends tightly together.
— Place in oven, with about 1 inch space between.
— Cook no more than 4 ears of fresh corn at a time, for 6 to 7 minutes, or until tender.
— For frozen corn, wrap each ear in a piece of waxed paper and twist ends together.
— Microwave for about 12 minutes on high.

CORN CUSTARD

2 tablespoons butter or margarine
2 eggs, slightly beaten
1 cup milk
1 can (12 oz.) cream-style corn
2 tablespoons all-purpose flour
1 teaspoon salt
½ teaspoon pepper

— Place butter in 1-quart casserole.
— Microwave on medium for 1 minute or until butter melts.
— Add remaining ingredients.
— Cover with glass lid or plastic wrap.
— Microwave on medium for 9 minutes. Stir and continue cooking on medium for 7 to 8 minutes or until custard is slightly soft in center.
— Let stand, covered, 5 minutes or until custard is set in center.

(4-6 servings)

SWEET AND SOUR CABBAGE

4 cups shredded cabbage
2 strips bacon — cut up
2 apples, peeled, cored, and finely chopped
½ cup brown sugar
½ cup butter
¼ cup vinegar
Salt and pepper to taste

— Place cabbage in a 1 ½-quart glass casserole
— Combine remaining ingredients. Pour over cabbage.
— Cook, covered, for 6 to 7 minutes, on high or until cabbage is tender.
— Stir once during cooking period.
— Add salt and pepper to taste.

PARMESAN ZUCCHINI

4 zucchini, not pared, sliced lengthwise
4 tablespoons butter or margarine
1 cup tomato sauce
½ teaspoon pepper
Parmesan cheese
Salt to taste

— Place zucchini in a microwave proof baking dish, cut side up.
— Pour tomato sauce over zucchini.
— Season with salt and pepper.
— Dot top with butter.
— Sprinkle Parmesan cheese generously over zucchini.
— Cover with waxed paper, cook 12 to 14 minutes, on high or until done.

(4 servings)

BAKED SQUASH

1 medium acorn squash
2 tablespoons brown sugar
2 tablespoons butter or margarine

— Pierce squash with fork and place on a paper towel.
— Cook 8 minutes on high, or until fork-tender, turning once.
— Cut in half and remove seeds.
— Place one tablespoon sugar in each cavity.
— Dot with butter.
— Cook 2 to 3 minutes on high, or until butter and sugar are melted.

(2 servings)

CAULIFLOWER

— Remove outer leaves and stalks from 1 medium head of caulifflower.
— Separate into flowerets.
— Place in a 1 ½-quart casserole.
— Add 2 to 3 tablespoons water.
— Microwave for 7 to 8 minutes, on high, or until cauliflower is tender.
—Stir once during cooking period.

(3-4 servings)

BEETS

— Wash well and cut stems and root ends from 1 bunch ((4 to 5 medium) beets.
— Place in a deep 2 ½-quart mixing bowl with water to cover.
— Cover with plastic wrap.
— Microwave for 20 to 25 minutes, on high, or until beets can be easily pierced with the point of a sharp knife.
— Drain and slip off skins. Serve whole or sliced.

(4 servings)

CHEESED CAULIFLOWER

1 medium head cauliflower
3 tablespoons oil
1 large onion, diced
¼ teaspoon salt
Dash of pepper
¼ cup grated Cheddar cheese

— Remove outer leaves and stalks from cauliflower.
— Separate into flowerets. Place in glass dish and microwave for 7 to 8 minutes on high or until cauliflower is tender.
— Put oil in a 1-quart casserole.
— Add onion.
— Cook, uncovered, for about 4 minutes, on high or until onions are limp and tender.
— Stir once or twice during cooking period.
— Add salt, pepper, and bread crumbs.
— Drain cauliflower and leave in original casserole.
— Top with hot onion mixture.
— Sprinkle cheese over top.
— Microwave on high, uncovered, for 1 ½ to 2 minutes, or until cheese is melted and cauliflower is piping hot.

(4 servings)

ONION BAKE

¼ cup chopped almonds
1 teaspoon butter
1 pkg. (10 oz.) frozen creamed onions
¼ cup grated Cheddar cheese
Chopped parsley
¼ can (3 ½ oz.) French-fried onion rings

— Combined onions, cheese and parsley in a glass casserole.
— Cook, covered, 5 minutes, on high, stirring twice.
— Add almonds and butter.
— Cook, uncovered, 3 minutes, on high, stirring once.
— Sprinkle onion rings on top.

(3 servings)

CHEESE CREAM ONIONS

2 jars (16 oz. each) onions, drained
1 jar (8 oz.) process cheese spread
1 tablespoon dried parsley flakes
¼ cup buttered dry bread crumbs

— Combine onions, cheese and parsley flakes in 1 ½-quart glass casserole. Cover with glass lid or plastic wrap.
— Microwave on medium for 4 minutes. Stir; sprinkle with buttered crumbs, and continue cooking on medium for 3 to 4 minutes or until hot. Let stand, covered, 3 minutes before serving.

(3-4 servings)

SUCCOTASH

2 (10-oz.) package frozen lima beans, thawed
2 (10-oz.) packages frozen whole kernel corn, thawed
⅓ cup chopped canned pimiento
2 teaspoons salt
½ teaspoon sugar
¼ teaspoon pepper
6 tablespoons butter or margarine
½ cup light cream

— Place lima beans and corn in a large, heat-resistant, non-metallic bowl.
— Heat, covered, on high 12 minutes or until vegetables are hot.
— Add remaining ingredients and stir to combine. Heat, uncovered, on medium 5 minutes or until heated through.

(6 servings)

PICKLED BEETS

1 can (1 lb.) sliced beets
⅓ cup sugar
⅓ cup vinegar
1 teaspoon pickling spice

— Drain beets, reserving ⅓ cup of the beet liquid.
— Place beets in a 1-quart casserole with sugar, beet liquid, and vinegar.
— Tie pickling spice in a small square of cheesecloth and add to beets.
— Microwave, covered, for 4 to 5 minutes, on high, or until mixture comes to a boil.
— Cool and remove bag of spices.
— Refrigerate up to 2 weeks.

BRAISED CELERY

2 cups celery, cut diagonally in ½-inch pieces
½ teaspoon basil
¼ teaspoon thyme
¼ cup red wine, or ¼ teaspoon instant beef bouillon dissolved in ¼ cup hot water

— Place celery in 1-quart casserole.
— Season with basil and thyme.
— Pour wine over celery.
— Cover.
— Microwave 5 to 7 minutes on high, or until celery is tender crisp.

(4 servings)

HARVARD BEETS

1 can ((1 lb.) diced or sliced beets
¼ cup sugar
1½ tablespoon cornstarch
½ teaspoon salt
Freshly ground pepper to taste
¼ cup vinegar
¼ cup orange juice

— Drain beets, reserving liquid.
— Pour beet liquid into a 1-cup measure and add enough water to make 1 cup of liquid.
— Combine sugar, cornstarch, salt, pepper, and vinegar in a 1-quart casserole or bowl. Stir in beet liquid.
— Microwave, uncovered, for 2½ to 3 minutes, on high stirring occasionally, until mixture thickens and is clear.
— Add beets and stir lightly.
— Cook, covered, for about 3 minutes, on high or until beets are piping hot.

(4 servings)

SAUERKRAUT WITH APPLES

1 tablespoon butter or margarine
1 small onion, chopped
1 can (1-lb.) sauerkraut, drained
1 cup tart apples, thinly sliced
1 tablespoon flour
½ cup apple juice
½ tablespoon vinegar
⅛ teaspoon caraway seed

—Combine butter and onion in 1-quart casserole.
— Microwave on high until butter melts.
— Stir in sauerkraut and apples.
— Sprinkle with flour.
— Pour in bouillon.
—Add vinegar and caraway seed.
— Mix gently.
— Cover.
— Microwave 3 to 5 minutes on high, or until apple is tender and sauce slightly thickened.

(4 servings)

CAULIFLOWER CONFETTI

2 lb. cauliflower (frozen)
1 zucchini, sliced
¼ cup finely chopped onion
2 tablespoons butter
1 cup soft cheese spread
1 cup grated cheddar cheese
2 tomatoes, cut into 8 wedges each
½ teaspoon salt
⅛ teaspoon thyme leaves, crushed

— Cook cauliflower on high for 7-8 minutes or until thawed.
— In a deep, 2-quart, heat-resistant, non-metalic casserole place zucchini, onion and butter and heat, uncovered, on high 3 minutes or until zucchini and onion are tender.
— Add cauliflower and cheese sauce and tomatoes to onion-zucchini mixture.
— Add salt and thyme leaves to mixture.
— Cook, covered, on high 5 minutes or until tomatoes are tender.

(6 servings)

SCALLOPED POTATOES

6 cups potatoes, peeled and thinly sliced
3 onions, sliced
Salt and pepper to taste
4½ tablespoons grated Parmesan cheese, divided
3½ tablespoons all-purpose flour, divided
4 tablespoons butter or margarine
3½ cups milk
Paprika

— Place ⅓ of potatoes in 3-quart casserole and cover with one-third of the onion.
— Add salt and pepper to taste, 1 tablespoon cheese, and 1 tablespoon flour.
— Repeat process twice with remaining potatoes, onion, seasonings, cheese, and flour.
— Dot with butter.
— Pour milk over top.
— Sprinkle with paprika.
— Cook, covered, for 25 minutes, rotating casserole every 10 minutes.
— Remove from oven and let stand at least 5 minutes before serving.

(6-8 servings)

BOILED POTATOES

— The potatoes should all be about the same size for uniform cooking.
— Peel 4 medium potatoes and cut up in approximately 1½-inch squares. The more uniform, the better the results.
— Place in a 1½-quart casserole.
— Cover with water and add ½ teaspoon salt.
— Cook, covered, for 10 minutes on high, or until potatoes are tender.

(4 servings)

ORANGE-POTATO SHELLS

2 oranges, reserve 2 tablespoons juice.
1 can (23-oz.) sweet potatoes
4 portions instant mashed potatoes, prepared according to package directions.
¼ cup miniature marshmallows

— Cut oranges in half, making a sawtooth pattern.
— Free fruit from shell carefully.
— Reserve juice.
— Stir in 2 tablespoons reserved orange juice.
— Blend in mashed potatoes.
— Mix well.
— Fill orange shells with potato mixture, using a pastry tube or spoon.
— Top with marshmallows.
— Microwave 1 minute on high, or until marshmallows soften.

(4 servings)

HASHED POTATOES

⅓ cup butter or margarine
½ cup coarsely chopped onions
4 baked potatoes, cold
Salt and pepper to taste

— In a 1½-quart casserole put butter and onion.
— Cook, uncovered, for 6 minutes on high, stirring occasionally.
— Peel potatoes and cut in small chunks.
— Stir into onion in casserole.
— Season to taste.
— Microwave, uncovered, for 4 to 5 minutes, on high, stirring occasionally.

(4 servings)

BEETS A L' ORANGE

1 can (1 lb.) diced beets
1 tablespoon cornstarch
1 ½ tablespoons sugar
¼ cup orange juice
2 tablespoons lemon juice
1 tablespoon butter or margarine

— Drain beets, reserving liquid.
— Pour liquid into a measuring cup and add enough water to make ½ cup liquid.
— Combine cornstarch, salt, sugar, and orange juice in a 1-quart bowl. Stir in beet liquid.
— Microwave, uncovered, for 2½ to 3 minutes, on high, or until mixture comes to a boil and is clear.
— Add lemon juice, orange peel, and butter.
— Stir to melt butter.
— Add beets.
— Cook, uncovered, for about 3 minutes on high or until beets are piping hot.

(4 servings)

PEACHEY YAMS

1 can (17 oz.) vacuum packed yams or sweet potatoes, mashed
1 can ((28 oz.) peach halves, undrained
3 tablespoons packed brown sugar
2½ tablespoons butter or margarine
3 tablespoons brandy or brandy flavoring
1 tablespoon grated orange peel
¼ teaspoon salt

— Place peach halves, cut side up, on glass serving platter.
— Combine 4 tablespoons peach syrup and remaining ingredients in mixing bowl; mix well.
— Spoon mixture into peach halves.
— Microwave on Reheat for 6 to 7 minutes on high, or until hot. Let stand for 3 minutes before serving.

(6 servings)

TIP: Make ahead and reheat at serving time.

BROCCOLI

— Clean 1½ lbs. broccoli.
— Split stems about 1-inch up to make for faster, more even cooking.
— Place in a 1½-quart casserole with the split stem ends arranged toward the outside of the dish. Add ¼ cup water.
— Microwave, covered, for 7 to 9 minutes on high or until broccoli is tender.

(4 servings)

TWICE BAKED POTATOES

4 medium baking potatoes
2 tablespoons butter or marggarine
½ cup milk
Salt and pepper
1 cup Cheddar cheese, grated

— Prick potatoes and place in oven.
— Microwave on high for 10 to 12 minutes or until fork-tender.
— Cut potatoes in half.
— Carefully scoop cooked potato out of shells and put into mixing bowl.
— Add butter, milk, salt and pepper to taste; mash until lump-free.
— Fill potato shells; top with cheese and place on glass serving platter.
— Continue cooking on high for 4 to 5 minutes or until hot. Let stand 3 minutes before serving.

(4-8 servings)

SWEET POTATOES BRULEE

1 can (17 oz.) vacuum packed sweet potatoes, mashed
2 tablespoons butter or margarine
3 tablespoons orange juice
Salt
⅛ teaspoon cinnamon
3 tablespoons chopped nuts
¼ cup packed brown sugar

— Combine potatoes, butter, orange juice, salt and cinnamon in 1-quart glass casserole
— Sprinkle top with nuts and brown sugar.
— Cover with glass lid or pastic wrap.
— Microwavve on low for 6 to 7 minutes or until hot.
— Let stand, covered, 3 minutes before serving.

(4-5 servings)

INDONESIAN ASPARAGUS

3 tablespoons butter
3 tablespoons chopped peanuts
10 oz. frozen chopped asparagus
1 celery stalk, sliced
1 tablespoon soy sauce

— Place butter and peanuts in a baking dish.
— Cook 3 minutes on high, stirring every 1 minute.
— Remove peanuts.
— Add asparagus and celery, and cook, covered, 6 minutes on high.
— Pour in soy sauce and sprinkle with peanuts. Cook, covered, 30 seconds on high.

(4 servings)

ORIENTAL ASPARAGUS

2 tablespoons butter
2 tablespoons slivered almonds
1 package (10-oz.) frozen cut asparagus
½ cup thinly sliced celery
1 can (5-oz.) water chestnuts, drained and sliced
2 tablespoons soy sauce

— Combine butter and almonds in 1-quart glass casserole.
— Microwave on high for 3 to 4 minutes or until tender-crisp.
— Stir in soy sauce and almonds.
— Let stand, covered, 3 minutes before serving.

(4 servings)

BROCCOLI CHEESE GRATIN

10 oz. broccoli
2 tablespoons butter
1 cup fresh cream
¼ cup Swiss cheese
3 tablespoons flour
1 stock cube
½ teaspoon salt
Dash of pepper and paprika

— Place broccoli stalk side up in water for 10 minutes.
— Separate all the branches.
— Wrap, undrained, and cook 5 minutes on high.
— Put butter in a casserole and mix with fresh cream, Swiss cheese, flour, salt and pepper.
— Add 1 stock cube dissolved in 1 cup water.
— Put cooked broccoli in the casserole and cook, covered, 9 minutes on high, stirring every 3 minutes.
— Let stand several minutes.
— Sprinkle with paprika and serve.

(4 servings)

HONEY SWEETENED SQUASH

4 cups (2-lb.) 1-inch cubed Hubbard squash
⅓ cup butter
⅓ honey
½ teaspoon salt
1 tablespoon grated orange peel

— Combine all ingredients in 2-quart glass casserole.
— Cover with glass lid or plastic wrap.
— Microwave on high for 5 minutes.
— Stir and continue cooking on high for 4 to 5 minutes or until fork-tender.
— Let stand, covered, 3 minutes before serving.

(4-5 servings)

LEMON BROCCOLI

½ cup slivered almonds
1 tablespoon butter or margarine
2 packages (10-oz. each) frozen broccoli spears
1 package (8-oz.) cream cheese
⅓ cup milk
1 teaspoon grated lemon juice
½ teaspoon ground ginger
¼ teaspoon salt

— Combine almonds and butter in small glass bowl.
— Microwave on medium for 3 minutes. Stir and continue cooking on medium 2 to 3 minutes or until almonds are light brown; set aside.
— Place frozen broccoli in 2-quart glass casserole. Cover with glass lid or plastic wrap.
— Microwave on high for 4 to 5 minutes or until broccoli is tender. Cover, and continue cooking on high for 6 to 7 minutes or until tender-crisp.
— Let stand, covered.
— Place cream cheese in 2-cup glass measure, Microwave on low for about 4 minutes or until softened.
— Cream until smooth.
— Stir in remaining ingredients.
— Microwave on medium for 3 to 4 minutes or until hot.
— Place broccoli spears on serving platter and pour sauce over.
— Sprinkle with almonds and serve.

(6-8 servings)

MINTED PEAS

2 tablespoons butter
1 tablespoon chopped mint leaves
1 teaspoon sugar
1 package (10-oz.) frozen peas
½ teaspoon salt

— Place butter in 1-cup measure. Microwave on High until butter melts.
— Stir in mint leaves and sugar.
— Place frozen peas in 1-quart casserole. Sprinkle with salt.
— Pour minted butter over peas.
— Cover.
— Microwave 3 to 5 minutes on High, or
— Stir well to coat with sauce.

(3-4 servings)

BRUSSEL SPROUTS AU GRATIN

2 packages (10-oz. each) frozen brussel sprouts, cooked and drained
½ cup sharp cheese spread
¼ cup butter
¼ cup crushed dry bread crumbs
⅓ cup chopped nuts

— Place hot cooked brussel sprouts in 1 ½-quart casserole. Dot with cheese spread. Set aside.
— Place butter in 1-cup measure. Microwave on high until butter melts.
— Stir in bread crumbs and nuts. Toss to coat. Scatter crumb mixture over brussel sprouts.
— Microwave 30 seconds to 1 minute on high, or until cheese melts.

(6-8 servings)

CANDIED CARROTS

4 large carrots
⅓ cup butter or margarine
½ cup sugar
1 teaspoon salt
⅓ teaspoon cinnamon
1 tablespoon water

— Peel and cut carrots into thin strips.
— Place carrots in a 1 ½-quart casserole.
—Set aside.
— In a small bowl combine remaining ingredients.
— Heat, uncovered, on high 1 minute or until butter is melted.
— Spoon butter-sugar mixture over carrots.
— Heat, covered, on high 7 minutes.
— Spoon sauce over carrots and heat, uncovered, on high an additional 3 minutes.

(4 servings)

GLAZED CARROTS 'N APPLES

4 to 5 medium carrots, sliced
1 tart cooking apple, peeled, cored and chopped
3 tablespoons packed brown sugar
2 tablespoons butter or margarine
2 tablespoons water
¼ teaspoon salt

— Combine all ingredients in 1-quart glass casserole.
— Cover with glass lid or plastic wrap.
— Microwave on high for 5 minutes.
— Stir and continue cooking on high for 3 to 4 minutes or until carrots are tender-crisp.
— Let stand, covered, 3 minutes before serving.

(5-6 servings)

TANGY GLAZED CARROTS

6 carrots
½ cup orange juice
2 tablespoons sugar
½ teaspoon ground cloves
¼ teaspoon salt
½ jar (5-oz.) pineapple cheese spread

— Peel carrots. Slice.
— Cook, covered, in a 1 ½-quart glass dish for 7 minutes on high.
— Combine juice, sugar, cloves, salt, and cheese spread.
— Blend thoroughly. Pour mixture over hot cooked carrots.
— Cook, uncovered, for about 1 ½ minutes, on high until cheese melts and mixture is piping hot.

(5-6 servings)

CHEESE BROCCOLI

2 tablespoons butter or margarine
2 tablespoons all-purpose flour
½ teaspoon salt
1 cup milk
1 ½ cup shredded Cheddar cheese
2 package (10-oz. each) frozen broccoli spears
1 medium tomato, sliced

— Place butter in 2-cup glass measure.
— Microwave on medium for 2 minutes. Stir and continue cooking on high for about 1 minute or until melted. Blend in flour, salt and milk.
— Microwave on high for 1 to 2 minutes or until mixture thickens.
— Stir in cheese until melted.
— Place broccoli on glass serving platter. Cover with plastic wrap.
— Microwave on high for 6 minutes.
— Rearrange spears and continue cooking on high 6 to 8 minutes or until broccoli is tender-crisp.
— Drain well.
— Top with cheese sauce and garnish with tomato slices.
— Microwave on high for 2 to 3 minutes until hot.

(6 to 8 servings)

SPINACH CASSEROLE

2 packages ((10-oz. each) frozen chopped spinach
1 can (10¾-oz.) cream of mushroom soup
1 small onion, finely chopped
2 tablespoons butter

— Place spinach in a 2-quart casserole.
— Cover and cook 6 minutes, or until spinach is defrosted throughout.
— Drain well.
— Stir in soup and onion. Dot with butter.
— Cover and cook 8 minutes, or until hot.

(6-8 servings)

EGGPLANT WITH STUFFING

2 medium eggplants
2 medium onions, chopped
1 tablespoon butter
1 lb. ground beef
1 beef bouillon cube
1 can (8 oz.) tomato sauce
½ teaspoon oregano
2 tablespoons chopped parsley
½ teaspoon salt
¼ teaspoon pepper

— Cut eggplant in half lengthwise.
— Scoop out insides, leaving a shell 1-inch thick.
— Chop pulp into medium size chunks.
— Place onion and butter in a casserole.
— Crumble in beef. Cook, covered, 5 minutes.
— Drain off fat.
— Dissolve bouillon cube in ½ cup hot water. Add to cooked beef with 3 tablespoons tomato sauce and chopped eggplant.
— Microwave, covered, 5 minutes, stirring occasionally.
— Add oregano, parsley, salt and pepper. Fill eggplant halves with mixture.
— Top with bread crumbs and spread remaining sauce over crumbs.
— Place eggplant halves in a glass dish.
— Microwave, uncovered, 8 minutes.

(4 servings)

SPINACH SOUFLE

2 packages (10 oz. each) frozen, chopped spinach
¼ cup butter or margarine
2 cups cooked rice
2 cups shredded cheese
⅔ cup milk
4 eggs
½ cup finely chopped onion
2 tablespoons parsley flakes
1 teaspoon salt
¼ teaspoon thyme
½ teaspoon nutmeg

— Place frozen spinach in 2-quart glass casserole. Cover with glass lid or plastic wrap.
— Microwave on high for 8 to 10 minutes.
— Drain well through sieve.
— Stir in butter until melted.
— Add rice and cheese.
— Combine milk and eggs in 4-cup glass measure.
— Blend in remaining ingredients.
— Stir into spinach mixture until well blended.
— Cover with glass lid or plastic wrap.
— Microwave on medium for 25 minutes or until knife inserted near center comes out clean. Let stand, covered, 5 minutes before serving.

(6-8 servings)

SPINACH DELISH

1 package (10-oz. frozen chopped spinach)
½ cup sour cream
2 tablespoons dry onion soup mix

— Place spinach, icy side up, in 1-quart glass casserole.
— Cover with glass lid or plastic wrap.
— Microwave on high for 4 minutes.
— Stir and continue cooking on high for about 3 minutes or until tender-crisp.
— Stir in sour cream and onion soup mix; recover.
— Microwave on medium for 1 to 2 minutes or until hot.
— Let stand, covered, 2 minutes before serving.

(3-4 servings)

PASTA, RICE AND CEREALS CHART

Item	Pasta, Rice or Cereal—Quantity	Amount Water	Setting #1 And Time	Setting #2 And Time
Macaroni, Spaghetti, or Egg Noodles	2 cups	2½ cups	high 5 to 6 minutes	medium 8 to 9 minutes
Lasagna Noodles	½ lb.	4 cups	high 5 to 6 minutes	medium 8 to 9 minutes
Noodles Romanoff	6¼ oz. pkg.	4 cups	high 5 to 6 minutes	medium 8 to 9 minutes
Short Grain White Rice	1 cup	2 cups	high 4 to 5 minutes	low 15 to 16 minutes
Long Grain White Rice	1 cup	2 cups	high 4 to 5 minutes	low 15 to 18 minutes
White and Wild Rice Mix	6 oz. pkg	2½ cups	high 5 to 6 minutes	low 30 to 35 minutes
Brown Rice	1 cup	3 cups	high 6 to 7 minutes	low 25 to 30 minutes
Wild Rice soaked in water 3 hours	1 cup raw or 2 cups soaked	3 cups	high 6 to 7 minutes	low 50 to 60 minutes
Quick-Cooking Rice	1 cup	1 cup	high 3 to 5 minutes	Rest, covered, 5 minutes or until all water absorbs
Quick-Cooking Cereal, 1 serving	⅓ cup	¾ cup	medium 1 to 1½ minutes	

***high — 100% power : medium — 60% power : low — 30% power.

PASTAS, RICE & CEREALS

PERFECT EGG NOODLES

1 ½ quarts water
1 teaspoon salt
1 teaspoon oil
1 package (8 oz.) egg noodles (approx. 4 cups)

— Pour water into casserole.
— Cover.
— Microwave 5-7 minutes on high until water is boiling.
— Stir in salt, oil and noodles. (Do not cover.)
— Microwave 6-8 minutes on high until tender. Drain. Rinse if desired.

(4-6 servings)

MACARONI SAUTE

½ cup vegetable oil
1 (8-oz.) box or 2 cups uncooked elbow macaroni
½ cup finely chopped onion
½ cup finely chopped green pepper
1 clove garlic, peeled and crushed
1 (20-oz.) can tomato juice
1 teaspoon salt
¼ teaspoon pepper
2 tablespoons Worcestershire sauce

— In a 1 ½-quart casserole, place vegetable oil, macaroni, onion, green pepper and garlic
— Heat, uncovered, on high 5 minutes or until macaroni turns slightly yellow. Stir occasionally. Set aside.
— In a 1-quart measuring cup, heat tomato juice, uncovered, on high for 6 minutes or until tomato juice comes to a boil.
— Add salt, pepper and Worcestershire sauce to tomato juice. Stir to combine.
— Pour tomato juice mixture into macaroni mixture.
— Heat, uncovered, on medium for 15 minutes or until macaroni is tender.

(6 servings)

BAKED ZITI

1 (8-oz.) package ziti, cooked conventionally
Italian Tomato Sauce
¾ cup shredded Mozzarella cheese

— In a deep, 2-quart casserole combine ziti, tomato sauce and ⅓ cup shredded cheese
— Sprinkle remainder of cheese on top of casserole and heat, uncovered, on medium for 7 to 10 minutes or until cheese is melted and sauce is bubbly.

(4 servings)

LASAGNA

1 lb. ground beef
1 teaspoon salt
1 package (1 oz.) spaghetti sauce mix
1 can (16 oz.) tomato sauce
1 can (4 oz.) mushroom stems and pieces, drained
1 package (8 oz.) lasagna noodles, cooked
1 carton (12 oz.) creamed cottage cheese
1 package (6 oz.) sliced Mozzarella cheese
½ cup grated Parmesan cheese

— Crumble ground beef in 2-quart glass baking dish. Cover with glass lid or plastic wrap.
— Microwave on high for 5 minutes
— Drain and stir in salt, spaghetti sauce mix, tomato sauce and mushrooms; mix well.
— Assemble in 2-quart glass baking dish by layers: ⅓ cooked noodles, ⅓ meat mixture, ½ cottage cheese and ½ Mozzarella cheese; repeat layers.
— On third layer of noodles spread last ⅓ of meat mixture and sprinkle with Parmesan cheese. Cover with plastic wrap.
— Microwave on medium for 15 to 18 minutes or until hot in center.
— Let stand, covered, 5 minutes before serving.

(6-8 servings)

MANICOTTI

1 package (8-oz.) manicotti noodles, cooked and drained
1 package (1 lb.) ricotta cheese
½ pound mozzarella cheese, grated
Parmesan cheese
3 tablespoons chopped parsley
3 teaspoons sugar
1 egg, lightly beaten
Salt and pepper to taste
2 sweet Italian sausages
1 clove minced garlic
1 medium minced onion
1 lb. ground beef
1 can (12 oz.) tomatoes, mashed
1 can (16 oz.) tomato sauce
½ teaspoon basil

— Combine ricotta, mozzarella, 3 tablespoons Parmesan cheese, 1 tablespoon parsley, 2 teaspoons sugar, egg, and salt and pepper to taste. Blend well and reserve

— Remove sausage from casings. Crumble into a 2- or 3-quart casserole.

— Add garlic, onion, and 2 tablespoons chopped parsley.

— Microwave, covered, for about 3 minutes on high stirring once during cooking time.

— Crumble ground beef on top of sausage meat and toss lightly. Microwave, covered, for 5 minutes on high, stirring and breaking up meat at least once during cooking time.

— Add tomatoes, tomato sauce, basil, 1 teaspoon sugar, and salt and pepper to taste

— Microwave, covered, for 10 minutes on high, stirring occasionally.

— Pour a thin layer of meat sauce on the bottom of two 2-quart baking dishes or flat casseroles.

— Fill cooked manicotti tubes with cheese mixture. Place 10 filled tubes close together in each casserole. Cover with remaining meat sauce.

— Microwave, covered tightly, for 20 minutes on high.

— Remove cover, sprinkle top of casserole with ¼ cup grated Parmesan.

— Microwave for 2 to 3 minutes on high, or just until cheese is melted.
(This recipe makes 2 casseroles).

(8-10 servings)

GREEN NOODLES

¼ cup butter
¼ cup flour
½ teaspoon salt
¼ teaspoon hot sauce
2½ cups milk
1 cup diced sharp Cheddar cheese
¼ cup grated Parmesan cheese
3 cups cooked green noodles
3 hard-cooked eggs, halved

— Put butter in a 1½-quart casserole.

— Microwave, covered, for 1 minute on high, or until butter is melted.

— Remove and stir in flour, salt, and hot sauce to make a smooth paste.

— Microwave for 1 minute on high.

— Gradually stir in milk.

— Microwave, covered, for 5 to 6 minutes on high stirring occasionally during last half of cooking time.

— Remove and stir briskly to make a smooth sauce.

— Add Cheddar cheese and Parmesan cheese and stir until cheese is melted.

— Add noodles and toss until well coated.

— Microwave, covered, for 5 minutes on high.

— Top with egg halves.

— Microwave, covered, for 3 minutes on high. or until piping hot.

(6 servings)

NOODLES ROMANOFF

3 cups cooked egg noodles
1 cup cottage cheese
1 cup sour cream
¼ cup finely chopped onion
1 clove garlic, peeled and crushed
1½ teaspoon Worcestershire sauce
Few drops Tabasco sauce
½ teaspoon salt
½ cup grated sharp Cheddar cheese

— Combine all of the ingredients except the Cheddar cheese in a greased (8x8-inch) square baking dish.

— Sprinkle the grated cheese over the top and cook, uncovered, for 14-16 minutes on high. until cheese melts.

(6 servings)

MACARONI, SPAGHETTI OR NOODLES

4 cups hot water
2 cups macaroni, noodles, etc.
½ teaspoon salt

— Mix water and salt in deep, 3-quart, heat-resistant, non-metallic casserole.
— Bring water to a boil (approximately 6 to 8 minutes on high power.)
— Add pasta and stir.
— Cook on high 15 minutes or until cooked completely.
— Drain in a colander.

NOODLES ROMANO

1 package (8-oz.) medium noodles, cooked and drained
¼ cup butter
½ cup whipping cream
1 egg yolk, slightly beaten
½ cup freshly grated romano or parmesan cheese
1 tablespoon snipped parsley

— Place butter in 2-cup measure.
— Microwave on high 1 minute until butter melts.
— Stir in cream.
— Microwave 1 minute on high, or until cream is warm.
— Stir a little of the cream mixture in beaten egg yolk, stirring with fork. Pour hot egg mixture into cream mixture and blend well.
— Pour sauce over steaming hot noodles.
— Sprinkle with cheese.
— Toss gently to ccat well.
— Garnish with parsley.

(4 servings)

NOODLES ALMONDINE

1 package (7-oz.) egg noodles, cooked and drained
3 tablespoons butter
¼ cup slivered almonds

— Place noodles in 1-quart casserole.
— Combine butter with almonds in 1-cup measure.
— Microwave 5 minutes on high, or until almonds are golden, stirring once.
— Pour over noodles.
— Microwave 3 minutes on high, or until butter is bubbly and noodles are hot.

(6-8 servings)

POLENTA

1 recipe Cornmeal Mush
1 cup grated sharp Cheddar cheese
⅛ teaspoon paprika
Cayenne pepper

— Add cheese, paprika, sprinkle of cayenne pepper to cooked cornmeal mush.
— Heat on medium for 2 minutes; let stand, covered, 5 minutes.
— Pour mixture into a (8x8-inch) square cake dish.
— Cover closely with wax paper. Chill.
— Cut Polenta into slices.
— Coat each slice lightly with flour.
— Saute slowly in hot bacon drippings or oil.
— Serve with syrup if desired.

(6 servings)

PRE-COOKED RICE

1 teaspoon salt
1¼ cups water
1¼ cups pre-cooked rice

— Combine water, rice and salt in a 2-quart casserole.
— Heat, covered, on high 4 minutes, or until water boils.
— Allow to stand 6 to 8 minutes before serving.

(3-4 servings)

FRIED RICE

2 tablespoons chopped onion
2 tablespoons butter
2 cups pre-cooked rice
1⅔ cups water
2 beef bouillon cubes
½ teaspoon salt
Dash pepper
2 eggs, slightly beaten
¼ cup green onion, chopped
2 teaspoons soy sauce

— Saute 2 tablespoons chopped onion in butter on high for 2 minutes, using a 2-quart casserole.
— Add rice, bouillon cubes, salt and pepper.
— Bring to a rolling boil on high 5 minutes. Stir well, cover, and cook on high 2 additional minutes.
— Stir and let stand, covered, 5 minutes until water is absorbed.
— Add eggs and chopped green onion.
— Heat on medium for 2½ minutes, stirring several times until edges are set.
— Stir in soy sauce.

(4-5 servings)

INSTANT OATMEAL

Individual package instant oatmeal
Water as called for on package directions

— Pour oatmeal into a 10-ounce bowl. Add water and stir to combine.
— Heat, covered, on high for 1 ½ minutes or until water boils.
— Stir and heat, covered, an additional 1 minute on high.
— Let stand 3 to 5 minutes to finish cooking.

(1 serving)

INSTANT CREAM OF WHEAT

1 package instant cream of wheat. Water as called for on package directions.

— Pour water into a 10-oz. bowl.
— Add 1 package of instant cream of wheat.
— Heat, covered, on high 1 ½ minutes.
— Let stand 2 minutes.

(1 serving)

OATMEAL

1 ½ cups hot water
½ teaspoon salt
⅔ cups oats

— Place water and salt into a deep, 2-quart casserole. (Be sure to use a large container as oatmeal increases in volume substantially.
— Heat, uncovered, on high for 3 ½ minutes or until boiling.
— Add oats and cook on high for 3 ½ minutes.
— Cover and let stand for a few minutes before serving.

(2 servings)

QUICK SHRIMP RICE

3 cups hot cooked rice
1 can (8-oz.) small cooked shrimp
1 can (6-oz.) water chestnuts, sliced
½ cup finely chopped onion
½ cup chopped celery
⅓ cup butter, cut in bits
¼ cup dry sherry
1 clove garlic, pressed or finely chopped
½ teaspoon salt

— Combine all ingredients in a 1 ½-quart casserole. Mix well.
— Cover.
— Microwave 4 minutes on high, or until heated through, stirring after 2 minutes.

(4-6 servings)

MACARONI AND CHEESE

1 ½ cups cooked macaroni
2 tablespoons butter
2 tablespoons flour
¼ teaspoon salt
½ teaspoon Worcestershire sauce
½ teaspoon prepared mustard
Freshly ground pepper to taste
1 cup milk
2 cups shredded sharp Cheddar cheese
¼ cup cracker crumbs
Tomato slices (optional)

— Melt butter in a 2-quart casserole for 30 seconds on high.
— Stir in flour, salt, Worcestershire, mustard, and pepper. Microwave, uncovered, for 30 seconds on high.
— Gradually stir in milk.
— Microwave, uncovered, for 2 ½ to 3 minutes on high, stirring occasionally during last half of cooking time.
— Stir in 1 ½ cups shredded cheese and continue stirring until cheese is melted. If cheese is not melted, cook for an additional 30 seconds, on high or just until cheese is melted.
— Stir cooked macaroni into sauce.
— Top with remaining cheese and cracker crumbs, and with tomato slices if desired.
— Microwave, uncovered, for 3 to 4 minutes on high, or until cheese is melted and macaroni is piping hot.
— Let stand about 4 minutes before serving.

(4 servings)

WILD RICE CASSEROLE

1 package (12 oz.) frozen white and wild rice
4 ounces mushrooms, chopped
1 medium onion, chopped
2 tablespoons butter or margarine

— Place pouch of rice in oven. Microwave 5 minutes on high, or until hot, flexing pouch after 3 minutes. Set aside.
— Combine mushrooms, onions and butter in casserole with butter on top. Microwave 2 minutes, 30 seconds to 3 minutes on high, stirring after 1 minute.
— Add rice to mushroom mixture. If necesary, Microwave 30 seconds on high to warm.

(4-6 servings)

RICE VERDE

¼ cup butter or margarine
1 small onion, finely chopped
1 cup hot cooked rice
1 package (10-oz) chopped spinach, defrosted
1 cup milk
1 egg, slightly beaten
½ teaspoon salt
1 cup grated cheddar cheese

— Combine butter and onion in 1½-quart casserole. Microwave 2 to 3 minutes on high, or until onion is transparent.
— Stir in rice, spinach, milk, beaten egg, salt and cheddar cheese, mixing well with fork.
— Cover.
— Microwave 4 to 6 minutes on high, or until mixture is hot and cheese is melted.

(3-4 servings)

RICE PILAF

¼ cup butter
¾ cup chopped onion
1 cup chopped celery
1 envelope (1¾ oz.) chicken noodle soup mix
2½ cups water
½ teaspoon salt
¼ teaspoon pepper
¼ teaspoon ground sage
¼ teaspoon ground thyme
1 cup long grain white rice

— Combine butter, onion and celery in 2-quart glass casserole.
— Microwave on medium for 5 minutes or until onions and celery are partly cooked.
— Stir in remaining ingredients, except rice; mix well. Cover with glass lid or plastic wrap.
— Microwave on high for 5 to 6 minutes or until boiling. Stir in rice; recover.
— Microwave on low for 15-18 minutes or until rice is tender. Let stand, covered, 5 minutes before serving.

(5-6 servings)

LONG GRAIN RICE

2½ cups water
1 teaspoon salt
1 teaspoon butter
1 cup long grain rice

— Combine all ingredients in 2-quart casserole. Stir. Cover.
— Microwave 5 minutes on high.
— Microwave 10 to 12 minutes on medium, or until rice is tender and water is absorbed.

(4-6 servings)

CAKE MIX COOKING GUIDE

Type of Cake	Package Size	Container Size	Setting #1 and Time	Setting #2 and Time
Yellow or White Cake Mix	1 lb. 2½ oz.	9-inch round	medium 6 minutes	high 3 to 4 minutes
		3-quart (13 x 9) baking dish	medium 9 minutes	high 6 to 7 minutes
Chocolate Cake Mix	1 lb. 2½ oz.	9-inch round	medium 6 minutes	high 6 to 7 minutes
Bundt Cake Mix	26¼ oz.	10 cup non-metalic bundt cake dish	medium 9 minutes	high 6 to 7 minutes
Snacking Cake	15½ oz.	9-inch round	medium 6 minutes	high 3 to 4 minutes
Gingerbread Mix	15 oz.	2-quart (8 x 8-inch) baking dish	medium 6 minutes	high 3 to 4 minutes
Cupcakes From Mix		Paper cupcake		
2		liners	medium 2 to 2½ minutes	
4			medium 3 to 3½ minutes	
6			medium 4 to 4½ minutes	

***high — 100% power : medium — 60% power : low — 30% power.

DESSERTS

COOKING HINTS

Cake baking can be more creative than ever in your Microwave Oven. You can bake cakes in dessert dishes, mixing bowls or even ice cream cones. Microwave baked cakes will not fall even if the oven door is opened. White and yellow cakes will not brown as in conventional cooking; however, because they are usually frosted, there is no noticeable difference. Cake batter may be prepared in advance and refrigerated or frozen. You may want to cook one layer and keep another in the freezer for unexpected company.

The simplest and easiest way to prepare cake pans, line the bottom of each pan with waxed paper. You will not need to grease the pan if this method is used. You may also use the conventional method of preparing your cake pans by lightly greasing the bottom and sides of the dish with vegetable shortening and lightly dust with flour.

Cake dishes should not be filled over half full. Microwave baked cakes increase substantially in volume and the texture is somewhat lighter than conventionally baked cakes. Save extra batter and use for cupcakes.

Bake one layer at a time and allow each to cool no longer than 5 minutes before removing from pan, unless otherwise noted in receipe.

Overcooked cakes will be dry and slightly hard or tough. It is always better to undercook and check for doneness frequently toward the end of the cooking period.

If you desire a cake with a heavier texture, place plastic wrap over the top of the cake batter.

Cake may be warmed or leftover cake may be freshened by heating in the Microwave Oven on medium for a few seconds.

Most cakes are less porous in texture and give best results when cooked at about 70% power. Thus, many receipes in this section recommend baking on medium.

Commercially frozen layer cakes may be defrosted on low. A 17-ounce cake defrosts in 1 minute, 15 seconds on low.

Pies of all types can also be made in your Microwave Oven. The cooking time of fruit fillings may vary according to the ripeness and amount of fruit used. Test the fruit with a fork to determine doneness. To recapture that just from the oven taste, reheat individual slices of pie on high for 30 seconds per slice. Pie a la mode can even be made in your Microwave Oven by placing a hard scoop of ice cream on a piece of pie and heating it on high for 45 seconds. The pie will be hot and the ice cream will be just the right consistency.

SNACK CAKE MIX

1 (14 1/2-ounce) package snack cake mix
ingredients as called for on package

— In either an 8-inch square glass cake dish or a 9-inch round glass cake pan, prepare mix according to package directions.
— Heat, uncovered, on high 8 to 9 minutes or until cake begins to pull away from the edges of the pan and a toothpick inserted in the center comes out clean.
— Allow to cool. Serve from baking dish.

STREUSEL COFFEE CAKE

1 package (14 1/2-ounces) streusel coffee cake mix

— Prepare coffee cake as directed on package.
— Pour all the batter into (8 x 8-inch) baking dish.
— Sprinkle all streusel topping on top. Microwave 8 to 10 minutes on medium or until wooden pick inserted in center comes out clean, rotating dish once one half turn.
— Let stand 5 minutes.

(9 servings)

FEINBERG SPICE CAKE

2 eggs
1 cup sugar
2 tablespoons molasses
2 cups sifted all-purpose flour
1 teaspoon ground cinnamon
1 teaspoon ground cloves
½ teaspoon ground allspice
¼ teaspoon salt
2 teaspoons baking powder
1 teaspoon baking soda
1 cup buttermilk
⅔ cup cooking oil

— Beat eggs until thick and lemon-colored.
— Beat in sugar and molasses until well blended.
— Sift together flour, spices, salt, baking powder, and baking soda.
— Add to egg mixture alternately with buttermilk, mixing well after each addition.
— Stir in oil.
— Pour batter into a lightly greased (12x8x2-inch) baking dish.
— Microwave for 9 minutes on medium.
— Microwave again for 6 minutes on high, or until done, rotating dish every 2 minutes.
— Cake is done when a toothpick inserted in center comes out clean
— Let cool before serving.

(12 servings)

PINEAPPLE UPSIDE DOWN CAKE

¼ cup butter or margarine
½ cup packed brown sugar
6 slices canned pineapple, drained
6 maraschino cherries
1 package (9 oz.) yellow cake mix

— Place butter in 9-inch round glass baking dish.
— Microwave on medium for about 2 minutes or until melted.
— Stir in brown sugar.
— Arrange pineapple on top.
— Place a cherry in center of each pineapple slice.
— Prepare cake mix as directed on package.
— Pour over pineapple.
— Microwave on low for 7 minutes.
— Microwave on high for 3 to 4 minutes or until toothpick inserted near center comes out clean.
— Let stand 1 minute.
— Turn out onto platter and serve warm or cool.

(4-6 servings)

DEVIL'S FOOD CAKE

2 cups sifted all-purpose flour
1¼ teaspoons baking soda
¼ teaspoon salt
½ cup shortening
2 cups sugar
½ cup cocoa
1 teaspoon vanilla extract
½ cup buttermilk
2 eggs lightly beaten

— Line the bottoms of two 9-inch round glass cake pans with waxed paper.
— Sift together flour, baking soda, and salt; set aside.
— Cream together shortening, Sugar, cocoa, and vanilla until light and fluffy.
— Measure 1 cup water in a 2-cup measing cup
— Microwave for about 2½ minutes, or until water comes to a boil.
— Let stand.
— Stir boiling water, buttermilk, and eggs into creamed mixture and beat well.
— Add sifted dry ingredients all at once and beat well.
— Divide mixture between prepared cake dishes.
— Microwave, uncovered, one layer at a time for about 6 minutes on medium and 3 minutes on high.
— Remove from oven and let stand until cake layers are cool.
— Turn out of dishes and cool thoroughly.
— Repeat cooking procedure for second layer. Frost as desired.

(2 9-inch layers)

KANT BUNDT CAKE MIX

1 (27½-ounce or 23¼-ounce) package bundt cake mix
Ingredients as called for on package

— Lightly grease and flour a 10 cup heat-resistant, non-metallic bundt pan.
— Prepare bundt cake mix according to package directions.
— Pour batter into prepared bundt pan until ⅔ full.
— Microwave, uncovered, on medium for 11 to 12 minutes or until a toothpick inserted comes out clean.
— Allow cake to cool for 5 to 10 minutes before removing from pan.

SPICY APPLESAUCE CAKE

½ cup shortening
2 cups sugar
2 eggs
2 ½ cups flour
1 ½ teaspoons soda
½ teaspoon salt
1 teaspoon baking powder
1 teaspoon cinnamon
¼ teaspoon nutmeg
1 cup raisins
½ cup chopped walnuts
1 ½ cups applesauce
½ cup water
1 teaspoon vanilla

— Cream shortening and sugar together.
— Beat in eggs.
— Add flour, soda, salt, baking powder, cinnamon, cloves, nutmeg, raisins and nuts.
— Stir in applesauce, vanilla and water.
— Place half of the batter into a 9-inch cake dish lined with waxed paper. Microwave 6 ½ to 7 minutes on medium and 2 ½ to 3 minutes on high, or until cake springs back when lightly touched.
— Let cake stand 5 minutes before turning onto cake rack.
— Repeat with second layer.

(2 layer cake)

STRASSLER PUMPKIN PIE

2 eggs, lightly beaten
1 ½ cups solid-pack cooked pumpkin
¾ cup sugar
½ teaspoon salt
teaspoon ground cinnamon
½ teaspoon ground ginger
¼ teaspoon ground cloves
1 can (14 ½ ounces) evaporated milk
1 9-inch baked pastry shell

— Combine eggs, pumpkin, sugar, salt, and spices and blend well.
— Stir in milk and make a smooth mixture.
— Remove ⅔ cup of this mixture and set aside
— Pour remaining mixture into baked pastry shell.
— Cook for 4 minutes on high.
— Stir very carefully to move the cooked portion from edge of pie to the center.
— Microwave for 6 to 8 minutes more on medium, or until a knife inserted near the center comes out clean.
— Let cool before cutting.
— Serve with flavored whipped cream.
(Pour reserved pumpkin mixture into custard cups, filling them three-quarters full. Microwave for about 4 minutes on medium, or until a knife inserted near the center comes out clean.)

BLACK BOTTOM PIE

1 9-inch baked chocolate wafer crumb crust
½ cup sugar
1 tablespoon corn starch
2 cups milk or cream
4 egg yolks, slightly beaten
1 package (6-ounces) semi-sweet chocolate bits
1 teaspoon vanilla
1 tablespoon unflavored gelatin
¼ cup cold water
4 egg whites
½ cup sugar
1 cup whipping cream, whipped
Shaved bitter chocolate

— Combine sugar and corn starch in 2-quart bowl.
—Gradually stir in milk.
— Microwave 6 minutes on high or until slightly thickened, stirring twice with wire whip.
— Stir half the hot mixture into egg yolks.
— Blend warmed yolks into hot mixture. Microwave 1 ½ to 2 ½ minutes on high or until mixture lightly coats a metal spoon, stirring once.
— Pour 1 cup of the hot custard into 1-quart measure.
— Add chocolate bits to custard in measure.
— Stir until chocolate melts.
—Stir in vanilla.
— Pour into baked crumb crust. Chill.
— Soften gelatin in cold water and add to remaining hot custard.
— Stir until gelatin is completely dissolved. Cool.
— Beat egg whites until foamy.
— Gradually beat in sugar.
— Continue beating until stiff peaks form.
— Fold into cooled custard-gelatin mixture.
— Spread over chilled chocolate layer.
— Refrigerate pie until set.
— Top with whipped cream and shaved chocolate just before serving.

(9 inch pie)

VANILLA CREAM PIE

1 9-inch baked pastry shell
¾ cup sugar
3 tablespoons corn starch
Pinch salt
2 cups milk or light cream
3 egg yolks, slightly beaten
2 tablespoons butter
1 teaspoon vanilla
3 egg whites
¼ teaspoon cream of tartar
6 tablespoons sugar

— Combine sugar, corn starch and salt in 2-quart bowl.
— Gradually stir in milk.
— Microwave 6 minutes on high or until thickened, stirring three times with wire whip
— Stir a little of the hot mixture into egg yolk. Blend warmed yolk into hot mixture.
— Microwave 1½ minutes on high, or until custard coats a metal spoon, stirring twice.
— Stir in butter and vanilla until butter melts; cool. Pour into baked pie shell.
— Beat egg whites with cream of tartar until foamy.
— Gradually beat in sugar.
— Continue beating until stiff peaks form
— Gently spread meringue over cream filling, sealing meringue to edges of crust.
— Brown under conventional broiler

Variations:

BANANA CREAM PIE

— Slice 2 ripe bananas into bottom of baked pie shell, or graham cracker crust.
— Pour Vanilla Cream filling over bananas.
— Top with meringue.

CHOCOLATE CREAM PIE

— Follow above recipe, but increase sugar to 1 cup.
— Melt 2 squares (1-ounce each) unsweetened chocolate.
— Add with vanilla.

COCONUT CREAM PIE

— Stir in 1 cup flaked coconut with butter.
— Sprinkle ⅓ cup coconut over meringue before browning.

BUTTERSCOTCH PIE

— Substitute ¾ cup firmly packed brown sugar for granulated sugar.
— Increase butter to ⅓ cup.

DALTON RUM CAKE

1 (18½-ounce) package devil's food cake mix
Ingredients as called for on package label
3 egg whites, at room temperature
¼ teaspoon salt
6 tablespoons sugar
1 cup plus 2 tablespoons light corn syrup
2 teaspoons vanilla extract
Apricot preserves
Rum

— Line two 9-inch round, heat-resistant non-metallic cake pans with waxed paper, set aside.
— Prepare cake mix according to package directions.
— Pour 2⅔ cups of the batter into each prepared pan.
— Bake on medium for 9 minutes.
— Repeat above for second pan.
— Allow cakes to cool in pan for 5 minutes before inverting onto cooling rack.
— While cakes are cooling, prepare frosting.
— In a small mixing bowl, beat egg whites with salt until foamy.
— Add sugar, 1 tablespoon at a time, beating until stiff peaks form.
— Pour corn syrup into a 2-cup measuring cup
— Microwave corn syrup, uncovered, on high 2 minutes or until corn syrup comes to a boil.
— Gradually pour boiling mixture over egg whites, beating constantly until frosting is cool and very stiff.
— Beat in vanilla.
— Pour rum over the tops of both cake layers.
— Spread apricot preserves over one of the cooled layers, then spread some of the frosting on it.
— Place second layer on top of first layer and spread entire cake with frosting.

(8 servings)

PACKAGED CAKE MIX

1 (17 to 18½-ounce) package cake mix
Ingredients as called for on package

— Line the bottom of two 9-inch round glass cake pans with waxed paper.
— Prepare cake mix according to package directions.
— Pour 2⅔ cup batter into each prepared cake pan.
— Cook one layer at a time, uncovered, on medium for 9 to 10 minutes or until toothpick inserted in center comes out clean.
— Allow cake to cool for 5 minutes before removing from pan.

WAIKIKI PINEAPPLE PIE

9-inch baked pastry shell
1 tablespoon flour
1 can (15 ½-ounces) crushed pineapple and juice
3 tablespoons corn starch
2 tablespoons sugar
1 tablespoon grated lemon rind
1 tablespoon lemon juice
¼ teaspoon salt
1 tablespoon butter

— Dust baked pie shall with flour. Set aside.
— Combine pineapple and juice in 1 ½-quart bowl.
— Microwave 4 minutes on high, or until mixture is hot.
— Add corn starch, sugar, lemon rind, lemon juice and salt.
— Microwave 3 minutes on high, or until mixture thickens, stirring every minute.
— Stir in butter.
— Let stand 15 minutes.
— Pour into baked pie shell.

(6-8 servings)

PALKO'S PECAN PIE

1 9-inch baked pastry shell
3 eggs, slightly beaten
⅔ cup sugar
½ teaspoon salt
⅓ cup butter or margarine, melted
1 cup light corn syrup
1 cup pecan halves

— Beat eggs, sugar, salt, butter and corn syrup in medium bowl using a rotary beater.
— Stir in pecan halves.
— Pour into 9-inch baked pastry shell. Microwave 6 to 7 minutes on medium, or until filling is set,, rotating dish ½ turn after 3 minutes.
— Let cool.
— Garnish with whipped cream if desired.

(9 inch pie)

MIXED FRUIT AMBROSIA

½ cup flaked coconut
2 tablespoons graham cracker crumbs
1 can (20 oz.) pineapple chunks, drained
1 can (16 oz.) sliced peaches, drained
1 can (11 oz.) mandarin oranges, drained
6 maraschino cherries, halved

— Combine all ingredients in 2-quart glass casserole; mix well.
— Microwave on low for 6 to 7 minutes or until hot.

(6-8 servings)

CREME DE MENTHE PIE

⅓ cup butter
1 ½ cups chocolate cookie crumbs (about 24 cookies yield 1 ½ cups)
½ cup sugar
3 cups miniature marshmallows
½ cup milk or light cream
3 tablespoons while creme de cocoa
3 tablespoons green creme de menthe
1 cup chilled heavy cream, whipped
Chocolate curls

— In a 9-inch pie pan, melt butter on high 1 minute.
— Combine cookie crumbs and sugar in a small bowl until well blended.
— Stir cookie mixture into butter.
— Press mixture onto bottom and sides of pie pan.
— Cook, uncovered, on medium for 3 minutes or until crust has a crunchy texture.
— Allow to cool while preparing filling.
— In a large bowl, combine marshmallows and milk.
— Microwave, uncovered, on medium for 3 minutes or until marshmallows begin to puff.
—Stir to blend.
— If not completely melted, return to Microwave Oven and heat on medium an additional 30 seconds.
— Stir in creme de cocoa and creme de menthe.
— Chill until thickened but not set, about 20 minutes.
— Fold in whipped cream.
— Pour mixture into crust.
— Refrigerate at least 4 hours.
— Serve garnished with chocolate curls.

(8 servings)

MONA'S GINGER PEARS

6 canned Bartlett pear halves, drained
¼ teaspoon ginger
¼ teaspoon nutmeg
¼ teaspoon cinnamon
2 tablespoons butter or margarine
2 tablespoons sugar

— Arrange pears in a single layer, cut sides up, in a 1-quart casserole.
— Combine ginger, nutmeg and cinnamon.
— Sprinkle over pears.
— Cream butter and sugar together.
— Divide evenly between pears, placing mixture in cavities.
— Microwave 2 minutes on high, or until butter is melted and pears hot.
— Garnish with whipped cream and maraschino cherries, if desired.

(6 servings)

BOSTON CREAM PIE

⅓ cup sugar
2 tablespoons flour
1 egg, well-beaten
¾ cup milk
1 tablespoon rum
½ cup light corn syrup
1 (6-ounce) package semi-sweet chocolate pieces
1 tablespoon butter
¼ cup half and half or milk
¼ teaspoon vanilla extract
1 (18½-ounce) package yellow cake mix
Ingredients as called for on package label

— Sift together sugar and flour into a medium-sized bowl.
— Add well-beaten egg, ¾ cup milk and rum.
— Mix thoroughly using an egg beater or hand mixer.
— Cook, uncovered, on medium for 3 minutes.
— Stir.
— Cook on medium an additional 1 minute. stirring once.
— Place in refrigerator to chill.
— In a 1-quart measuring cup, combine corn syrup, chocolate pieces and butter.
— Cook, uncovered, on medium for 2 minutes.
— Stir. If chocolate is not completely melted, heat on medium an additional 30 seconds.
— Gradually stir in half and half and vanilla.
— Blend well.
— Cook, uncovered, on medium for 2 minutes.
— Chill in refrigerator.
— While custard and topping are cooling, prepare cake mix according to package directions.
— Line bottoms of two 9-inch round, glass cake pans with waxed paper. Pour 2⅔ cups batter into each prepared cake pan.
— Bake one layer at a time on medium for 9 to 10 minutes or until toothpick inserted in center comes out clean.
— Allow cake to cool for 5 minutes then invert onto cooling rack.
— Peel off waxed paper.
— When cake has cooled, place one layer on serving plate. Spread chilled custard on top.
— Place other layer on top of custard and spread chilled chocolate sauce over top and let drizzle down sides.
— Chill in refrigerator for 1 hour before serving.

(8 servings)

EASY BOSTON CREAM PIE MIX

1 package Boston cream pie mix

— Prepare pudding in package according to package directions. Set aside.
— Grease the bottom of a 9-inch round cake dish. Place 2 circles of waxed paper on bottom of pan.
— Prepare cake mix according to package directions, reducing liquid by 1 tablespoon.
— Microwave, uncovered, on high for 3½ to 4 minutes, or until cake starts to come away from sides of pan and cake tester comes out clean.
— Cool in pan about 3 minutes. Turn out of pan onto cake cooler and peel off waxed paper.
— Assemble finished cake according to package directions.

CHOCOLATE CHIP DATE NUT BARS

¼ cup boiling water
½ cup chopped dates
½ cup sugar
⅓ cup butter at room temperature
1 egg.
1 cup flour, sifted
¼ teaspoon salt
½ teaspoon baking powder
2 teaspoons unsweetened cocoa
¼ cup sugar
¾ cup semi-sweet chocolate bits
¼ cup nuts

— In a small bowl pour ¼ cup boiling water over chopped dates. Let cool.
— Lightly grease and flour an (8x8-inch) square baking pan. Set aside.
— Cream ½ cup sugar and ⅓ cup butter until light and fluffy.
— Add egg to creamed sugar mixture. Blend well.
— Sift together flour, salt, baking powder and powdered cocoa.
— Add date and flour mixture alternately to creamed butter and sugar mixture.
— Pour batter into prepared pan.
— Smooth top of batter with spatula.
— In small bowl combine ¼ cup sugar, semi-sweet chocolate bits and nuts.
— Sprinkle topping mixture on top of batter and press topping into batter.
— Cook on medium for 7 minutes or until a toothpick inserted in center comes out clean. Let cook in pan 5 minutes.

(8 servings)

APPLE PIE

7 medium cooking apples
3/4 cup sugar
2 tablespoons flour
1/8 teaspoon salt
1 teaspoon cinnamon
1/4 teaspoon nutmeg
1 mixed, uncooked pie crust (rolled into 2 layers)
1 to 2 teaspoons lemon juice
2 tablespoons butter

— Pare and slice apples. Mix in a bowl with sugar, flour, salt, cinnamon, and nutmeg; set aside.
— Fit one pie crust layer in the bottom of a 9-inch pie dish.
— Put apples in pie crust..
— Sprinkle lemon juice over top if apples are not too tart. Dot with butter.
— Put the remaining pie crust layer over apples. Seal edges and cut slits in top of pie
— Microwave, uncovered, for about 10 minutes, on high or until apples are tender.
— While apples are cooking, preheat conventional oven to 450°.
— When apples are tender, bake pie in conventional oven 12 to 14 minutes, or until crust is golden brown.
— Serve warm or cold.

BROWNIES

2 squares or envelopes unsweetened chocolate
1/3 cup butter
1 cup sugar
2 eggs
1 cup unsifted flour
1/4 teaspoon baking powder
1/4 teaspoon salt
1/2 teaspoon vanilla
1/2 cup chopped nuts

— Combine chocolate and butter in medium glass mixing bowl.
— Microwave on medium for 1 1/2 to 2 minutes or until melted.
— Stir in sugar; beat in eggs.
— Stir in remaining ingredients. Spread batter into 2-quart glass baking dish.
— Microwave on low for 7 minutes.
— Microwave on high for 3 to 4 minutes or until puffed and dry on top.
— Cool until set; cut into bars.

(24 bars)

LEMON MERINGUE PIE

1 9-inch baked pastry shell or graham cracker crust
1 1/2 cups sugar
1/3 cup corn starch
1 1/2 cups boiling water
3 egg yolks, slightly beaten
3 tablespoons butter
1 tablespoon grated lemon rind
3 tablespoons lemon juice
3 egg whites
1/4 teaspoon cream of tartar
6 tablespoons sugar

— Combine sugar, corn starch and boiling water in a 1 quart measure.
— Microwave 3 to 4 minutes on high, or until thick and clear, stirring once.
— Stir a little of the mixture into egg yolks.
— Add warmed yolks to hot filling.
— Microwave 1 minute on high.
— Add butter, lemon rind and lemon juice. Cool.
— Pour into baked pie shell.
— Beat egg whites with cream of tartar until foamy.
— Gradually beat in sugar.
— Continue beating until stiff peaks form.
— Gently spread meringue over lemon filling, sealing meringue to edges of crust.
— Brown in conventional broiler.

CUPCAKES

1 package (8-oz.) yellow cake mix

— Place paper liners in 8 custard cups.
— Prepare cake mix according to package directions, reducing liquid by 1 tablespoon.
— Pour mixture into lined custard cups.
— Place 4 cupcakes at a time in the oven, spaced about 1 inch apart. (Eight is too many and will not bake properly.)
— Microwave, uncovered, on high for 2 to 2 1/2 minutes, rotating once.
— Remove from oven and let stand; allow tops to dry out slightly.
— Frost as desired.

Variation:
— Lightly grease the bottoms of 6 custard cups. Pour batter into cups.
— Microwave, uncovered, on high for 2 1/2 to 3 minutes.
— Remove from oven. Let stand 2 minutes.
— Turn cupcakes out and let cool upside down.
— Frost in this position.

(8 cupcakes)

APRICOT CHEESECAKE

¼ cup butter
⅔ cup graham cracker crumbs (about 12 crackers)
2 tablespoons flour
2 tablespoons sugar
¼ teaspoon cinnamon
1 package cream cheese
1 can (16 oz.) apricot halves
⅓ cup sugar
2 eggs
1 tablespoon lemon juice
1 can (16 oz.) apricot halves
1 envelope unflavored gelatin

— Place butter in 9-inch round glass baking dish.
— Microwave on medium for about 1½ minutes or unti melted.
— Stir in cracker crumbs, flour, sugar and cinnamon.
— Press mixture over bottom and halfway up sides of dish; set aside.
— Place cream cheese in medium glass mixing bowl.
— Microwave on low for 3 to 5 minutes or until cheese is softened; beat until light and fluffy.
— Drain 1 can apricots and reserve juice.
— Puree apricot halves in blender or food mill.
— Stir into cream cheese along with sugar, eggs and lemon juice; beat until smooth.
— Pour into prepared crust.
— Microwave on medium setting for 23 to 25 minutes or until almost set in center. Chill 1 hour.
— Drain second can of apricots and reserve juice. Arrange apricots on cheesecake.
— Pour gelatin and apricot juice from both cans in 4-cup glass measure; let stand 5 minutes.
— Microwave on high for 3 to 3½ minutes or until gelatin is dissolved; stir.
— Chill until consistency of unbeaten egg white, about 30 minutes.
— Spoon over cheesecake.
— Refrigerate about 4 hours before serving.

(10-12 servings)

LAYERED CREAM TORTE

1 box (11¼ oz.) frozen baked pound cake, thawed
2 packages ((3 oz. each) cream cheese
½ cup strawberry preserves
2 tablespoons sliced almonds

— Split cake in thirds horizontally.
— Place on glass platter; set aside.
— Place cream cheese in 2-cup glass measure.
— Microwave on low for 3 to 3½ minutes or until softened.
— Beat cheese until smooth. Spread between cake layer and place one on top of the other.
— Spread jam over top of cake.
— Microwave on medium for 2 or 3 minutes or until heated through. Sprinkle with almonds and serve.

(6-8 servings)

PUMPKIN NUT TORTE

1 cup flour
¼ cup brown sugar, packed
½ cup chopped walnuts
1 package (3-oz.) cream cheese
1 egg
1 can (1-lb.) pumpkin
1 can (14-oz.) sweetened condensed milk
1 teaspoon pumpkin pie spice
½ teaspoon salt
1 cup hot water
Whipped cream

— Combine flour and sugar.
— Add butter and using pastry blender or fork, work mixture until it resembles coarse meal, add nuts.
— Press firmly in an even layer oven bottom of an 8x8 inch square baking dish.
— Microwave, uncovered, on high 4 minutes and set aside.
— Meanwhile soften cream cheese in a medium size glass bowl, (Microwave 45 seconds on high or until softened).
— Beat in egg.
— Add pumpkin, condensed milk, spice and salt. Beat until smooth.
— Stir in hot water.
— Pour into a baked nut crust.
— Microwave 20 minutes on high, or until filling is barely set in center.
— Cool thoroughly before serving.
— Garnish each piece with whipped cream.

BANANAS FOSTER

2 tablespoons butter or margarine
2 large bananas, quartered
2 tablespoons brown sugar
2 tablespoons banana or orange liqueur
2 tablespoons rum

— Place butter in 1-quart casserole.
— Microwave on high until butter melts.
— Roll bananas in butter.
— Mix brown sugar and cinnamon together.
— Sprinkle over bananas.
— Microwave 2 minutes, 30 seconds to 3 minutes on high, or until sugar begins to melt.
— Remove from oven.
— Pour liqueur and rum over hot bananas. Ignite.
— When flame dies down serve bananas and sauce on ice cream or a thin slice of pound cake.

STRAWBERRY MACAROON TORTE

½ cup butter
1 package (13-oz.) coconut macaroon mix
1 package yellow cake mix
Strawberry cream filling

— Melt butter in a medium size glass bowl.
— Microwave 2 to 3 minutes on high or until dissolved.
— Blend butter with macaroon mix.
— Press one quarter of mixture firmly and evenly in bottom of a 9-inch cake dish. Set remaining mixture aside.
— Prepare cake mix according to package instructions.
— Pour half the batter over macaroon mixture in a cake dish.
— Sprinkle one quarter of macaroon mixture evenly over batter, making sure it goes all the way to the edge.
— Microwave 4 to 4½ minutes on high, or until a wooden pick in the center comes out clean.
— Turn out on cake rack and cool.
— Repeat procedure for the second layer.
— Place one layer on serving dish, and spread a layer of strawberry cream filling on top of it.
— Put the second layer of cake on top and put the remaining filling on top.

(8 servings)

QUICK PEACH DELIGHT

4 large canned peach halves
1¼ teaspoons butter or margarine
4 teaspoons brown sugar
Vanilla ice cream

— Drain peaches thoroughly.
— Place in a 1-quart glass baking dish.
— Put ¼ teaspoon butter in center of each peach.
— Sprinkle 1 teaspoon brown sugar on each peach half.
— Bake, uncovered, on high for 3 minutes, or until piping hot.
— Serve warm with a small scoop of ice cream in center of each peach half.

(4 servings)

BRANDIED PEACHES

1 (29-oz.) can peach halves, undrained
⅔ cup pineapple preserves
⅓ cup brandy
1 teaspoon lemon juice
¼ cup toasted coconut

— Drain peach halves and reserve ½ cup syrup
— In a small bowl, combine reserved syrup, pineapple preserves, brandy and lemon juice
— Arrange peaches in a shallow, glass baking dish.
— Pour sauce over peaches. Sprinkle with coconut.
— Cook, uncovered, on high 4 to 5 minutes.
— Serve either warm or chilled.

(4 servings)

BLUEBERRY BUCKLE

¾ cup sugar
¼ cup soft shortening
1 egg
½ cup milk
1 ½ cups all-purpose flour, sifted
2 teaspoons baking powder
½ teaspoon salt
2 cups blueberries, drained
1 cup firmly packed dark brown sugar
1 teaspoon ground cinnamon
½ cup soft butter

— In a large mixing bowl, mix sugar, shortening and egg thoroughly.
— Stir in milk.
— Blend in dry ingredients.
— Fold in blueberries.
— Allow batter to stand 15 minutes.
— Lightly grease and flour an (8x8-inch) square glass baking dish. Pour batter into baking dish.
— In a smal bowl combine remaining ingredients until well blended. Sprinkle topping mixture on top of batter.
— Microwave, uncovered, on medium for 15 minutes or until toothpick inserted in center comes out clean.

(8-10 servings)

TAPIOCA PUDDING

2 egg yolks
3 tablespoons sugar
⅛ teaspoon salt
2 cups milk
3 tablespoons minute tapioca
2 egg whites
2 tablespoons sugar
1 teaspoon vanilla

— Combine egg yolks, 3 tablespoons sugar, salt, milk and tapioca in a 1 ½ quart casserole.
— Let stand a few minutes to soften tapioca.
— Beat egg whites in a 2 quart bowl until foamy. Gradually beat in sugar and vanilla.
— Continue beating until egg whites hold soft peaks and set aside.
— Place tapioca mixture in microwave and cook 5 ½ minutes or until mixture bubbles.
— Take tapioca out of oven and put beaten egg white mixture on top. Chill until cooled, about 1 hour.

(4-6 servings)

RICE PUDDING

1 cup cooked rice
2 cups milk
2 eggs, beaten
½ cup sugar
⅛ teaspoon salt
½ cup raisins
¼ teaspoon cinnamon
½ teaspoon vanilla

— Heat milk in a 1-quart measure, cooking 2 to 3 minutes on high, or until almost boiling.
— Combine eggs, sugar and salt in a 2 quart casserole.
— Stir in scalded milk.
— Mix with rice, raisins, cinnamon and vanilla.
— Microwave 6 to 8 minutes on low power, or until set.

(4 servings)

LEMON SOUFFLE

½ cup sugar
1 tablespoon unflavored gelatin
¼ teaspoon salt
1 cup water
3 eggs, separated
1 tablespoon grated lemon peel
4 tablespoons lemon juice
⅓ cup sugar
1 cup cream, whipped

— Mix ½ cup sugar, gelatin, salt and water in 4-cup measure.
— Separate eggs, placing whites in a mixing bowl and adding yolks to gelatin mixture.
— Beat in yolks until blended well.
— Microwave, uncovered, on high 3 minutes or until mixture just begins to boil, stirring occasionally.
— Stir in lemon peel and juice.
— Cool until mixture thickens.
— Beat egg whites well until foamy.
— Beat in ⅓ cup sugar until mixture forms stiff peaks.
— Fold in lemon mixture and whipped cream.
— Pour into a 4-cup glass or ceramic souffle.
— Refrigerate at least 5 hours.
— Remove wax paper from souffle dish before serving.
— Spoon into individual serving dishes and top with whipped cream.
— Cointreau or other liqueur may be added before serving.

(6 servings)

STRAWBERRY SOUFFLE

2 pints fresh strawberries, washed and hulled
2 envelopes unflavored gelatine
¼ cup water
⅔ cup sugar
4 egg yolks, well beaten
⅛ teaspoon salt
1 tablespoon lemon juice
4 egg whites, at room temperature
½ cup sugar
1 cup heavy cream, chilled and whipped
2 to 3 drops red food coloring (optional)
Sweetened whipped cream (optional)

— Puree strawberries in an electric blender or press through a sieve or food mill.
— In a 1-quart measuring cup, combine 1 cup of strawberry puree, gelatine, water, the ½ cup sugar, egg yolk and salt.
— Stir to combine.
— Microwave, uncovered, on medium for 4 minutes or until mixture just begins to boil. Stir frequently.
— Cool mixture slightly.
— Add remaining strawberries and lemon juice.
— Chill mixture until it is consistency of unbeaten egg whites.
— While mixture is chilling, beat egg whites in a large bowl until stiff peaks form.
— Add the ½ cup sugar, 1 tablespoon at a time, beating constantly until egg whites are stiff and glossy.
— Fold whipped cream and chilled berry mixture into egg whites. Add food coloring until desired color is reached.
— Pour mixture in a 2-quart mold.
— Chill at least 3 to 4 hours to set.
— Unmold, if desired.
— Garnish with whipped cream, if desired.

(6-8 servings)

DRIED FRUIT COMPOTE IN SHERRY

1 cup dried apricots
1 cup dried prunes
1½ cups water
½ cup cream sherry
½ teaspoon cloves

— Place fruit in a 2 quart casserole.
— Add sugar, water, sherry and spices. Stir.
— Cover and cook 15 to 20 minutes on high or until fruit is tender and flavors have married.
— Let stand 10 minutes.
— This is excellent served over pound cake, or spooned over vanilla ice cream, or over waffles or pancakes.

(6 servings)

WINSLOW EGG CUSTARD

1 tablespoon unflavored gelatin
⅔ cup sugar
Dash of salt
2 cups milk
4 eggs
2 tablespoons orange flavored liqueur
1 tablespoon brandy
2 cups whipped cream

— Mix gelatin, sugar, salt, milk and eggs in a casserole.
— Beat well until blended. Make a few slits in top of mixture.
— Microwave, covered, 5 minutes on high or until mixture bubbles, stirring occasionally
— Cool until mixture thickens.
— Add orange flavored liqueur and brandy and fold in whipped cream.
— Pour into 8-cup jello mold. Chill in the refrigerator until set.
— Unmold and serve.

(8 servings)

AUTHENTIC INDIAN PUDDING

2 cups milk
¼ cup yellow cornmeal
2 tablespoons sugar
½ teaspoon salt
½ teaspoon cinnamon
¼ teaspoon ginger
1 egg, beaten
¼ cup molasses
1 tablespoon melted butter
Vanilla ice cream

— Pour 1½ cups milk into a 1½-quart casserole. Heat for 3½ minutes on high.
— Combine cornmeal, sugar, salt, cinnamon, and ginger. Stir into hot milk.
— Microwave, uncovered, on high for about 2 minutes, stirring at least once during cooking time.
— Beat together egg, molasses, and butter. Stir a small amount of hot milk mixture into egg mixture. Return to casserole. Stir well.
— Microwave, uncoverd, on high for 4 minutes. stirring every 2 minutes.
— Pour remaining ½ cup cold milk carefully over top of pudding. Do not stir. Microwave, uncovered, for 3 minutes on high, or until set.
— Let stand 10 to 15 minutes before serving.
— Serve warm topped with vanilla ice cream.

(4-6 servings)

BAKED CUSTARD

1 3/4 cup milk
1/4 cup sugar
3 eggs
1/4 teaspoon salt
1/2 teaspoon vanilla
Nutmeg

— Combine all ingredients, except nutmeg, in 4-cup measure.
— Beat well with rotary beater.
— Pour into four 6-oz. glass custard cups, filling each 3/4 full.
— Sprinkle with nutmeg.
— Microwave on low setting for 15 to 16 minutes or until knife inserted near center comes out clean.
— Let stand 5 minutes before serving.

(4 custards)

RHUBARB PUDDING

6 cups diced fresh rhubarb
1 1/4 cups sugar
2 1/2 tablespoons quick-cooking tapioca
1 teaspoon grated lemon peel
1 tablespoon grated orange peel
2 3/4 cups soft bread cubes
1/3 cup butter
1 teaspoon vanilla or lemon extract

— Mix together rhubarb, sugar, tapioca, lemon peel and orange peel in a bowl and set aside
— Place bread cubes in another bowl.
— Melt butter, covered, 30 seconds on high in a measuring cup.
— Pour butter over bread cubes. Add vanilla and mix lightly.
— In a casserole, layer rhubarb and bread-cube mixture alternately, ending with buttered bread cubes on top.
— Microwave, covered, 12 minutes on high, or until rhubarb is cooked. Serve warm or chilled.
— Regular tapioca may be used, cooking first with 1/2 cup water for 5 minutes.

(6 servings)

NEW ENGLAND BAKED APPLES

6 baking apples
Lemon juice
1/2 cup slivered almonds
1/4 cup raisins
1/4 cup brown sugar
2 teaspoons ground cinnamon
6 teaspoons butter

— Remove cores from washed apples, making a large cavity in each apple.
— Peel thin circle around cavity and sprinkle with lemon juice.
— Mix together almonds, raisins, brown sugar and cinnamon.
— Place in cavities and put each apple in a small custard dish with 2 tablespoons of water in dish around apple.
— Dot each apple with 1 teaspoon of butter.
— Microwave for 5 minutes on high. Let stand 2 to 3 minutes and serve.
— Fresh apples may be used, filling centers with butter and sugar and cooking each apple for 3 minutes on high.
— If the above receipe is too sweet, decrease brown sugar to 1 tablespoon.

(6 servings)

CREAMY CARAMEL APPLES

1 package (14 oz.) caramels
2 tablespoons hot water
6 medium apples
6 wooden sticks

— Place unwrapped caramels in buttered deep medium-size glass bowl.
— Add water.
— Cover with plastic wrap.
— Microwave on medium for 3 minutes.
— Stir and continue cooking on medium for about 2 minutes or until melted.
— Skewer each apple with wooden sticks.
— Dip each apple in melted caramel mixture; turn to coat evenly.
— Place dipped apples on buttered cookie sheet or buttered wax paper.

(6 apples)

(If caramel mixture thickens while dipping apples, return to oven and re-soften, covered, on medium. Buttering cookie sheet or wax paper keeps caramel from sticking to cooling surface and pulling off apple.)

BEAUTIFUL BAKED APPLE

1 cooking apple
1 to 1 ½ tablespoons brown sugar
2 teaspoons butter or margarine
Cinnamon

— Peel a rim of apple skin from top of apple.
— Core apple.
— Combine brown sugar and butter.
— Fill cavity with brown sugar mixture.
— Place apple in custard cup.
— Springle cinnamon over cavity and peeled portion of apple.
— Microwave 2 minutes on high, or until apple is almost tender.
— Let stand 5 minutes to complete cooking.

NOTE: When cooking several apples at a time add 1 additional minute per apple.

(1 serving)

CHERRIES JUBILEE

1 lb. fresh cherries, cut in half and remove pits
1 tablespoon cornstarch
¼ cup sugar
⅓ cup water
¼ cup cherry brandy, brandy, Cointreau or other liqueur
Vanilla ice cream

— Mix cornstarch, sugar, water and cherries in a glass casserole serving dish.
— Microwave, uncovered, 6 minutes on high or until mixture thickens, stirring occasionally.
— Microwave brandy in a dish 30 seconds. Ignite brandy and pour over cherries.
— Serve over ice cream when flame dies down.

(8 servings)

COOKIES CHART

Cookie	Package Size	Number of Cookies	Setting #1 and Time	Setting #2 and Time
Brownie Mix	16 oz.		medium 6 minutes	high 3 to 4 minutes
	22½ oz.		medium 6 minutes	high 4 to 5 minutes
Date Bar Mix	14 oz.			
Filling			high 2 minutes	
Bars			medium 12 minutes	high 2 minutes
Peanut Butter Chocolate Chip Bar Mix	21 oz.		medium 7 minutes	high 3 to 4 minutes
Chocolate Cookie Mix	10 oz.	4	medium 2 to 2½ minutes	
		6	medium 3 to 3½ minutes	
		12	medium 5 to 5½ minutes	
Home made Cookies		4	medium 2 to 3 minutes	
		6	medium 3 to 4 minutes	
		12	medium 5 to 6 minutes	

***high — 100% power : medium — 60% power : low — 30% power.

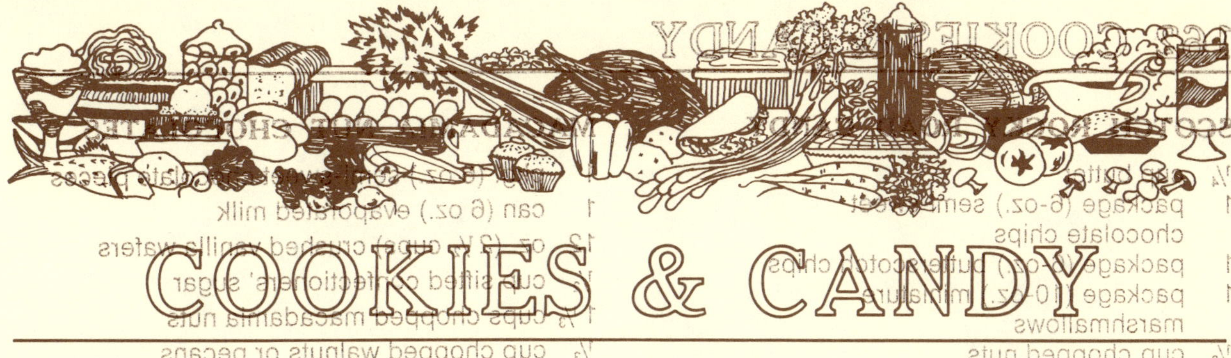

COOKIES & CANDY

NATURE'S OWN CANDY

½ cup (1 stick butter)
¾ cup firmly packed light brown sugar
1 ½ cups quick-cooking oatmeal
1 cup flaked coconut
1 cup coarsely chopped walnuts
½ cup wheat germ
⅓ cup sesame seeds
½ cup snipped dried apricots
⅓ cup honey
1 teaspoon cinnamon

— Combine butter and brown sugar in a glass (10 x 8-inch) baking dish.
— Microwave 1 minute, 30 seconds on high uncovered, or until melted.
— Add all remaining ingredients and mix thoroughly. Spread evenly in the baking dish.
— Microwave 6 minutes on high, or until bubbly, stirring every 2 minutes.
— Turn mixture out onto a sheet of waxed paper. Spread evenly to 1-inch thickness.
— Allow candy to cool completely and break into bite-sized pieces, or cool only until mixture can be handled comfortably.
— Form into 1-inch balls. Cool.

(5 dozen pieces)

FRUIT BRULE

1 can (16-oz.) pitted black cherries, drained
1 can (17-oz.) figs, drained
1 can (16-oz.) pears, drained
1 can (16-oz.) apricots, drained
Juice and grated rind of one orange
Juice and grated rind of one lemon
1 ½ cups firmly packed brown sugar

— Combine fruits, juices and rinds in (10 x 6-inch) baking dish. Sprinkle brown sugar over top.
— Microwave, uncovered, 15 minutes on high, or until mixture is hot, stirring once after 7 minutes.
— Serve hot or cold.

(6-8 servings)

FUDGE

½ cup butter
½ cup cocoa
1 package (1-lb.) confectioners sugar
½ cup milk
½ cup chopped nuts
1 teaspoon vanilla

— Place butter and cocoa in a medium size mixing bowl.
— Microwave, uncovered, 3 to 4 minutes on high, or until butter melts and becomes bubbly.
— Stir cocoa and butter until well blended.
— Add sugar and milk a little at a time, beating after each addition. If batter is too stiff you may add a little more milk.
— Stir in nuts and vanilla.
— Spread fudge evenly in a greased 1½ quart baking dish.
— Refrigerate 1 hour.

(24 squares)

PEANUT BUTTER CANDY

½ cup butter
2 cups sugar
1 tablespoon molasses
⅛ teaspoon salt
½ cup milk
3 cups quick-cooking rolled oats
½ cup shredded coconut
½ cup chopped peanuts
½ cup peanut butter
2 teaspoons vanilla

— Melt butter in a 2-quart glass mixing bowl by cooking on medium for 2 minutes.
— Add sugar molasses, salt and milk. Blend well.
— Microwave, uncovered, 5 minutes on high stirring once after 2 minutes.
— Stir in remaining ingredients.
— Pour into greased pan.
— Chill for several hours in refrigerator.
— Cut into squares.

(60 squares)

SCOTCH ROCKY ROAD CANDY

¼ cup butter
1 package (6-oz.) semi-sweet chocolate chips
1 package (6-oz.) butterscotch chips
1 package (10-oz.) miniature marshmallows
½ cup chopped nuts

— Combine butter, chocolate and butterscotch chips in 1-quart glass measure.
— Microwave, uncovered, 2 to 3 minutes on high, or until chips have softened and can be stirred easily.
— Beat with a fork until well blended.
— Mix marshmallows and nuts in 2-quart, shallow casserole.
— Pour in melted mixture.
— Mix thoroughly.
— Drop by spoonfuls onto waxed paper.
— Refrigerate until firm.

(24 pieces)

TEACAKES

1 cup butter
2 eggs
½ cup powdered sugar
1 teaspoon vanilla
2⅓ cups unsifted flour
1 cup finely chopped nuts
2 pkgs. (5¾ oz. each) milk chocolate kisses
Powdered sugar for sprinkling

— Soften butter in mixing bowl.
— Cream eggs and powdered sugar. Add vanilla and beat until fluffy. Mix in flour and nuts.
— Shape dough (about the size of a walnut) around each chocolate kiss.
— Microwave 10 at a time, uncovered, on a paper towel for about 1 minute, 30 seconds on high, or until surface is no longer doughy looking.
— Sprinkle powdered sugar on warm cookies.

(50 cookies)

BROWNIES

1 package (13-oz.) brownie mix

— Prepare batter as directed on package. Spread into (8 x 8-inch) baking dish.
— Microwave 7 minutes to 8 minutes, 30 seconds on medium, or until firm to touch.
— Cool.
— Cut in 2-inch squares.

(16-18 squares)

MACADAMIA NUT CHOCOLATES

1 pkg. (6 oz.) semi-sweet chocolate pieces
1 can (6 oz.) evaporated milk
12 oz. (2½ cups) crushed vanilla wafers
½ cup sifted confectioners' sugar
1⅓ cups chopped macadamia nuts
⅓ cup chopped walnuts or pecans
⅓ cup orange juice

— Place chocolate pieces and evaporated milk in a deep 1½-quart cooking dish.
— Microwave, uncovered, 2 minutes on high, until chocolate melts, stirring after 1 minute.
— Stir in crushed wafers, sugar, macadamia nuts (⅓ cup), walnuts and orange juice.
— Mix until well-blended. Let stand at room temperature about 1 hour.
— Drop chocolate mixture by half-teaspoons onto dish with remaining macadamia nuts (1 cup).
— Roll to coat with nuts and make balls.
— Refrigerate to harden.

(64 pieces)

DINNERMAN PEANUT BRITTLE

2 cups sugar
1 cup light corn syrup
1 cup water
2 cups shelled unroasted peanuts
¼ teaspoon salt
1 teaspoon butter
1 teaspoon soda

— Combine sugar, corn syrup and water in a glass 2 quart bowl.
— Microwave 18 to 20 minutes, on high, or until a small amount dropped in very cold water forms a soft ball (240°F).
— Stir in peanuts and salt.
— Microwave, uncovered, 7 to 9 minutes, on high or until a small amount dropped in very cold water separates into hard brittle threads (290°F).
— Immediately stir in butter and soda.
— Mix well.
— Spread evenly on large buttered cookie sheet.
— Cool, lifting occasionally with a spatula to prevent sticking. Break into pieces when cool.

SOTOLOFF WHITE FUDGE

2 tablespoons butter
½ cup chopped toasted almonds
2 cups sugar
½ cup butter or margarine
1 cup evaporated milk
1 (8-oz.) bar white chocolate, with whole almonds
1 cup miniature marshmallows
1 teaspoon vanilla extract

— In a shallow baking dish melt the 2 tablespoons butter on high 30 seconds.
— Add ½ cup almonds and heat, uncovered, on high 3 to 4 minutes, or until almonds are toasted.
— Stir each minute of heating. Set aside.
— In a deep, 3-quart casserole combine sugar, the ½ cup butter and evaporated milk.
— Microwave, uncovered, on medium for 18 to 20 minutes, or until mixture reaches 234°F with candy thermometer.
— Add broken pieces of white chocolate and miniature marshmallows. Beat until melted.
— Add toasted almonds and vanilla.
— Beat until candy thickens.
— Pour candy into a buttered, shallow baking dish.
— Cool before cutting into squares.

(1 ½ pounds)

COOPER RAISIN BROWNIES

¼ cup brandy
¼ cup raisins
⅓ cup butter or margarine
2 squares bitter chocolate
2 eggs
1 cup sugar
1 cup baking powder
1 cup unsifted all-purpose flour
Dash of salt
½ cup chopped nuts
A few drops vanilla
Ice cream

— Soak raisins in brandy. Set aside.
— Melt butter and chocolate in a bowl 1 minute, 30 seconds, on high, uncovered.
— Stir in eggs and sugar.
— Sift in baking powder and flour.
— Add raisins, salt and nuts and stir well.
— Add vanilla.
— Spread cookie mixture in a rectangular (10 x 6-inches) baking dish.
— Microwave, covered, 5 minutes on high.
— Slice into pieces of desired size when cool.
— Serve with ice cream on top.

(20 bars)

CURRIED FRUIT

1 package (12-oz.) mixed dried fruits
1 can (20-oz.) pineapple chunks
1 can (21-oz.) strawberry or cherry pie filling
¼ cup dry sherry
½ cup water
1 to 2 teaspoons curry powder

— Combine dried fruits, pineapple chunks and juice in 2-quart casserole.
— Combine pie filling, sherry, water and curry powder in 1-quart measure and pour over fruits. Cover with plastic wrap.
— Microwave 13 minutes on high, or until fruits are fork tender, stirring after 5 minutes.
— Let stand 15 minutes before serving with pork, ham or poultry.

(8 servings)

FANTASTIC FUDGE

¾ cup evaporated milk or light cream
1 tablespoon butter
1 ½ cups sugar
1 ½ cups miniature marshmallows
1 package (6-oz.) chocolate chips
1 cup chopped nuts
1 teaspoon vanilla

— Combine evaporated milk, butter, sugar and marshmallows in 2-quart bowl.
— Microwave, uncovered, 2 to 3 minutes on high, or until marshmallows puff and mixture begins to boil. Stir.
— Reduce setting. Microwave 2 ½ to 3 ½ minutes on medium, uncovered, or until mixture boils and sugar dissolves completely.
— Stir in chocolate chips, nuts and vanilla.
— Beat until smooth.
— Spread in buttered (8 x 8-inch) baking dish. Cool.
— Cut into 1-inch squares.

(64 pieces)

BUTTERSCOTCH CRISPS

1 package (12-oz.) butterscotch bits
3 cups crisp unsweetened cereal

— Pour butterscotch bits into large mixing bowl.
— Microwave 2 minutes, 30 seconds on high, uncovered, or until very soft.
— Stir in cereal gently but thoroughly.
— Spread in well-buttered rectangular pan.
— Refrigerate until completely cooled and set.
— Cut into squares.

(2 dozen squares)

INSTANT CHOCOLATE FONDUE

1 tablespoon butter
2 squares semi-sweet baking chocolate
2 cups marshmallow creme
½ cup Kahlua
Assorted fresh fruits and pound cake squares

— Place butter and chocolate in 1-quart bowl.
— Microwave 45 seconds to 1 minute on high, uncovered, or until butter and chocolate are melted.
— Add marshmallow creme.
— Microwave, uncovered, 35 to 40 seconds on high, or until melted.
— Stir in Kahlua until smooth.
— Serve with chunks of fresh fruit or cake squares on forks.

(2½ cups sauce)

MARBLE BARS

½ cup rum
1 cup raisins
½ cup butter or margarine
1½ cups Graham cracker crumbs
1 cup semi-sweet chocolate chips
⅔ cup crushed peanuts
1½ cups sweetened condensed milk
⅔ cup coconut

— Soak raisins in half cup of rum. Set aside.
— Grease a rectangular (12 x 7 inches) baking dish with butter. Heat 40 seconds in microwave on high until butter melts.
— Sprinkle with cracker crumbs.
— Sprinkle rum raisins on cracker crumbs.
— Spread chocolate on top.
— Scatter peanuts over chocolate.
— Pour on half of the milk, sprinkle with coconut and then finally pour on remaining milk.
— Microwave, uncovered, 8 minutes on high.
— Cool and slice into desired pieces.

(1 bar)

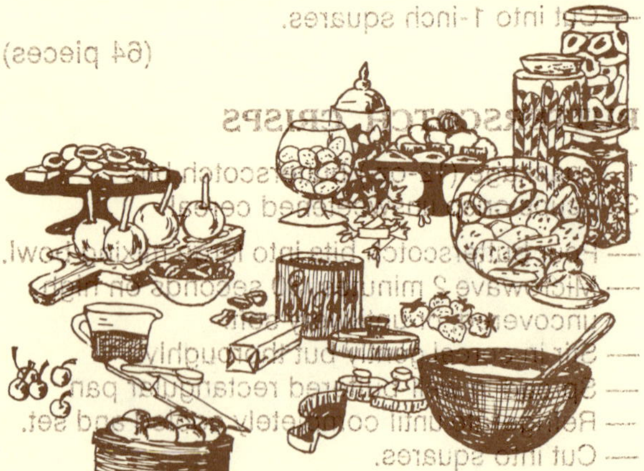

FONDANT

2 cups sugar
1½ cups, plus 2 tablespoons water
⅛ teaspoon cream of tartar
2 tablespoons light corn syrup
1 tablespoon butter
1 teaspoon vanilla

— Butter the sides of a deep 3½-quart glass casserole.
— Combine sugar, water, cream of tartar and corn syrup in casserole.
— Microwave 22 to 26 minutes on high, uncovered, or until a small amount dropped in very cold water forms a soft ball (238°F).
— Immediately pour syrup into large platters. Let cool until warm to touch.
— Using a wooden spoon, work fondant from outside toward center until it forms a creamy white mass.
— Work in butter and vanilla. Continue working until fondant begins to harden.
— Drop by teaspoonfuls onto wax paper.
— Let stand until firm. Store in closed container

NOTE: Do not use candy thermometer in the microwave oven.

(4 dozen pieces)

SUNSHINE DIVINITY

2 cups sugar
½ cup light corn syrup
⅓ cup water
2 egg whites
1 teaspoon vanilla
¾ cup finely chopped candied cherries
¾ cup chopped nuts

— Combine sugar, corn syrup and water in a deep glass 3-quart bowl. Stir until sugar dissolves.
— Microwave 5 minutes on high, uncovered, or until mixture is clear.
— Stir thoroughly.
— Microwave 8 minutes on high, uncovered, or until a small amount dropped in very cold water forms a hard ball (260°F).
— While syrup is cooking, beat egg whites until stiff peaks form.
— When syrup is ready, beat egg whites with electric mixer while slowly pouring in a thin stream of hot syrup. Add vanilla.
— Beat until candy loses its gloss. (About 6 to 8 minutes). Fold in fruit and nuts.
— Drop from buttered teaspoon onto waxed paper or spread in a buttered (10 x 8-inch) pan.
— Cut into squares when cooled.

(2½ dozen pieces)

TUPPI'S TOFFEE TEMPTERS

¼ cup butter or margarine, softened
¼ cup vegetable shortening
½ cup firmly packed brown sugar
1 cup flour
1 package (6-oz.) semi-sweet chocolate pieces
½ cup chopped nuts (optional)

— Thoroughly mix butter, shortening and sugar in medium bowl.
— Blend in flour.
— Spread evenly in (8 x 8-inch) glass baking dish.
— Microwave 2 minutes, 30 seconds on high, or until set.
— Immediately sprinkle chocolate pieces on crust.
— Let stand 2 to 3 minutes until chocolate softens.
— Spread evenly.
Sprinkle with nuts, if desired.
— Cut into squares while warm.

(16 small pieces)

FROSTED OATMEAL SQUARES

4 cups quick-cooking rolled oats
1 cup firmly packed brown sugar
1 cup softened butter or margarine
½ cup white corn syrup, molasses or honey
1 pkg. (6 oz.) semi-sweet chocolate pieces
¾ cup chunky peanut butter

— Mix oats, brown sugar, margarine and syrup thoroughly.
— Divide the mixture between two 2-quart glass utility dishes.
— Press evenly into dishes and bake each separately for 3 minutes, 30 seconds on high, uncovered, until entire top is bubbly.
— Cool.
— In a bowl, melt chocolate pieces and peanut butter for 1 minute, 30 seconds, on high, uncover, stirring midway through cooking time.
— Stir until smooth and spread on top of oatmeal mixture.
— Keep in refrigerator.
— The squares will seem too hard to cut, but after a few minutes at room temperature, they will soften.
— Cut each dish into 24 squares.

(24 squares)

ALMOND COOKIES

1 cup butter or margarine
1 egg
1 cup sugar
1 teaspoon cream of tartar
1 teaspoon baking soda
2 cups flour
1 teaspoon almond extract

— Melt butter in a large bowl 30 seconds on high.
— Add egg and sugar.
— Mix well with a whisk until fluffy and creamy.
— Add cream of tartar, soda, sifted flour and almond extract.
— Mix well.
— Form mixture into 1-inch balls.
— Place 8 or 9 balls in a baking dish lined with wax paper. Chill.
— Flatten chilled balls by pressing softy with palms which have been dipped in sugar.
— Microwave, uncovered, 2 minutes, 30 seconds on high.
— Repeat the process with remaining mixture.

(50 cookies)

CHOCOLATE BUTTER COOKIES

¾ cup butter or margarine
1 egg
¾ cup sugar
1¾ cups all-purpose flour
1 teaspoon baking powder
2 tablespoons grated bitter chocolate
⅓ cup choped nuts
½ teaspoon salt
½ teaspoon vanilla
Pinch of sugar

— Place butter in a fairly large bowl and microwave on high 25 seconds until melted.
— Add egg and sugar.
— Whisk until egg mixture bubbles.
— Sift in flour and baking power.
— Mix in chocolate, nuts, salt and vanilla.
— Refrigerate 30 minutes until the mixture rises.
— Form mixture into balls 1 inch in diameter.
— Put wax paper in another baking dish. Arrange 11 to 12 sugared balls in it. Leave a 1½ inch space between balls.
— Dip the bottom of wine glass in sugar. Flatten the balls with the glass.
— Microwave, uncovered, 3 minutes, 30 seconds on high.
— Microwave remaining cookies in the same way.

(22-24 cookies)

PEANUT BUTTER COOKIES

1 pkg. (10 oz.) pie crust mix
1 1/4 cups brown sugar
1/2 cup peanut butter
3 tablespoons water
2/3 cup chocolate pieces
1/4 cup chopped peanuts

— Place pie crust mix, brown sugar, peanut butter and water in a bowl.
— Mix well.
— Spread and flatten mixture in a shallow 2-quart glass baking dish.
— Microwave, uncovered, 4 minutes, 30 seconds on high, or until dough becomes puffy.
— Sprinkle with chocolate pieces and chopped peanuts.
— Microwave, uncovered, about 30 more seconds on high, or until chocolate pieces melt.
— Spread melted chocolate to mix together with peanuts.
— Cut into squares after cooled.

(40 cookies)

LARGO'S CHOCOLATE BOURBON BALLS

1 cup finely chopped pecans
1/4 cup bourbon
1/2 cup butter or margarine
4 cups sifted confectioners' sugar
3 (8-oz.) packages semi-sweet chocolate bits

— Combine chopped pecans with bourbon and refrigerate overnight.
— Melt butter in small, heat-resistant, non-metallic bowl on high 1 minute, uncovered.
— Add confectioners' sugar, 1 cup at a time, to melted butter. Add nuts and bourbon, mixing well.
— Place in refrigerator to harden.
— Mixture should be stiff enough to hold its shape for dipping.
— If necessary, more confectioners' sugar may be added to obtain the desired stiffness.
— In a medum-sized, heat-resistant, non-metallic bowl, place the chocolate bits.
— Microwave, uncovered, on high 4 minutes or until melted.
— While chocolate is melting, shape candy into balls. Dip balls into melted chocolate.
— Place on tray with waxed paper and return to refrigerator to harden.

(1 1/2 dozen)

(Dip only a few bourbon balls at a time, leaving the rest in the refrigerator. If balls become to soft, return to the refrigerator to harden. If chocolate becomes too stiff, return to Microwave Oven for 1 minute to soften.)

PRINCE LEMON COOKIES

1/4 lemon
4 tablespoons butter or margarine
1/2 cup sugar
1 egg
1 1/3 cups all-purpose flour (sifted)
Granulated sugar
Salad oil

— Squeeze lemon and grate lemon peel.
— Whisk butter until creamy.
— Add sugar and whisk until mixture turns white.
— Add beaten egg, lemon juice, grated lemon peel and sifted flour.
— Mix well.
— Flatten dough to a thickness of 1/4 inch on a board coated with flour.
— Coat one side with granulated sugar.
— Grease paper with salad oil and arrange half of cookies on it with sugared side up. Microwave, uncovered, 3 minutes, 30 seconds on high.
— Repeat with remaining half.

(40-50 cookies)

PALKO GINGER PEOPLE

2 1/2 cups all-purpose flour
1 teaspoon salt
1 teaspoon ginger
1/4 teaspoon nutmeg
1/4 teaspoon cloves
1/2 teaspoon cinnamon
1/2 cup margarine or vegetable shortening
1/2 cup sugar
1/2 cup molasses
1/4 cup water

— Combine flour, salt, ginger, nutmeg, cloves and cinnamon in 1-quart glass measure.
— Mix together lightly. Set aside.
— In large mixing bowl. Cream shortening and sugar together until light and fluffy.
— Stir in molasses and water. Blend in flour mixture until smooth.
— Chill dough at least 3 hours.
— Roll dough 1/8-inch thick on floured pastry cloth.
— Cut into gingerbread boys or girls with 3 to 4-inch cookie cutters.
— Place sheet of waxed paper on inverted glass (12 x 8-inch) baking dish. 4 at a time.
— Microwave, uncovered, 3 to 5 minutes on high or until cookies are set.
— Cool.
— Decorate as desired.

(2 dozen)

SHA'S SUGAR COOKIES

1 cup butter or margarine
1 cup sugar
2 eggs
3 cups unsifted all-purpose flour
1 teaspoon cream of tartar
½ teaspoon soda
½ teaspoon salt
1 teaspoon almond extract

— Cream butter in large mixer bowl until fluffy.
— Beat in sugar and eggs until well blended.
— Stir in remaining ingredients and chill.
— Shape into 1-inch balls; place on wax paper, 1 inch apart; flatten with glass dipped in water, then sugar.
— Place cookies on wax paper in the oven.
— Microwave, uncovered, on low until tops have dry appearance:
4 cookies — 2 to 3 minutes
6 cookies — 3 to 4 minutes
12 cookies — 5 to 6 minutes
— Cool on wax paper; remove, and store in tightly covered container.

(48 cookies)

GINGER JOY

½ cup vegetable shortening
½ cup sugar
½ cup light molasses
1 ½ teaspoons vinegar
1 egg, well beaten
3 cups all-purpose flour
½ teaspoon soda
½ teaspoon ginger
½ teaspoon cinnamon
¼ teaspoon salt

— Blend shortening, sugar molasses and vinegar together in 1-quart glass casserole.
— Microwave, uncovered, 2 minutes on high or until mixture begins to boil, stirring once after 1 minute.
— Let stand ½ hour to cool.
— Stir in egg.
— Combine flour, soda, ginger, cinnamon and salt in 1-quart measure.
— Mix together lightly.
— Stir into cooled molasses mixture.
— Mix thoroughly.
— Refrigerate several hours.
— Place a sheet of waxed paper on inverted glass (12 x 8-inch) baking dish.
— Form dough in 1-inch balls.
— Place 6 to 8 on waxed paper.
— Microwave, uncovered, 2 minutes on high, on until set.
— Let stand 1 minute. Cool.

(3-4 dozen)

COCOA COOKIES

7 tablespoons shortening
7 tablespoons sugar
1 egg, separated
⅓ teaspoon vanilla
½ teaspoon nutmeg
Dash of cinnamon
1 ½ cups all-purpose flour
½ teaspoon baking powder
¼ teaspoon salt
2 tablespoons cocoa

— Combine shortening and sugar.
— Add egg yolk and stir well.
— Beat egg white well.
— Add vanilla.
— Sift together nutmeg, cinnamon, all-purpose flour, baking powder, salt and cocoa.
— Mix all ingredients and form 1 inch thick sticks
— Wrap and refrigerate about 1 hour, 30 minutes
— Cut chilled sticks to make ¼ inch thick cookies. Arrange half of the cookies on waxed paper in a baking dish.
— Microwave, uncovered, 3 minutes, 30 seconds on high.
— Remove and place on wire rack to cool.
— Repeat with remaining half.

(40-50 cookies)

SANTA'S FAVORITE COOKIES

¼ cup butter
¾ cup sugar
2 eggs, beaten
½ cup molasses
1 ¾ cups sifted flour
¾ teaspoon salt
1 teaspoon baking powder
½ teaspoon each: cinnamon, allspice, nutmeg and cloves
2 tablespoons bourbon
1 cup chopped nuts
4 oz. chopped citron
½ oz. sweet chocolate, melted and cooled

— Cream butter and sugar until fluffy.
— Add eggs and molasses.
— Beat thoroughly.
— Sift dry ingredients and add to mixture.
— Mix well.
— Add bourbon, pecans, citron and chocolate.
— Drop from teaspoon on ungreased cookie sheet.
— Microwave on medium 5 to 6 minutes, or until lightly browned.

PINEAPPLE COOKIES

½ cup sugar
½ cup brown sugar firmly packed
½ cup butter
½ cup crushed pineapple, drained
½ cup chopped nuts
1 egg, beaten
1 tablespoon pineapple juice
2 cups flour
½ tablespoon baking soda
¼ teaspoon salt
1 teaspoon baking powder

— Cream butter and sugars.
— Add beaten egg, pineapple juice, pineapple and nuts.
— Sift dry ingredients together and add to creamed mixture.
— Drop by tablespoon on greased cookie sheet.
— Microwave on medium 5 to 6 minutes, or until done.

(4 dozen cookies)

JOHNNY'S ANGEL PUFFS

4 egg whites
1 cup sugar
1 teaspoon vanilla
2 oz. unsweetened chocolate, finely grated
1 cup semisweet chocolate bits
3 tablespoons milk
¾ cup chopped pistachio nuts

— Beat egg whites stiff.
— Gradually fold in sugar.
— Fold in vanilla and grated chocolate.
— Drop by teaspoonfuls on ungreased cookie sheet covered with paper.
— Microwave on medium 5 to 6 minutes, or until done.
— Cool.
— Melt semisweet chocolate adding milk gradually to the chocolate to make a thick paste.
— Dip tops of puffs into chocolate paste, then dip into chopped nuts.

(3-4 dozen cookies)

JELLIES, JAMS & FRIUTS

APPLE BETTY

⅓ cup melted butter or margarine
2 cups fresh bread crumbs
6 cups sliced, peeled, and cored cooking apples
½ cup firmly packed brown sugar
½ teaspoon ground nutmeg
¼ teaspoon ground cinnamon
1 tablespoon grated lemon peel (optional)
2 tablespoons lemon juice

— Toss melted butter with bread crumbs.
— Put one-third of the buttered bread crumbs in a 2-quart casserole.
— Combine apples with brown sugar, nutmeg, cinnamon, and lemon peel. Put half of the apple mixture on bread crumbs layer.
— Cover with one-third of the crumbs.
— Add remaining apples.
— Combine lemon juice and ¼ cup water.
— Pour over apples.
— Top with remaining buttered crumbs.
— Microwave, covered, for 12 minutes on high.
— Remove cover and Microwave again for 10 minutes on high, or until apples are tender.

(6 servings)

HOT GINGERED PEARS

2 cans (1-lb., 13-oz. each) pear halves
24 whole cloves
2 cinnamon sticks
¼ teaspoon nutmeg
4 teaspoons lemon juice
1 teaspoon grated lemon peel
1 teaspoon grated orange peel
2½ tablespoons chopped crystallized ginger
⅛ teaspoon ground ginger
2 tablespoons butter

— Drain pears well, reserving 1½ cups syrup.
— In 2-quart bowl, combine reserved syrup, 10 cloves, cinnamon sticks and nutmeg.
— Microwave 5 to 7 minutes on high, or until mixture boils.
— Reduce setting. Microwave 4 minutes on medium.
— Remove and discard cloves.
— Add lemon juice, lemon and orange peels, gingers and butter. Mix well.
— Microwave 5 to 7 minutes on medium, or until slightly thickened.
— Arrange pear halves in (12x8-inch) baking dish. Insert 1 or 2 cloves in each.
— Pour hot syrup over pears.
— Microwave 6 minutes on medium, basting pears with syrup several times.
— Serve hot or cold. Will keep in jars several days, refrigerated.

(two 3-pint jars)

GRAPE-AND-HERB JELLY

½ cup boiling water
¾ tablespoon dried basil
¼ teaspoon rosemary
1 tablespoon lemon juice
1½ cups grape juice
1 package (1¾-oz.) powdered fruit pectin
3¼ cups sugar

— Pour boiling water over basil and rosemary in small bowl. Cover.
— Let stand 5 to 10 minutes.
— Strain through cheese cloth into measuring cup. Add more water, if necessary, to make ½ cup.
— Combine basil water, grape juice, lemon juice and pectin in 2-quart bowl.
— Microwave 5 to 7 minutes on high, or until mixture boils. Stir in sugar.
— Reduce setting. Microwave 7 to 9 minutes on medium or until mixture is slightly thickened, stirring once to dissolve sugar; skim.
— Pour into hot sterilized jars. Seal.

(4 ½-pint jars)

EASY SPICED PEACHES

2 cans (1-lb., 13-oz. each) peach halves with juice
2 tablespoons cider vinegar
1 teaspoon whole allspice
1 teaspoon whole cloves
4 cinnamon sticks (2 ½-inches)

— Drain peaches well, reserving 1 ½ cups syrup.
— In 2-quart glass bowl, combine reserved syrup, vinegar, allspice, cloves and cinnamon sticks.
— Microwave, uncovered, 4 to 6 minutes on high, or until mixture boils.
— Reduce setting. Microwave 5 minutes on medium, uncovered.
— Remove and discard cloves.
— Arrange peach halves in (12x8-inch) glass baking dish. Pour hot syrup over peaches.
— Microwave 6 minutes on medium, uncovered, basting peaches several times.
— Serve hot or cold. Peaches will keep in 3-pint jars several days, refrigerated.

(two 3-pint jars)

MILD PEACH CHUTNEY

1 large unpeeled apple, cored and chopped
1 cup chopped celery
¼ cup chopped green pepper
1 tablespoon finely chopped onion
2 cans (16-oz. each) sliced cling peaches with juice
½ cup seedless raisins
¾ cup cider vinegar
½ cup sugar
½ teaspoon salt
¼ teaspoon ginger
Dash cayenne pepper

— Combine all ingredients in a 3-quart glass casserole.
— Stir well. Cover.
— Microwave 5 minutes on high, or until mixture boils.
— Reduce setting. Microwave 45 minutes on medium, or untl syrup is thickened and chutney is to the desired consistency, stirring after every 15 minutes.
— Ladle into hot sterilized 1-pint jars.
— Cover tightly. Cool.
— Store in refrigerator.
— Serve with meats.

(Two 1-pint jars)

ARISTOCRATIC APPLE JELLY

2 cups apple juice
1 package (1 ¾-oz.) powdered fruit pectin
1 tablespoon aromatic bitters
2 tablespoons lemon juice
Red food color
3 ½ cups sugar

— Stir apple juice and pectin together in 2-quart glass bowl. Microwave 5 to 7 minutes, uncovered, on high, or until mixture boils.
— Add bitters, lemon juice and a few drops red food color.
— Stir in sugar.
— Reduce setting. Microwave 7 to 9 minutes uncovered, on medium, until mixture is slightly thickened, stirring once to dissolve sugar. Skim.
— Pour into hot sterilized ½-pint jars. Seal.

(Four ½-pint jars)

ANTIPASTO RELISH

½ small head cauliflower, cut in flowerets and sliced
2 carrots, pared, cut in 2-inch strips
2 stems celery, cut diagonally in 1-inch pieces (1 cup)
1 small onion, cut in ¾-inch squares
1 green pepper, cut in 2-inch strips
1 jar (3-oz.) stuffed green olives, drained
¾ cup wine vinegar
½ cup olive or salad oil
1 tablespoons sugar
1 teaspoon salt
½ teaspoon oregano leaves
¼ teaspoon pepper
¼ cup water

— Combine all ingredients in 3-quart casserole.
— Microwave 8 to 10 minutes on high, or until mixture has come to a rapid boil, stirring twice.
— Reduce setting. Microwave 5 to 7 minutes on medium. Cool.
— Refrigerate at least 24 hours.
— Drain well before serving.
— Will keep several days in refrigerator, covered. Serve as appetizer, salad, or garnish for meats.

NOTE: Pitted ripe olives, medium zucchini cut in 1-inch pieces, or other crisp, fresh vegetables may be substituted for part of ingredients above.

(6 servings)

GRAPEFRUIT AND SAVORY JELLY

½ cup boiling water
2 teaspoons dried summer savory
1 cup grapefruit juice
1 package (1¾-oz.) powdered fruit pectin
Green food color
3¼ cups sugar

— Pour boiling water over savory in small bowl.
— Cover. Let stand 15 minutes.
— Strain through cheese cloth into a glass measuring cup.
— Add more water, if needed, to make ½ cup.
— Combine savory water, grapefruit juice and pectin in 2-quart bowl.
— Microwave, uncovered, 5 to 7 minutes on high, or until mixture boils.
— Tint light green with food color.
— Stir in sugar.
— Reduce setting. Microwave 7 to 9 minutes on medium or until slightly thickened, stirring once to dissolve sugar. Skim.
— Pour into hot sterilized jars and seal.

(Three ½-pint jars)

APPLE JAM

2 medium-sized apples, washed, cored and peeled
1½ cups sugar
1 teaspoon lemon juice

— In a medium-sized bowl, place the 2 apples.
— Add sugar.
— Do not mix.
— Microwave, uncovered, on high for 5 minutes.
— With electric mixer beat apples until apples and sugar are well blended.
— Microwave, uncovered, on high for 3 minutes.
— Stir in 1 teaspoon lemon juice.
— Cool before serving.

(1 cup)

RHODE ISLAND RASPBERRY JAM

2 (10-oz.) packages frozen raspberries
3½ tablespoons liquid pectin
2½ cups sugar
1 tablespoon lemon juice

— Place 2 packages of frozen raspberries in a deep 3-quart, heat-resistant, non-metallic mixing bowl.
— Microwave, uncovered, on high 4 minutes.
— Stir in liquid pectin and mix well.
— Microwave, uncovered, on high 4 minutes.
— Stir and heat for an additional 2½ minutes on high.
— Add sugar and lemon juice.
— Cook, uncovered, on high 2 minutes.
— Stir and heat an additional 4 minutes on high, or until the jellying point has been reached.
— Pour into sterilized jars and seal.

(3 cups)

Test for jellying point:
Dip a large metal spoon into the boiling syrup; tilt spoon until syrup runs from the side of the spoon. When the jellying point is reached, liquid will not flow in a stream, but will divide into distinct drops which run together and flake or sheet from the spoon.

OTHER IDEAS

Kind of Flower	Number	Setting	Time
Roses	1	high	2 minutes
	2	high	3 minutes
	3	high	4 minutes
Chrysanthemums	1	high	2 minutes
	2	high	3 minutes
	3	high	4 minutes
Carnations	1	high	3 minutes
	2	high	4½ minutes
	3	high	6 minutes
Daisies	1	high	1½ minutes
(3 cups)	2	high	2½ minutes
	3	high	3½ minutes
Leaves	2	high	1½ minutes
	4	high	2½ minutes

*high — 100% power   medium — 60% power   :   low — 60% power.

CONVERT FAVORITE RECIPES TO MICROWAVE COOKING

As your experience with the microwave oven grows, you will want to try doing some of your old family favorites the speedy microwave way. Many recipes can be changed with very little effort and experimentation. The following guidelines will help you to make the conversion from conventional to microwave cooking a little easier.

— Look in this cookbook for a recipe that is similar to yours. In most recipes you can use the ingredients called for and combine them in the usual way. However, sensitive ingredients need special considerations and adjustments to the recipe may be needed such as:

- Reducing the amount of liquids in stews, sauces and fillings thickened with cornstarch;
- Decreasing the quantity of herbs and spices in casseroles and stews;
- Using half the listed amount of baking powder and soda when baking cakes, quick breads and cookies.

— Compare the cooking utensils your conventional recipe asks for with those suggested for use in the microwave oven. Often you can use the same casserole or baking dish in both methods of cooking as long as the container is heat-resistant and non-metalic.

— Adjust the cooking time, using the microwave recipe as a guide. Remember that although a cup of water boils in 2½ minutes, a half-dozen rolls take only seconds to heat in the microwave. The food's starting temperature, shape, volume and density are all factors that can vary the cooking times and should be considered when converting recipes.

OTHER IDEAS

FLOWER DRYING

A microwave oven is one of the most versatile appliances that you can own. Tasty foods can be made and the microwave oven has been known to be used for reheating coffee, warming baby bottles, softening hard ice-cream, making croutons, drying herbs and spices, cracking nuts, softening hardened brown sugar, crisping soggy potato chips or pretzels, and for defrosting frozen concentrated fruit juice. You will find that a microwave is also a great way to quick-dry fresh flowers. The directions below will show you how easy and fun this craft can be.

Drying flowers, like many crafts, requires time and practice to achieve perfection. In 30 minutes a microwave oven can give your dried flowers a professional look that may take up to 8 days to acquire using the conventional method.

To assure that you attain the best possible results, it is important to consider the color and kind of flower that you decide to dry. Some colors maintain their natural tones better than others. Yellow, gold, blue and white flowers hold their brilliance to a greater extent than colors like pink and red. Roses, chrysanthemums, carnations and daisies dry very well in the microwave. Try not to choose large, thin-petaled flowers like tulips, petunias and geraniums because they become very fragile when dried, making them difficult to handle.

The ease and speed in which you can dry flowers will encourage you to dry whole bouquets with beautiful and long lasting results. The equipment and procedure necessary for micro-dried flowers is given.

1 box (24 oz.) silica gel crystals
Florist wire
Florist tape
2 toothpicks
1 small paint brush
1 cup (8 oz.) water

— Dry flowers as soon as they have been picked, choosing those flowers that have not quite reached maturity.
— Cut blossoms so that ½ inch of stem is left.
— Remove leaves from the stem and reserve.
— Place ¾ inch of silica gel in a glass (9 x 5-inch) loaf pan.
— Put stem of flower in gel, blossom side up. (If drying more than one flower or leaf, leave 1 inch between them.)
— Carefully spoon remaining crystals around flower petals, gently filling in the space without forcing petals together or pressing them out of their natural shape.
— Continue to add crystals until flowers are completely covered.
— Put silica covered flowers and the cup of water (water should be in a separate glass container) in the microwave oven.
— Microwave, uncovered, on high according to times listed in the chart.
— Let flowers stand in the gel for ½ hour after being microwaved.
— Carefully remove blossoms, lifting them out with toothpicks. Blossoms should be flexible, but still firm enough to stand upright.
— Attach to florist wire by placing wire parallel to ½ inch stem. Wrap wire onto stem with florist tape.
— Repeat above directions for flower leaves.
— Connect to wire stem with florist tape.

NOTE: For best results, dry one kind of flower at a time.

INDEX